REDEMPTION

REDEMPTION

A STORY OF SISTERHOOD, SURVIVAL,
AND FINDING FREEDOM BEHIND BARS

STACEY LANNERT

and KRISTEN KEMP

CROWN PUBLISHERS

NEW YORK

Disclaimer: Some names and identifying characteristics of some of the people mentioned in this book have been changed in an effort to minimize intrusions on or protect their privacy.

Copyright © 2011 by Libre Diem, LLC

Published in the United States by Crown Publishers, an imprint of the Crown Publishing Group, a division of Random House, Inc., New York.
www.crownpublishing.com

CROWN and the Crown colophon are registered trademarks of Random House, Inc.

Library of Congress Cataloging-in-Publication Data is available upon request.

ISBN 978-0-307-59213-2
eISBN 978-0-307-59215-6

Printed in the United States of America

Book design by Gretchen Achilles
Jacket design by David Tran
Jacket photograph by Deborah Feingold

1   3   5   7   9   10   8   6   4   2

FIRST EDITION

To Matthew Blunt,

former governor of the state of Missouri,

for giving me a chance at redemption.

I would like to thank my attorneys,

Ellen Flottman and Mike Anderson,

for standing behind me and believing in me

even when I did not know how to believe in myself.

Without their unrelenting support and dedication,

I would not be free today.

WHERE THE EAGLE FLIES

Searching for a certain rare find,
a strength of heart and a peace of mind,
my guests all failed with desperate sighs
in trying to reach where the eagle flies.

Living a life of mere existence,
meeting with failure and much resistance,
I found that hate laughs and love cries,
in searching for where the eagle flies.

My journey has brought me to a strange place,
where all of my fears I am forced to face,
but here I have found in the cold winter skies
that within my soul is where the eagle flies.

Behind these walls, the iron doors locked tight,
I close my eyes and enjoy the flight,
soaring above the mountain highs,
reaching to where the eagle flies.

—JONATHAN C. BOYER, *January 6, 1992*

REDEMPTION

Second Chance

A second chance was never supposed to happen to me. I had a life sentence without the possibility of parole, yet in one magical stroke of a pen, the governor of Missouri, Matthew Blunt, ordered that the prison gates be opened for me. After eighteen years, I was allowed to be Stacey Ann Lannert instead of Offender #85704.

I'll never completely shed the number, but I did start over. The real world was pure magic. On the outside, I saw miracles everywhere: birds clustered in trees, snowflakes sticking to my windshield, a crossing guard guiding children across the intersection. I saw my breath as it hit the cold air outside. I don't get stunned easily, but seeing my reflection in a mirror did the trick.

Beginning at age eighteen, I spent a total of eighteen years locked up. At least the numbers are neat and tidy, because the rest was a mess. The trouble started in 1980 at age eight. In 1990, life as I knew it ended, for better and for worse. I had committed murder, ending the life of my sexually abusive father. My personal time warp had begun.

Under incarceration, a punishment I believe I deserved, I was sealed off in a world where hugs were not allowed, and the Internet had never been invented. I couldn't imagine a phone with no cord that fit in a pocket. I lived in a universe where I wasn't allowed to talk, walk, or pee without special rules and permission. My drab, worn-out clothes had to be approved. A gourmet meal was a can of Hormel beef chili, and I had to make sure I could afford to buy it. In the beginning of my sentence, my mind was too numb to cry and too shut off to care. I could check in and out of my emotions as if they were library books. To me, sadness and happiness were all the same. The jail of my own making—before and after I committed the crime—was as bleak as the one I was locked up in. My prison bars were ironclad, emotionally and physically.

Fast forward to February 2009. I was thirty-six, and the bars had been completely removed. I'd been shown an act of mercy and grace. I had been delivered from sin. I had sacrificed all of my adult life purely in hopes of this redemption.

If I am fit for forgiveness, I want to live a worthy life. I just have to figure out how to make my way in this world. Get a job. Buy a car. Figure out how to use a cell phone, not to mention how to text. When did ordering coffee get so complicated? And why would anyone want to eat raw fish with rice?

The first time I walked into a department store after my release, for example, I was so overwhelmed that I began to sweat. I usually like to sweat—I teach step class—just not while shopping. Fabrics came in more colors and patterns than an LSD trip. The signs and sales and people bumped into me in every aisle. I needed bras, but the store was the size of a football field.

I left.

I decided I would have to live, once again, without the basic items I needed.

During my eighteen years in prison, shopping was sparse. I submitted a short list to the prison staffers whenever I wanted shoes, shirts, Hormel chili, or whatever. I paid for my goods because all prisoners have jobs, albeit with ridiculously low wages. In a few days or months, I'd go to a window, and workers would shove my order back at me. It wasn't even a store. The system was limited, and it sucked. But at least it was simple. I longed for more choices, and when I finally had them, I panicked.

I asked for help.

My mom volunteered to go shopping with me. It was a warm gesture, because we didn't shop together when I was growing up. She was always at school, at work, or on the phone with a friend. As a preteen, I picked out my own hair spray and headbands. Eventually, I bought most of the groceries, too. I used to shop a lot then, so what was my problem? I was going to figure it out.

With Mom.

A fresh start.

We browsed the aisles in a big Walmart. After fifteen minutes, she saw me sweating again, and she took action. I needed only two bras, and there were about 250,000 to choose from. The garments came with adjustable straps I'd never seen before. Some didn't have straps at all. They all promised miracles—perfect fits, lifts, pure comfort, flexibility, and control. Meanwhile, I didn't even know my size. When I was in prison, I wore only sports bras. Every time I ordered regular ones, they never fit right. If I ordered a small sports bra—just about any kind—I'd be all set.

My mom saw my eyes spinning. In two minutes, she dashed around and brought back five choices for me. She held up the bras and asked me to choose one. I could breathe. I stopped sweating. Five bras were doable; 250,000 were a panic attack. I picked one I liked; it didn't work. I went to the next option; it was not so good either. After three tries, we had a winner. Happiness was a bra that fit.

Then I glanced into the full-length mirror.

I froze. I stared. I had not seen my body since I was a teenager. We did not have full-length mirrors in the maximum-security state penitentiary. Primping wasn't exactly a priority. In all that time, I hadn't thought much about how I looked. Who was I going to impress? Prison guards, prisoners, or occasional visitors? Finally, at that moment, my looks mattered. I was thirty-six, and I wanted to see me.

Was that me?

Really?

How had some places gone soft when they used to be hard? My waist was squishier, and so were my thighs and breasts. Maybe if I'd seen my body even one time in the last decade, the difference wouldn't have been so drastic. I wanted to cry, and I felt tears coming on in the back of my eyes. I stopped myself, though.

This—everything—was ridiculous.

My mom was standing outside the dressing room. After a long silence, she peeked in to check on me. She read my face, and she was quiet for a few seconds. Then she said, "We all get older and go through changes." As she closed the curtain again, she added, "Things sag."

"I had no idea I'd get old in prison," I said, only half-joking. My friends used to say that prison preserves a person—an inmate's body doesn't get abused by alcohol, drugs, late nights, and other people. My friends had been wrong.

I couldn't get sad. I wouldn't allow it; I was free. There was no denying that while my world stood still, my body had grown older. But my body had also grown up, and my mind had grown wise.

Even though I've always been five feet, two inches and athletic, my middle had taken on a touch of fat. As a certified fitness instructor, I knew I'd have to exercise five hours a day to get rid of it. If I were still incarcerated, I could find those hours—and more—to work out. But then I would not have a full-length mirror to admire my tummy. I knew which option was better. I would love my flab and French fries too—we weren't allowed to have them in prison.

Most important, after so many years, I would love my mother. She's the only parent I have.

Clemency had granted me a deep look at myself—in a mirror. I thought about my life's journey. How did I get here? I wondered where God would lead me next. I planned to use all that I'd learned to make my world, and the world around me, a better place. If I was worthy of a second chance, I hoped I could fulfill that promise. Could I finally become the person I dreamed of being?

I was set free on January 16, 2009.

I was given a shot at redemption, and I didn't intend to waste it. My life would have meaning; I would make sure of that.

I am living proof that anyone—even a convicted felon sentenced to life in prison without parole—can walk a spiritual journey. I am proof that people can change. I am proof that people can learn and love and keep on living. Even the most troubled person can transform her life, just as an artist can turn raw materials into an entirely new creation. A glassblower, through persistence, care, and skill, can convert a few shards of glass into a gleaming thing of beauty. Not a lightweight, fragile object, but a well-formed, solid work of art worth saving, collecting, and protecting.

We are all worth saving and protecting.

In the Beginning

Most people do not take another person's life. The act is ugly, off limits, appropriate only in scary movies. But many people do use the words, "I'm going to kill you." A wife might say it to a husband when he brings home a new Ford truck without asking. A father might say it to a son after he wrecks that new truck. The words are normal when they're meaningless. Thankfully, the line "I'll kill you" isn't usually backed up by much threat.

Usually.

But what about when those words are said to a woman or girl who is in pain? A girl who is abused? A girl who is told she is a worthless whore almost every day of her life? I was that girl. The threat, "Be quiet, or I'll kill you," was real. So I stayed quiet. I made as little noise as possible almost all of the time. At the same time, my shame, isolation, and rage built up over the years while I prayed for an end to my problems. I prayed to be left alone, to be left unviolated for any short length of time. People like me are the caged birds.

My cage was my house.

My cage was my own bed.

Ending a life is the most grisly, uncivilized way of solving a problem. But it doesn't happen in a vacuum when otherwise sane people are involved. Instead, tension builds over time in a domestic pressure cooker. Is my abuser going to push too hard the next time and kill me? Should I kill myself so I don't have to feel the hurt anymore?

To people with these experiences, killing is real. Anyone can be

dead with the snap of the fingers. More often than not, victims consider suicide. But sometimes—guilt-ridden—we fantasize about the
deaths of our abusers. We don't necessarily want to do it ourselves.
In our fantasies, he goes quickly in a car crash; it makes sense because he drives drunk all the time. Or maybe he starts a fight with
someone who actually can—and does—kick his ass. But what if, hy-
pothetically thinking, the abuser gets into a fight with his victim,
and she magically overpowers him and gets away? She runs off to a
happier life where she can get a full night's rest. She goes to a place
where shadows don't scare her half to death. In dreams, that sce-
nario could be true.

In reality, overpowering a strong man usually takes a weapon.
So the hypothesizing continues: What if, in some way, she's able to
get that weapon? What if she uses it? What if she kills him herself?
That's how the words "I'll kill you" become warped reality.

Women aren't known for homicides—according to the Justice
Department, females commit only 10 percent of murders. When
they do kill, they take the life of an intimate partner or family member one-third of the time. Criminology researchers have found that
women usually didn't mean to do the crime; they didn't even think
they were capable, and they didn't plan their attacks for more than
a few seconds. Male murderers more commonly act deliberately instead of impulsively. They know exactly what is about to happen long
in advance. Men don't disassociate from their crimes, either. But a
woman, especially a victim of abuse, may not remember exactly how
she did it. If she remembers clearly, she can't find breath—only bile
rising in her chest. She'll have a panic attack or a breakdown. She's
in too much pain over what she did—and why she did it—to remember the details, according to researcher Jack Levin at Northeastern
University. More often than not, women kill because they're afraid
they'll be killed.

Most people don't have these thoughts about death, but I did for
most of my life.

Killing is best left to animals like the bald eagle. They must hunt to feed themselves and their young, and they do not have to be taught. My hometown of St. Louis is known for the bald eagles in the wintertime. People don't realize it, but Missouri can be cold. We get snow, ice, and sleet. That's when the eagles appear.

Snow days away from school were fun for most kids. But as I grew older, they were less exciting for me. Staying home was not a vacation; it was often a punishment. I wanted to be a bald eagle—big and strong with a sharp, pointy beak for protection. I wished for wings to take me to some other place during the different seasons. When it was coldest outside, I'd catch sight of them near the Mississippi River. The birds liked to hang out in the areas surrounding its muddy waters. Apparently, that's the best place to find food and build nests in sycamore trees. Bald eagles hunt fish, reptiles, mammals, and human picnic food. They don't care if the food is dead or alive when they swoop down with their lethal talons. They learn how to adapt and survive. These muscular creatures are tough, scrappy scavengers. When I was a kid, they were on the endangered species list. So if I caught sight of one, I was excited.

If I had been a different kid with a different family, I would have seen the eagle as noble in a patriotic way. I would have focused on its plumage and beauty instead of on how the awesome creature managed to stay alive. I saw the bird as a tough victim of our human invasion—clawing and clutching for its survival. That's exactly how I felt I lived, too, from age nine onward. With so much taken away from me, I wasn't free to think about kickball and BFFs and bracelets made out of embroidery floss. I took refuge in sports, and in my imagination. I found comfort in our cat, Buttercup; my dog, Prince; the track team; and my schoolwork.

Before age eight, my life was way better. I saw the eagles more innocently. I smiled more often because I wanted to—not just for other people's benefit. Born on May 28, 1972, just outside of St. Louis, Missouri, I was a happy baby with a stay-at-home mom who loved me and took care of me. I had a dad who came home after work, though he was often studying, tucked away behind his office door.

My mom held everything together for as long as she could.

She was used to life's difficulties—she'd grown up with enough of them. Her maiden name was Deborah Paulson, and she was born on October 17, 1951, in Granite City, Illinois. She was the oldest of five kids, and she longed to leave the rural countryside where she grew up. The first house she remembers had two bedrooms. The kids shared one, and her parents shared the other. When my mom was seven, she came down with rheumatic fever and was in the hospital for a long stretch. Then she had to stay out of school for more than a year. She had to take it easy and couldn't even walk to the second floor of the house. She slept on a rollaway bed in the living room. Her mom brought her a bedpan because the house's one bathroom was upstairs. The doctor said Debbie would never have children, and she might even come down with the dreaded rheumatic fever again later in life. With great worry and care, my grandmother waited on Debbie hand and foot. During that time my grandmother was really good to my mother.

Debbie recovered fully and took on responsibilities of her own. She was often in charge of her siblings, especially the littlest one, Deanna, who was thirteen years younger. By then, the family had moved into a three-bedroom house closer to the small downtown. They needed to be near my grandfather's work. Debbie was just happy she had fewer siblings to bunk with in a slightly larger house. Privacy was another matter—she still hoped for more of that. But her family was what it was. They had rules, like they stuck together no matter what. Debbie's parents were strict, and it wasn't easy for Debbie to be herself, to have friends, and to get out.

My maternal grandfather was Richard Paulson. My mother told me his story. He grew up picking cotton in Pearl, Mississippi, along-side his mother. He had to quit school to earn money when he was in the eighth grade. The oldest of eight children, he became the man of the house when his own father, a drunk, walked out on the family. Richard led a tough life with one goal: survival. When he grew up he headed to Illinois, looking for better work. He landed in Granite City, the small town just outside St. Louis that my grandmother, Marilyn, called home. Marilyn was the baby in a family that included seven children. By the time she was six, her father had hit the road, so she barely knew him. Richard and Marilyn had a lot in common. They both craved a bond they didn't get growing up, and they both knew that surviving in this world was hard, and took hard work. Neither had gotten a proper education. Marilyn dropped out of high school for Richard, skipping her senior year. She married him when she was seventeen on October 27, 1950. They shared the notion that a marriage should stay together no matter what. A man should always be in the family. A couple should never, under any circumstances, abandon their children.

Richard had strong opinions about things, too, and he was tough on his children, especially Debbie. One of Richard's younger sisters had gotten pregnant as a teenager, which had been a great source of shame and embarrassment for him. As a result, even at age eighteen, Debbie was not allowed to go out on the weekends without special permission. And she was rarely allowed to go out on both Friday and Saturday nights—she had to pick one activity and stay home the next night with her parents. That was only proper. After all, she was the oldest, and it was up to her to set a good example for the others. But some of the rules made absolutely no sense. For example, Debbie was allowed to close the bathroom door, but she couldn't lock it when she showered. She surely wasn't allowed to say no to her father for any reason. He gave her countless bloody noses with the back of his hand. One time, the last slice of pie in the house had disappeared. Richard lined up the children—Daniel, Daphne, Derek, and Debbie—and demanded to know who had eaten it. No one owned up, so he beat each of them with a belt until one of them claimed guilt. Then that child got dragged down to the basement and was beaten worse.

He might use and abuse his daughters, but no one else would— Richard was fiercely protective of his family. It wouldn't be a surprise to see him sitting on the front porch with a gun if any of his children were ever threatened.

Despite his sternness, Richard was not a larger-than-life personality. He was tall and thin, even though he liked to eat. He was actually a shy, soft-spoken man who didn't have much of a life out-side of his two occupations: cotton picker and local truck driver. He didn't have a lot of social skills, and he was self-conscious about his eighth-grade education. The only time he could really talk was when he drank beer—then he could be funnier, more opinionated, and feel more important. So he started going to the tavern, where he could become a whole new person, more and more often. He'd also drink simply to relax after a hard day of work. To Marilyn's dismay, he'd come home drunk. The drinking repulsed my mother as well. To this day, she can't stand alcohol. She especially cannot stand the smell of beer; it makes her sick.

Richard started sexually abusing Debbie when she was thirteen. Mom didn't tell me about specific incidents, but I overheard the con-versations she had with my dad. Over the years, I picked up on what happened to her. She eventually went public with the abuse in an affidavit to support my legal case.

She stated in an affidavit that Grandpa Paulson had fondled her. He might have abused his other daughters, too; I'm not sure what he did to each one. I do know my mother suffered at his hands from the time she was thirteen until she started dating my father. My mother was so ashamed she didn't even tell her closest sister. Years later, they confessed to each other and found out their father had abused them simultaneously.

When Mom was sixteen, all of the children were sleeping on pal-lets in the living room because their bedrooms were too hot—there was no air conditioning. Richard crept over to her and started fon-dling her.

"Stop it, Dad!" she yelled. "Stop!"

Marilyn woke up and asked her husband what was going on.

"Nothing," he said.

Marilyn asked Debbie for an explanation.

"Dad won't leave me alone. He keeps touching me," she said, crying.

At those words, Richard jerked my mother up from the prone position and hit her as hard as he could in the face. He flew into a violent rage, and Marilyn ran next door to the neighbor's house, where the police were called. Debbie suffered a black eye, dislocated shoulder, and swollen jaw. The police did not question Debbie, and Richard convinced the cops that he had been so violent only because someone had slipped a mickey in his drink at the lodge. Marilyn believed her husband.

But Mom and her siblings knew better. Richard was mean. Marilyn could see the physical violence, but what about the sexual abuse? I know my mother told her about everything when she was an adult and could finally speak the words. Marilyn said, "I wish you would have told me sooner." Marilyn, who was short and pretty, put up with a lot from her husband. The drinking was bad. But the sexual abuse going on under her roof was never acknowledged. She knew about some of the fondling because the girls complained to her, even as kids. But because allegations weren't made—the words "I am being molested" were never spoken—the situation could be quietly ignored. Marilyn always excused Richard's advances, saying, "Dad is just like that."

Marilyn didn't have the time to fuss and fret. By this time, she had five kids to take care of, and when money got tight, she got a job in a department store in Granite City to help out. She was a busy person. My mom says Marilyn would iron clothes in the kitchen while she served her kids breakfast. She washed clothes with a wringer washer long after many mothers had machines. Debbie remembers hearing about how Marilyn climbed to the roof of their two-bedroom house to drive nails into some loose shingles when she was eight months pregnant. She did what she thought needed to be done.

Debbie was ready to get out. And she did. She attracted men easily—she was cute, with her dusty blond hair, green eyes, and thin, womanly body. She's five feet, two inches tall and back then weighed barely a hundred pounds. It's too bad she always thought she was ugly. More proof that she wasn't: she got asked out on dates often, despite being allowed only one date per weekend. Men liked her soft, gentle voice, a voice that was understanding and submissive. That voice could be both quietly disagreeable and flirty. She was feisty and vulnerable wrapped into a kind package. It was no accident that she ended up with my father.

They met when she was eighteen. He was twenty-three, and they both worked at General American Life Insurance in St. Louis. She was a transcriber and copy girl, and he, Thomas Lannert, was on his way to becoming an actuary. My father was sitting with his work buddy when he first saw her across the company cafeteria. He nudged his friend and said, "That's the woman I'm going to marry." After that, he never stopped believing that my mother was beautiful. He used to sit me on his lap and get wistful talking about her. He probably told me the story of meeting her a hundred times. Forever in his mind, other women would pale in comparison to Debbie.

The way she tells the story about the day they met is a bit different: she certainly saw Tom wave at her that day at work, but she smiled back because she thought his friend was cute.

In her eyes, Tom was just okay at first. He wore these baggy flannel pants with pleats in the front. He was distinguished and handsome, but Debbie thought he really needed to learn how to dress. His clothes were put together, but in an old-man kind of way. He always wore a mustache, too, which made him look even older—much older than the mere five years that separated them.

He'd often come by her desk in the copy room and ask her to copy pages for him. He'd also dictate letters to clients and bring them over to Debbie on little red disks for transcription. She'd call him on the company phone when his documents were ready. One day, he asked her if she'd like to have a cup of coffee.

Debbie said no. First of all, she was in the middle of a transcription. And second, she just didn't drink coffee. Five minutes later, my mother told a coworker what had happened. Her friend nudged her, saying, "Maybe you could have said you'd like some hot chocolate some other time." Then it dawned on Debbie that he seemed nice. But then again, she just didn't drink coffee. And what about those ugly pants?

My dad never took no for an answer.

He asked her out a second time, and she told him, "I have a previous commitment." Debbie explained that she had a date with a boy on Friday, and she just couldn't commit to anything on Saturday. It was all true—she just didn't tell him that she had to get special permission from her parents to go out twice on a single weekend. She didn't even know if her parents would allow it if she asked. Debbie told Tom she'd let him know. It turned out that her parents did allow the date, and my parents went to dinner that Saturday evening in August of 1970. She found out he'd already been in the Marines, that his brother had died a few years back, and that he had gone to Tahiti after college graduation. She was impressed. And he was handsome, with deep, shocking blue eyes.

They had been together just three months when Tom asked her to marry him. Debbie had wanted to wait—to get to know him a little better. But he kept pushing the issue. He said he had to get married quickly because he was trying to get his fellowship in the Society of Actuaries. That meant he'd be able to get his license and practice. The society offered the test only every six months, and he had just failed one. He told Debbie he just couldn't keep going on like this because he had to study so much. Flirting with her and worrying about her made him too distracted to pass. He needed to focus for three to four hours every night. He just couldn't afford to fail the next test, he told Debbie. If he failed, it would be her fault, and he had a whole career riding on this.

So they had to get married. Debbie said they could tie the knot in June of 1971. Tom said it had to be that November. She thought they would end up married anyway, so she obliged; their anniversary date was November 27, 1970.

Debbie believed she was in love with him. After all, Tom didn't seem to be anything like Richard Paulson; he was a heck of a lot nicer. Her dad was a country man with backward beliefs and a vicious mean streak; Tom was worldly and smart. He was sweet about things. He had the kind of charisma that could make a person think the sky was not blue but fluorescent pink. Best of all, he knew what he wanted to do with his life. Tom Lannert was more determined and ambitious than any man she'd ever met.

He was a heck of a lot better than what she had grown up with. She couldn't take the fights, housework, drinking, and abuse at home. She had wanted out of her dad's house since she was thirteen. When she found an educated boyfriend, she wrote to her cousin in Mississippi that Tom was her "knight in shining armor."

Her knight was in love with her. But Debbie hadn't fallen madly, head-over-heels for him like so many other women had. Naturally, the more she held back, the more he wanted her. She didn't mind giving him a hard time. For one, she wanted him to wear different clothes. And she didn't like any drinking; she wanted a man who could provide for his family. She voiced her opinion as needed—in her soft, gentle voice. That soft voice meant business.

Her one dream in life was for joy. She hoped to get married and have children and live happily ever after, like in a fairy tale. She admired Tom's intellect and drive; he was looking at five years of difficult actuarial tests. My mother did everything a dutiful wife should do. She picked out stylish suits and took those suits to the dry cleaners. She did their grocery shopping, laundry, and every other chore while Tom pored over math equations. He'd come home from work to their two-bedroom apartment in St. Louis, eat dinner, then sit at his desk to study. Tom would disappear into a world of statistics and financial theory. All she had to do was chores. She quickly became lonely—and bored. When she complained, he told her she should go back to school. At the time, she wasn't interested. She said studying wasn't easy for her like it was for him. Maybe she'd attend college later. In the meantime, there was something else she wanted.

She wanted a baby.

He told her okay. But he pointed out that he had never wanted kids until he met Debbie. He would oblige for her. He reminded her that she was lucky she had said yes to that second date. He said he wouldn't have asked for a third.

Defying her childhood doctor's predictions, my mother had me without complications. She was twenty-one years old when I was born in May of 1972. I was going to be called Lisa Marie, but the Presleys got to that name first. My mom had been lobbying for the name Casey, but my dad said no—I was a baby and not a dog. He really liked the tough, troubled male actor Stacy Keach, but he saw the name *Stacy* as too masculine. It was Grandma Lannert who suggested Stacey with an *e*. She said the prettiest girl in her school went by that name. So the matter was settled. If I'd been a boy, I would've been Scott Thomas.

Even after she got her wish for a baby, my mom was always yearning for something more, never quite knowing what that something was. That yearning was apparent to me from the time I could remember, but only in a foggy little-kid kind of way. I sensed one thing instinctively: Tom loved her more than she loved him.

When I was young, she was a great mom, but I don't think my parents ever had a great marriage. In the beginning, they had stretches where they got along. But they bickered from as far back as I can remember. She was usually upset because he was gone so much, and they fought about his drinking, which continued despite her earlier insistence. I found it all very confusing.

I saw her cook, clean, shop, and do all the typical domestic chores. She didn't go out and party or run around with her friends. She wasn't unhappy then, but she wasn't completely satisfied either. She loved learning, and she liked teaching, too. She taught me the ABCs by age two. She showed me how to write my telephone number and name by age three. I could read before age four. My early education was thanks to her dedication. During her years of being a housewife, Mom made baby books for me, and later for my younger sister, Christy. She took us to those baby swimming classes. I have memories of a water-skiing trip with her when I was four, and Christy was almost three. When I see the photos, I barely recognize us because we look so happy. Momma—that's what I called her—taught us how to be tough and stand up for ourselves. She always said, "Anything boys can do, girls can do better." We had all of her attention in the early years. I wish we could have frozen time and just stayed in that place forever.

My dad, Thomas Lannert, was twenty-six when I was born. He was five feet nine and trim then, though he'd balloon up to three hundred pounds and then back to normal as I grew up. He was strong and in good shape. He was handsome, with a prominent nose and strong chin. He had a warm laugh and was bursting with charm. He wore his sandy brown hair with side chops in the 1980s. He had beautiful blue eyes that could melt or destroy me—it was his choice. He was the fun parent who would throw us way up in the air and catch us when we came back down. He would hold me on his lap for hours—late into the night—just talking and watching TV and being silly. We stayed up late together even when I was really little. He held me all the time when he finished work or studying.

My mom had the kind of intelligence that comes from years of being in charge of her own large—and largely dysfunctional—family. My dad was just plain smart. He made high grades at Missouri State University and was a proud alumnus. He liked to watch Mizzou football games and root for the Tigers. He studied math and decided he'd use it for an actuarial career. An actuary uses complicated math to predict good and bad outcomes, mostly bad. Actuaries help companies save money by figuring out their risks. For example, does it cost more to deal with the risk or to prevent the risk in the first place? Most actuaries, including my father, work for insurance companies. For instance, they compute how many people are likely to die, called mortality tables, or how many houses are likely to burn down in a given time frame. The work is more complicated than that, of course, but he always had a job with good pay. He easily tackled math that was too challenging for most people. He seemed to like his work, but despite his success, this wasn't the career path he had planned.

He wanted to fly planes and helicopters, but he had a condition called night blindness. He would never be allowed to man an aircraft, and he was always resentful of that fact. At age eighteen, he wanted to be like his older brother and join the military. Tom chose the Marines. His brother Bill, the uncle I never met, was in the air force. They both wanted to serve their country during the Vietnam War. They hoped to protect our freedom, show their patriotism, and play with guns. But things went badly. While on active duty, Uncle Bill was swimming recreationally and suffered an aneurysm. He was in a coma for seventy-two days. The family stood by his bedside all that time, completely devastated. No amount of praying could help Bill. He didn't make it.

My father was still in basic training, and he really didn't want to be there. He was discovering that the military wasn't everything he thought it would be. He just didn't like living by other people's rules. As he prepared for Bill's funeral, he decided he wouldn't go back to basic training.

The funeral was not without drama. The whole family was there. After the burial, my paternal grandmother, Una Mae Lannert, uttered these words to Tom: "Bill was always your father's favorite son."

Maybe she hadn't meant to be evil, but her words planted evil seeds in him. I believe she just wanted Tom to love her more than he loved his dad. My grandparents' marriage was deeply troubled. I can only guess that these were not the first unhealthy, unloving words my grandmother said to my dad. And it wasn't the first time Tom felt completely let down by his father.

As far back as I remember, my grandfather, Ken Lannert, was a nice, loving man. Like Mae, he grew up in Eminence, Missouri, a southern town with fewer than five hundred people. He was an only child, and short, but he was not poor. Quite the contrary—he was a brilliant, educated man from a decent background.

Mae was several years older than Ken, and she was several inches taller. At age twenty-four, Mae married Ken after his mother passed away. Grandma Lannert once told my mother that she married Ken because she felt sorry for him. She pitied him for losing his mom and for being so short. But Mae also radically changed her quality of life when she married Kenneth Lannert. She had grown up the oldest of eight kids in a two-room cabin with a dirt floor. Once she married my grandfather, she became well-to-do. As a young woman, she wore tasteful yet saucy black dresses. She was always stylish, and her hair was always done. She even got herself the most popular house of the time. It was common back then for couples to buy kit homes from stores like Sears and Roebuck and build their own dwellings. Mae and Ken spent $12,000 for their red brick cottage and settled in a nice St. Louis neighborhood called St. John. They finished it by 1941 or 1942. I stayed in that house many times; it was a place I loved dearly.

In that home, my grandparents' marriage was rife with sadness and problems. Their first child, Mary, arrived with the umbilical cord wrapped around her neck twice. If the death of their daughter wasn't heartbreaking enough, Mae couldn't hide her feelings—or lack thereof—for Ken. She told my mother she had never been in love with him.

She gave him a hard time about his job, though it provided them with money. Ken was an engineer. He designed assembly line machines for Hostess and other big companies. He traveled every Sunday through Friday evening, as he had to be on site while his creations were being built, used, and serviced. In the limited time he was home, he headed into the basement to tinker. He made transmitters and radios and other gadgets in the basement of the brick house he built himself. He smoked pipes filled with cherry tobacco.

He and Mae lived in that house until they died.

Mae couldn't get used to Ken's work schedule. Raising two boys was hard, and she didn't like doing it alone all week long. She'd tell her sons that Ken could've chosen to work closer to their home in St. Louis, but instead wanted to be away from them and to travel a lot. Tom loved his father, and he wanted love in return. He felt he wasn't getting it, so he grew up resenting Ken tremendously. It was bad enough that Ken wasn't around for track meets and baseball games. Mae's words, he chose a job requiring travel, stung worse.

While Ken was away, Mae believed he was cheating on her. She was probably right. A family story is that when Ken had a bad car accident, there was another lady in the car with him. He defended himself, saying he was just taking her home from a party. No one believed that, though. Mae would sometimes threaten to leave Ken, but Tom would tell her to stay. Tom told Mae he would never speak to her again if she ever left Ken.

My mother believes that Grandma Lannert did a lot of psychological damage to my father. Mae didn't intend to enrage my father or make him a monster. She wasn't a consciously cruel person; she was just desperate for her sons to love her. From the rumors I've always heard, her marriage certainly wasn't satisfying. And for whatever reason, she needed Tom to be totally dependent on her. She smothered him, and he was her baby. Tom grew up mad at his father and spoiled by his mother.

I don't know why my grandmother did the things she did—I saw only the wonderful side of her. Grandma Lannert was the sweetest person; she was like an older, wiser mother and I loved her very much. I called her Mee Maw and my grandpa Paw Paw.

When I was older, I recognized her fierce and frequent manipulative streak. To maintain her control, she would turn family members against each other. She'd bad-mouth loved ones behind their backs. She especially didn't like my mother after she left my dad. Through all the years, I never heard my father speak badly of Mee Maw. He didn't fault her. He didn't question her. He believed what she said and cared what she thought.

Tom's parents were complicated, and that might be why he grew up with little respect for authority. On paper, he was an excellent student, member of the student council, and top runner on the varsity track team. But in his 1964 senior yearbook, there are references to partying and mischief in almost all of his classmates' signatures.

One guy wrote: "Thanks for barfing all over my cabin. Keep blowing off."

Someone named Dianne was clearly dating him. Among other flirtations, she wrote, "Here's hoping that you stay with your word and stay off the booze . . . Take up women. I'll clue you in, they're a lot more fun."

My dad wanted everything to seem okay from the outside—he wanted teachers and adults to think he was squeaky clean. His classmates' opinions show a very different side of my father.

He wasn't just being a kid; some of his troubles were serious. In his senior year, he started hanging around with the wrong crowd—one boy in particular was bad news. He tried to get Tom to steal cars and commit petty crimes. He and Tom got into a fight one night. Apparently, Tom wanted out; he didn't want to be associated with the gang anymore. This one boy wouldn't allow Tom to leave that easily. He continued to bully Tom to do things he didn't want to do. Dad got sick of it. He swiped a gun from his parents' attic and threatened the boy with it at their next confrontation. They fought. My father shot the kid square in the shoulder and then ran away. He ditched the gun somewhere, hiding the evidence so his actions wouldn't come back to haunt him. As my dad suspected, the kid never reported the incident. Years later, after he was married, his parents confronted him about the missing gun. He acted like he didn't know what they were talking about. But that night, he told my mother the real story. That was the first time she was truly scared of her husband.

My dad told me about the incident, too. When I was younger, he'd use it as a warning to hang out with the good kids and stay on a straight path. When I was older, when things got really bad, Dad told me he had shot one kid, and he'd be happy to shoot me, too. There were two sides to my father, Good Dad and Bad Dad.

He told me how hard his life was growing up. He complained that his dad was never home. He told me that his father liked his brother better. Tom hated Ken sometimes. He hated Ken because he loved him—if that makes sense. My father held on to deep resentment while constantly striving for his father's approval. Ken rarely gave it. He was kind, but he did not know how to praise, acknowledge, or pat his son on the back. Tom could be an actuary ten times over, and it would still not be quite enough for Ken. At least, not in my father's eyes.

Tom did not think he could please Ken by staying in the military, so after his brother died, Tom left. My father used the sole surviving son military rule to get himself discharged. No questions were asked, and Tom was no longer a Marine. Ken called my dad The Baron, and the sarcasm must've stung. My dad would never be a pilot.

Once out of the Marines, my dad was a mess over Bill's death. To make him feel better, his parents bought him a cool convertible, a Plymouth Barracuda. But a car didn't do the trick. Tom took off for Tahiti, where he lost all control. He was a big drunk there, he admitted to my mother. He came home only when his visa expired and the country kicked him out. Then my father accepted the car, cleaned up his act, and enrolled at Mizzou. The rest is history.

I can remember Dad studying for the rigorous, infamously difficult actuarial exams, which he had to pass to get his license. Once he did, he immediately found jobs and worked his way up to partner in various actuarial companies. His career kept him out at all hours of the day and night. At least, that's what he told us—it was business that made him late all the time. I missed him terribly when he was gone.

I was a little girl, and I didn't know about his past. I just knew he was my daddy who hugged and kissed me. He lavished me with attention, and I could see no wrong in my father.

He was just *it* for me.

Happy Baby

I have a favorite photo album from when I was young. The cover is bright poppy red, and the edges are so dog-eared that brown cardboard pokes out underneath. The requisite words *Photo Album* are written in gold, 1970s-style cursive script that reminds me of *Charlie's Angels*. For long stretches of time, I haven't looked at the pictures. Sometimes I want to walk down memory lane, and sometimes I want to run away from it. Whether I look at the album or not, I keep it with me now that I'm out.

Like me, it's getting old. Some of the photos are crooked and loose because the sticky backing is worn out. Some of the plastic coverings are bent, scratched, or torn. I like them this way.

On days I decide to open the album, I can't help but wonder what might have happened to that blue-eyed baby—me—if things had been different. There were so many twists and turns as I grew up. What if, just one time, something bad that happened had been something good instead? Were there different options for my future? Could I have been an athlete for a college track team? That would have been fun. Maybe I would have become an English teacher. Would I have had a family? I could've had two kids, maybe four, by now. I'll never know.

I can't help but be wistful. Being wishful is a lot better than being angry about circumstances I cannot change. Acceptance isn't easy, but it's the only way. Thank God I was a happy baby, and I didn't have to wish for anything then.

I was a peanut of a kid. In one photo, I'm wearing a purple, ironed shirtdress decorated with duckies and lace around the edges. I'm so young that I must be propped up by a hidden hand or pillow. I'm wearing white patent leather shoes over thick, warm baby tights and have a great big smile. A baby's face can't lie. I look at the picture and see all the love and joy I felt. My chubby cheeks are filled with happiness, and I'm sure they were kissed often. It's almost like I remember it, and I can cling to the memory and feel it. But of course, I was only six months old. I'm just guessing.

During those years, in the early 1970s we lived in Cedar Rapids, Iowa. My mom loved being a mother. She carried me with her everywhere. I was bald except for a white-blond ring right on the top of my head. She'd brush it up and keep me in a kewpie curl, always. She gave up only when at age one I finally grew golden hair. It flew away from my head in soft, opinionated wisps. In one picture of me at eight months or so, she looks like she's dancing with me in our house in Iowa. My momma smiled wide as she carried me with her left arm, her right hand holding mine. Her long, straight blond hair matched the strands in my kewpie curl. The shade of our skin—pale and golden all at once—was exactly the same. Our smiles were similar, but the corners of my mouth turned down just slightly—a trait I inherited from Grandma Lannert. Our clothes also matched. She wore a blue dress with red and white dots. My pressed cotton outfit was patchwork-blue with white dots and yellow trim. She used to sew many of my clothes herself, and probably these outfits, too.

Maybe taken on the same day, there's another picture of me in that same patchwork dress. My dad looked so young and gentle as he held me out in front of him by my armpits. My hands waved out in the air, flapping in giggles. My smile, once again, was so much like my mom's. His expression was soft, and he looked like he might be melting. He had brown hair that was parted on the right side and combed neatly. His skin was perfect—smooth and healthy. His eyes were as blue as the ocean; they were clean and calm like a quiet lagoon. I can tell he was sober. I loved him when he looked like that—when he was so crystal clear.

My father hadn't been big on having kids, but he changed his mind once I came home from the hospital. He was proud of his baby. As far back as I can remember, he could hardly put me down when he got home from work.

I was his Little Kewpie. That's what they called me for my first few years.

Grandma Lannert also doted on me. I was her first grandchild, and she bought me more baby clothes than one kid could wear. She made a lot of them, too; she loved to sew. Mee Maw and Paw Paw meant the world to me then. They constantly fussed over me, more than the Paulson side of the family did. My mother had four siblings who started having kids at about the same time. The Paulsons helped Mom as much as they could, but they had other grandkids. The Lannerts had a lot more money to spoil us with. They helped us with down payments on our houses. My parents were just starting out, but when we lived in Iowa, Missouri, and Kansas, we always had nice places. I remember big one- or two-story homes, usually four or five bedrooms, always with basements.

Grandma and Grandpa's most important purchase, to me at least, was a Winnie-the-Pooh play set I loved—and eventually shared with my baby sister. The set included a vinyl chair, tiny table, and toy chest. It was white with gold and red checked Winnie-the-Pooh bears. I still dream about that play set, maybe because I'm next to it in so many of these old photographs.

From everything my mother says, all my needs were met and then some. Babies want to be dry, fed, and hugged, and I know that I was. I know for sure because I remember my mom taking such good care of my sister, and I remember how warm and close we all felt.

Life was wonderful then, and I still get lost in the thoughts of that time. As a very young child, I could mentally hold on to comfort. I could reach for my parents. I could soothe myself with the blankies and stuffed animals they gave me. If they fought when I was a toddler, I don't remember it. That stuff happened later. My babyhood was about bonding. We were a family there for a minute, through thick and thin. If my dad had a dark side, if he drank too much, I didn't know. My mother shielded me from his moods—she did this for years, while she was still around. She would send me off somewhere or give me something special to play with. Ignorance is bliss. I even like to think that my dad didn't drink much at that time. In my mind, he was a dad who was into his kids and wife—instead of alcohol.

A New Baby

I was two years old when Christy came along, and I was a proud big sister. We'd sit in our momma's lap together, and I'd hold her hand. I'd hold her hand as often as she'd let me, and my photo album is proof. In one picture, we're standing in front of the wood-paneled door to our house in Kansas—we had moved—and I'm leading her somewhere in my green and red polyester shirt with matching pants. She's wearing a purple polyester pantsuit, both sewn by either Mom or Grandma Lannert. She has chubby little cheeks just like mine. We both have the exact same little mole on the right side of our faces. I loved Christy with all my heart.

As she grew into a toddler, I'd hug her all the time. Christy was just so cute. Her blond hair was whiter than mine, and it matched her lightning personality. She never had a kewpie curl because she was born with thick hair all over her head. I had been kind of bald. She looked vibrant and healthy and perfect, even then. She smiled all the time, like nothing ever bothered her. She was so pretty that I called her my little doll. I'd just hold her and kiss her. That is, until she stopped letting me. She started shrugging and pushing me off. I was smothering her and making her feel like a little baby.

As much as I tried, we didn't always play together. We were two years apart, and some things—like our matching dolly carriages— were fun to play with as a team. But I didn't want to play with the toy xylophone with her; I had outgrown it. And she wasn't interested in my big-girl books. We played together half the time, and then we'd go our separate ways. I needed to be outside with other kids; Christy was more independent and often preferred to play alone. When we were together, one of our favorite things to do was make up games. For instance, we would put blankets on the floor and drive each other around on them for hours.

Sometimes, we could just be around each other doing nothing. Being sisters was fun, and it was enough—usually.

We'd also get on each other's nerves. When we fought, it was usually because I was bugging her. I was older, so I could grab a toy from her easily. I'd childishly slap her sometimes, like when she took my crayons. She could get even, though. She'd swipe my toys and zip down the hallway with them just for fun. I'd have to chase her to get my necklace or finger puppet back. She did that to me a lot.

Then, she got big enough to fend for herself and fight back. And it hurt. I decided I wasn't going to bug Christy anymore. Besides, she was my sister, and I didn't want us to hurt each other.

Davenport, Iowa

Iowa was awesome. I was in preschool and felt smart because I knew how to write my name. Life was pretty fantastic at that age. I loved my little sister. I even had a little boyfriend named Bobby. My mom and his mom were close friends, so we saw each other often. He wasn't really my boyfriend, but our moms would say stuff like that. We would hold hands, and the grown-ups would go on about how cute we were. I have mostly fond memories of that time. Mostly.

One day we were outside playing while our moms were inside doing mom stuff. Bobby didn't like whatever I was playing with, so he pushed me. I got mad. He had no right to push me; we were supposed to be having fun together. So I decided enough was enough, and I hit him as hard as my preschool self could. I think it was more of a shove than a punch, but either way, it was enough to scare Bobby and make him leave me alone.

What I remember most is how my mom reacted. She was so proud of me. She was glad I hadn't been scared. She said to his mom and the two of us, "I'm glad Stacey won't take anything off of a boy." She really believed that, as if shoving a boy would be the answer if a male attacked me.

No one was mad for long that day. The moms stayed friends, and so did Bobby and I. But I felt more powerful. My mom bought me a figurine with a girl holding a bat. At the bottom, it stated, "Anything boys can do, girls can do better."

I really didn't fight much. Mostly, I was just a little kid who liked to take bubble baths with Mr. Bubble—I could make the biggest bubble wigs in the bathtub that my mom had ever seen. Sometimes, Christy and I would take baths together. That stopped when I realized that she peed in the water.

We dressed alike, and we felt so pretty. Mee Maw bought us matching Easter outfits every year. And anytime we had special photos taken, she made sure we had new clothes. She loved to buy us things. We would get anything we wanted—toy phones, books, baby dolls, whatever. All we had to do was ask. She was so sweet to Christy and me. She was retired then, and wasn't involved in a lot of things outside of family. She just took care of Ken and watched *Wheel of Fortune*. I'm sure there was more to her life than that, but that's all I remember. She seemed to live for her grandchildren—and my dad. She spoiled us. Mee Maw knew Mom wouldn't let us have sugary cereal because we had cavities in our baby teeth, so when we got to her house, we'd get to choose a box from those six-packs of assorted sweet cereals. It was heaven. I loved visiting her, and I would do anything for her. I did do everything for her later, when I was a teenager.

Whenever we saw her, she'd say, "Oh, here are my baby girls!"

Grandpa didn't say much, and I don't remember him as the tanned, bespectacled, mechanical genius that he was. He had a damaging stroke before I turned five. Grandma Lannert had to devote her life to taking care of him. I don't think she liked it, but she didn't concern us with the situation as much as she did my parents. She complained to them.

My dad also liked sugary cereal, but unlike Grandma Lannert, he would not give us any. He ate Trix, but it was off limits to us.

Christy and I would beg him, "Let us have Trix!"

"Nope," he'd say from his spot on his bright orange velour chair.

We'd jump up and down. "Trix are for kids!"

"Trix are for Dad." He was smiling, but he wasn't kidding.

We girls got Kix instead. That was the bland, healthy stuff shaped like little balls. But sometimes, Mom would bring home a box of Trix for Dad, and we would get to it before either of them found out.

When he got home, he'd complain, "Who's been in my Trix?"

We would giggle and hide.

At least he let us eat his popcorn sometimes—but not out of his bowl. His famous bowl was the biggest, yellowest piece of Tupperware you can imagine. When he made popcorn, it was special. He stood over the stove shaking the metal pan as the kernels hopped around. He popped it on the stove using lots of oil and topped it with this salty, buttery, bright orange seasoning. When Dad made popcorn, he was happy.

My mom bought him one of those air poppers. She'd try to get him to use it because it was healthier. He didn't want any part of it; he wanted to pop it himself, and *shake it, shake it, shake it*. Sometimes he was just so much fun.

Mom was fun, too, but she was the serious parent. She was responsible for discipline because that's the way Dad thought it should be. When he was a kid, his mom had done the punishing while his father traveled, so Dad thought that discipline was the mother's job. Mom corrected us and did the spanking, rarely Dad. Instead, he was goofy. He'd take the whole box of Trix and mix it with his popcorn in his yellow bowl. Then he'd tease us with it. Eventually, he'd get out two little bowls, and we'd get a treat, too.

It was common for him to come home, have dinner, and then relax and eat popcorn while watching sports. Football and baseball were his picks; he didn't care for basketball. He spent Sunday afternoons in front of the TV. He loved his college team and other Midwestern teams. I sat on his lap and watched with him. We'd talk for hours and hours. Christy was usually with Mom; she'd sit still and color when I was with my dad.

If he wasn't watching TV, Dad was down on the floor playing with me. He wouldn't even take off his work clothes first—he'd be in his polo shirt and brown pants from a nice store called Famous Barr. He always wore the same leather loafers. Sometimes, he wore suits when he was working. I remember him shopping at a store called Grandpa Pigeon's, which despite the name, was surprisingly nice. The only time he dressed down was on the weekends. He wore ringer

T-shirts and shorts that were frayed on the ends and splattered with paint. He often wore his Marines jacket when he wasn't working. He usually looked more put together than other dads.

When I was a baby, I had a little ghost on a stick that he'd wiggle behind my head. He'd throw me high up in the air until I got too big; then he'd just hold me. I have a photo of him looking totally handsome and happy—baby Christy is sleeping in the crook of his right arm; I'm on the left, with his left arm around me, and I'm thrilled. I have both hands pressed against my cheeks. I'm smiling because I'm with Daddy.

Becoming a Tiger

Before I started kindergarten, we packed up and moved from Iowa to Manchester, Missouri. I was sad to leave Bobby, but Mom said I would make friends and learn to swim. She told me about the community pool that was just a few short blocks from our new ranch-style home. She also promised to paint my new room any color I wanted, and I told her I wanted purple. We had a new dog, a white toy poodle named Max, and I was in love with him. Of course, Mom told me Max was moving with us and would have a big fenced-in yard for playing. As sad as I was to leave the old place, I was even more excited about something new.

Our new house was beautiful, and I quickly made friends with a girl named Jennifer. Mom spent most of her time redecorating our new home, and that gave me plenty of time to play with my new buddy. I would get mad when Christy wanted to join us because she was just a baby who would mess up Candy Land and Chutes and Ladders. So Christy spent more time with Mom, helping her with all the household jobs.

Jenny and I even rode the same bus to kindergarten. We had the best bus driver in the entire world. His name was George, and he was at least sixty years old with shocking white hair, a wrinkled face, and kind blue eyes. He wore a uniform, a white oxford shirt and black pants, every day even though it was not required. He knew all kinds of kid music, and he would lead his troupe of five-year-olds in song as if we were his choir. My favorite was "The Wheels on the Bus." We could get loud, but George would just smile and sing.

Life was as ideal as it possibly could be, but then I began to have trouble with a boy on the bus. His name was Butch and he was mean to me every day. George would yell at him to stop, but he wouldn't. He would sit one seat in front of me and throw things at me, or sit behind me and pull my hair. I started wearing glasses, and one day, he threw a football in my face. It gave me a black eye. When I came home crying to Mom, she sat me down and told me, "Anything boys can do, girls can do better. Don't let any boy hurt you." I looked at my figurine and vowed to stand up for myself next time.

The next time came faster than I expected. The following day, Butch sat right in front of me and started up again. He leaned over the back of his seat and pulled one of my pigtails. I told him to stop, or I was going to hit him. He scoffed, shook his head, and leaned over to pull again. I cocked my arm back, balled up my fist, and let one fly. I caught him square in his eye. Butch started crying.

Terrified of what I'd done and whether I'd get in trouble, I looked into the rearview mirror, and I saw George's kind eyes looking straight at me. He smiled and nodded his head. I got the silent message that George was proud of me. But I still worried that I'd get into trouble.

Mom was waiting for me at the bus stop, and I immediately told her everything that had happened. George was still at the curb, and Mom stepped onto the bus to speak to him for a minute. When she returned, she took my hand and walked me home.

"Am I in trouble?" I asked.

"No, but we have to tell your father." She squeezed my hand, but I wasn't reassured.

I thought, *Uh-oh.*

I waited in the living room for Dad to come home. I was terrified. How would he react? Would he be mad? Would he spank me? He had never spanked me before. Why wasn't he home yet? He was usually home by now; what was taking so long?

He came home late and happy, with the faint smell of something heavy, sweet, and increasingly familiar on his breath. He scooped me up into his arms and hugged the giggles out of me. Mom came into the room, and I put on my somber face again.

"Tom, Stacey has something she needs to tell you," Mom said. He smiled.

I was still in his arms as I said, "I hit Butch today on the bus."

"Where did you hit him?" He put on his serious voice.

"In the eye." I was trembling. I felt bad about it.

He lowered me down to the ground and said, "Show me how."

I balled my fist, pulled back, and swung into the air. Then I looked into Daddy's face for a reaction.

"You are quite the little tiger, aren't you?" he said, smiling. I looked at Mom, and she smiled, too. We all just stood there smiling. I sighed heavily, very relieved.

Then the doorbell rang. Butch was standing on our front porch with his parents. He had a bright blue black eye. Mom and I went out on the porch to talk to them while Dad changed clothes. Mom draped her arm over my shoulder. With this new development, I still didn't know if I'd get in trouble or not. His parents wanted me disciplined; I could tell by their faces. Butch's Mom said something so low that I couldn't quite hear it, but my mom wasn't intimidated.

She said, "I'm not going to punish Stacey for standing up for herself."

His parents were hot, but there wasn't much they could do. They hadn't come looking for a fight; they just wanted to make sure I got scolded. And I didn't.

Whew.

Mom went on to tell Butch's mom: "George says your child picks on Stacey all the time. I'm proud of her this time." She gave me a little squeeze—a half hug—and I beamed. I couldn't help but smile and look up at her gratefully. I felt strong and brave and thankful. Both of my parents were proud of me.

When we walked back into the house my new nickname was born, "There's my Little Tiger. Come give me a hug," Daddy said.

I ran into my father's arms.

During the summer of that year I had another "fight," but this time it was with a girl. Her name was Kendra, and she was horrible. She was big and mean, and she called me names like butt face. I knew she wanted to fight me. This was bad. I ran into our house looking for backup. Maybe Christy could help me—she was especially feisty. Or at the very least, my parents might be able to tell me what I should do. It turned out that Christy was out with Mom, but at least I found my daddy. He was sleeping on the couch. I thought it would be okay to wake him up because Kendra's desire to whip my butt was important.

I shook him frantically.

"This girl outside says she's going to beat me up." I was panting and scared. I hadn't meant to start stuff with her—that's the kind of thing my sister did—but I didn't want to be a soft little flower petal either. I wanted Kendra off my back.

"Go fight her," he told me, still groggy. He seemed amused. I did not think this was funny.

"I can't do that," I said. I thought, *Do I hit her or slap her or kick her?* I had no clue, but none of the options sounded like fun to me. I did know how to mouth off, though, and that's exactly what had gotten me into hot water in the first place.

"Throw something at her, Tiger," he said as he rolled off the couch. I followed him into the kitchen where he handed me an egg.

I went back outside and threw that egg right at her—or somewhere in her vicinity. I thought I had been cool and tough, but actually, the egg had lobbed through the air like a badminton birdie. I totally missed Kendra, but I was proud of my effort. The only bad thing was, she was even more enraged. I decided it was best to run inside and hide.

A few minutes later, Kendra's dad came over, yelling as he knocked on our door. Gearing up for a fight of his own, my dad talked tough as he stalked to the front door. He told me to stay out of sight. I hid around the corner, expecting things to get ugly fast. To my surprise, though, he backed down quickly, apologized for the incident, and put on his charm. He talked Kendra's dad down, and they left our lawn.

When I asked him why he didn't fight, he told me Kendra's father was the assistant coach for St. Louis' football team. The man was very big, kind of like Kendra.

"Can I still be a tiger even though I lost?" I asked.

My dad answered, "There is one thing I have learned from the Mizzou Tigers, kid. Sometimes you may lose, but in your heart you are still a Tiger. You, Stacey, have the heart of a tiger." I think my dad and I both felt whipped, but we felt whipped together. We were a team, and that made everything okay.

The First Cracks

I truly believed we had an idyllic life in Manchester. We were happy, and I felt secure. I barely noticed the tiny cracks starting to show in the foundation of my family.

The first small break came when a police officer delivered my father to the front door. My father was boyish and happy even though he had just wrapped his car around a tree on a road we called Dead Man's Curve. He made a joke out of the crash.

He said, "A banana tree jumped right out in front of me. Good thing my car was there to save me."

I laughed because there weren't any banana trees on Dead Man's Curve. There weren't any banana trees in Missouri. My mother wasn't smiling as the tow truck pulled up with Dad's smashed Buick.

"My God, Tom, you should be dead," she said. Mom examined Dad and then the car. She was in disbelief at the wreckage. He should not have been able to walk away from that accident, but his body was so loose from the alcohol that he slithered right out of the car. He didn't even remember what had happened.

"He *should* be dead," said the police officer at our doorstep. "His blood alcohol level is so high that it would kill most people." My father laughed harder. Drunk driving laws weren't enforced back then, and the officer only issued my father a citation since no one was hurt. While he wasn't likely to get in legal trouble, he was definitely in Deborah trouble.

After the officer left, my parents fought the rest of the night. Daddy said he had to drink—he was out with the guys from work.

In a slurred voice, he explained, "This is the only way I can get promotions. I have to play the game."

I heard the whole thing, and I took his side; I didn't know any better. I thought Mom was nagging Dad because that's what he told me she was doing. She didn't say anything to me about the fight, but he would go on and on. "Tiger, it's not a big deal," he'd say, sitting on his chair. "Everything is going to be fine. Come here."

He came home two nights later with a brand new car—the bananamobile. He said he chose that big yellow station wagon with wood panels because it was a banana tree that destroyed his old Buick. "Look at this car, it will be perfect for towing the boat," he said with pride. Christy and I were excited. We ran to the car, exploring it inside and out. He was my superhero.

When we drove down Dead Man's Curve, Mom would shudder while Christy and I made a game out of guessing which one was the dreaded banana tree. It wasn't hard to figure out; it was the tree that looked like a Buick had been wrapped around it.

After the accident it seemed as if Mom began nagging Dad about his drinking more often. Every night, gauging the time he came home was like a litmus test. Would he be on time? Would he smell like alcohol? Some nights he passed inspection; some nights he didn't.

Dad and I began to bond more. On the nights he failed the test, Mom would barely speak to him. But I did. He would change out of his suit, and we would hang out together in his chair watching TV, hopefully eating popcorn. He would ask about my day and then tell me about his. I became closer to him and more distant from my mother.

My mother gave our dog, Max, away to her grandmother. I could not stand my great-grandma. She yelled at me and smelled like cigarettes. I did like her husband, George, probably because he had the same name as my favorite bus driver. He was my step-great-grandfather and not blood related. I didn't know what that meant, but I thought it was weird that I was supposed to call him by his first name. I hated the thought of Max going to live with them, and I didn't understand. I blamed Mom for giving him away, but I thought it was my fault.

I didn't want to use the bathroom at night because I had to walk past my parents' room. I was scared of waking them up and getting yelled at, so I peed in the air conditioning vent in my room. Mom smelled the urine and blamed it on Max. First, she banned him from my room. But she still smelled the pee. I didn't fess up; I was too scared I'd get in trouble. I also didn't want them to know I was terrified of waking them up. I don't remember why I didn't want to disturb them in the night.

All I understood at the time was that I begged her not to give the dog away—Max meant the world to me. But she got rid of him anyway. Sometimes, I was starting to see Mom as mean.

Twenty years later, I found out the truth. Mom wasn't mad about the air conditioning vents no matter who peed in them. She gave Max away because my dad would come home drunk, trip over my excited dog, and then kick Max. Mom felt awful when she heard the dog yelping in the hallway, and she wanted the dog to be safe. Meanwhile, there I was, almost eight years old, secretly hating her for taking my dog away.

Photo Album

In my photo album, I see pictures of a smiling, awkward, blond kid who laughed all the time.

In one photo, I am busy doing my favorite thing: waterskiing. Short and skinny and young. I am wearing my red life jacket. My white skis are held together with a huge black band so my legs will stay together. You can see that I was soaking up the rays of sun and smiling genuinely about it. My heart was happy. I remember how proud and exhilarated I was when I could finally stay up on those skis for ten whole minutes before falling down.

I learned how to water-ski when I was four. My parents bought matching life vests for the whole family—red with black toggles to close. Suiting up in that vest was one of the highlights of the summer. So was shopping for skis. We tried on so many pairs that the salespeople would try to hide their aggravation.

We loved going on trips in Dad's yellow bananamobile. Mom bought travel games that Christy and I played in the backseat. Sometimes we'd yell and scream and fuss at each other—the best fun was when we were cutting up.

We'd get threats from the front seat. Dad would warn, "Don't you make me pull over this car." But he was all talk on vacation.

We knew a fun vacation week was starting when the tarp came off Old Red. Our boat had red stripes, and it was just big enough for four people. Mom and Dad would keep us quiet in the car by telling us to watch Old Red. The boat dangled from the hitch on the back of the bananamobile, and they said it would fall off if we looked away. We caught on to that scam quickly. They also pulled "the quiet game" to see who could be silent for the longest. One of us would break after barely two minutes. Then we'd move on to the license plate game, seeing who could spot the most tags from the most states. When all else failed, Mom took out a piece of paper, and we played hangman or squares. She made dots, and we got points for connecting them.

Every year, we vacationed at Table Rock Lake in the Ozark Mountains, at a resort called Lone Pine. They had a pool, lots of fishing, a sandy lakeside, and tons of games. As I got older, I played shuffleboard and badminton.

Then there was the waterskiing. We'd get most excited when Old Red went in. We'd swish around in the boat asking to put on our skis, but we weren't allowed to until we had a thick, gooey layer of zinc oxide smeared on our noses. Mom and Dad had matching white beaks. We'd laugh at other people's white noses because we'd forget about our own. Dad manned the steering wheel of Old Red wearing his aviator sunglasses and a huge smile. We drank grape soda on vacation, and Dad drank beer.

When we first learned how to water-ski, Mom skied behind us. Both parents would check to make sure our life jackets were secure before Mom slipped into the water, and Dad lowered us into her arms. She would guide us to the rope and ski behind us until we were ready to stand on our own. When we fell, Dad would circle back to get us, and Mom would be right there in half a second.

We couldn't be on vacation all year long, though. Daily life continued to crumble—very slowly at first. There was another big, bad moment. I wish I could forget it. Mom had made a huge spaghetti dinner, and Dad was late again. We waited more than an hour for him to show up. Finally, we ate without him. She put all of the food away and started cleaning the house while Christy and I went into the living room to watch TV.

When Dad arrived home, purple-faced from gin martinis, he told Mom, "I want my dinner."

She wasn't looking for a fight with him. When he was drunk, she never won. If she told him later what he'd said or done, he wouldn't remember it; he wouldn't even believe that anything had happened.

Mom replied to him, "Go get it yourself." She told him where to find the French bread and pasta and sauce. Then she continued to run the sweeper. Christy and I had bad feelings in our stomachs. We pretended like we didn't know what was going on at first. We stayed fixated on the television.

That's when he pulled out the handle of the vacuum cleaner and bent it like a boomerang. Then he took out the bread, noodles, and sauce from the refrigerator. He heaved the food across the kitchen, hitting the tile backsplash behind the faucet. The glass dishes broke the tiles, and bits of our dinner splattered all over the room.

Next, he went for the ceramic fruit bowl on the kitchen table. He hurled it into the wall. My mom called Grandma Lannert, who at that time lived twenty minutes away.

"Mae," she said, "Tom's come home angry because I won't put dinner on the table. He's gone crazy, and I'm bringing the girls over." My grandmother talked him down on the phone. Meanwhile, Mom gathered me and Christy together, and we stayed at Grandma Lannert's for a few days. I didn't like what had happened. I was confused. How could the daddy I loved so much act so crazy? Maybe he was just having a bad day. Maybe, like Dad said, Mom had done something to make him behave that way.

I knew he'd been wrong. But it was over, I hoped. I just wanted Mom to stop talking about it and move on. I missed Daddy terribly. I was so lonesome for him that I became angry at Mom for taking him away.

Dad came to visit us at Grandma's. His mission was clear—he was there to sweet-talk Mom into coming home. Grandma convinced Dad to slow down on the drinking, and she talked Mom into giving him another chance.

When we did go back, we were making some real changes. We packed up the bananamobile and moved to Kansas City, Kansas.

We were going to start all over—fresh.

Kansas City

Life in Kansas started out great. We reconnected as a family and put the pain aside. We bought a beautiful two-story house that was so big we needed to buy more furniture. I picked out a cool Holly Hobbie bedroom set, and Christy wanted Mickey Mouse. We each had our own walk-in closet.

Shortly after moving, I outgrew my banana-seat bike. I was seven years old when Mom took me shopping for a new one. I begged her for a big, shiny ten-speed, but Mom thought it might be too grown-up for me. She said we'd have to ask Dad. That evening, he said yes, and I jumped up and down like it was Christmas.

Dad couldn't assemble it fast enough. When it was finally ready, I took it for its maiden voyage down our suburban street. The wind rushed through my hair as I pedaled and shifted gears. I was clueless about the gears, but I thought I could figure them out. Instead, I lost control and veered into the grass. The only problem was a large boulder five feet from my front tire. I tried not to panic; I simply slammed my feet backward to brake. But the brakes weren't on the pedals; they were on the handlebars.

I yelled, "Shit." Dad used that word when he was frustrated, and this seemed like an appropriate time for me to say it, too. I crashed headfirst into the huge rock. Mom and Dad ran down the street toward me. I wanted badly to cry, but I didn't because I had a big-girl bike, and big girls don't cry.

"Oh my God, are you okay? Maybe the bike is too much." Mom checked me from head to toe.

I lifted my chin and said, "I'm fine. I love my bike. Please let me keep it!"

Dad just laughed and rubbed my head. "Way to go, Crash."

I was afraid that Crash would be my new nickname, but luckily it wasn't. We walked the bike home, and Dad put the chain back on. We ended up putting that chain back on several times that summer. That summer was easy; it was magical.

Things were so good that I almost didn't notice when Dad started coming home late again in the fall. He wasn't around as much for me. Meanwhile, I had to quietly accept that Mom and Christy spent hours together cooking or doing crafts, and I didn't want to do those activities. So I went off on my own, playing in the backyard or riding my bike. I looked for other kids on the block to play games with or race.

If Dad was home, I would hang out with him. On the weekends, I liked to watch football or *Dr. Who* with Daddy. It seemed like—more and more—we were going separate ways. Mom and Christy hung out together. Dad and I went into the basement.

Looking back, Christy and I probably had the most functional relationship in our family. Sure, I was jealous of her because Mom gave her so much attention. Sure, we loved and hated each other in the routine business of being sisters. But at least we always knew where we stood. With Christy, there was no long story, and nothing got too complicated like it did with Mom and Dad. She was just Christy. When we fought, it was usually over one thing: she said I bossed her around. And I did. Mom often put me in charge. I considered Christy my little baby as much as Mom did, and that got on Christy's nerves. Ever since I can remember, I saw myself as being a mom one day. I practiced on Christy.

I was the oldest, just like Mom had been the oldest growing up. Mom had to watch her brothers and sisters, and she expected me to do the same from an early age. I had to make sure everything was okay—meaning Christy wasn't upset or getting herself into trouble. If something happened—a broken toy or a screaming match—I'd get in trouble because I was supposed to be keeping an eye on things. By age eight, I had even more responsibility for taking care of her and keeping her safe. I liked doing what Momma told me to do. I liked being the obedient daughter both of my parents could count on. But I didn't like getting in trouble. If something happened on my watch—even if I had nothing to do with it—Mom would yell at me for it. She didn't yell at Christy.

If I ever felt bad for not being Mom's favorite, Christy felt worse for not being Dad's. He'd yell at her like she was the devil. By the time I was eight and Christy was six, he'd smack her—sometimes in the back of the head at the dinner table. He never put his hands on me. He was cold and withdrawn toward her. For example, if she went down the stairs too slowly, he might say something like, "I should just push you down."

She didn't get to sit on his lap every night like I did, either. When he made popcorn, I got a bigger bowl. I think he treated her that way because she was the youngest, just like he had been the youngest. He would say he always got his older brother in trouble for everything. He saw Christy as being manipulative and sneaky. Maybe he saw Christy as himself. All I know is that when he talked to her, there was a tinge in his voice that wasn't there when he spoke to me. She didn't get the loving father treatment I got; she didn't have a nickname. The only times he made her really happy were when he shared his popcorn. She soaked up any leftover bits of affection she could get from him.

There was another side of my dad that I did not like—he could be a total bigot. He would use racial slurs, downgrading people of different races and creeds. Mom was the opposite. She taught me to accept people for who they were, not what they were. My best friend in Kansas City was Jewish, and Dad didn't want me to play with her. He told me to find a new friend. So I did, and she was black. He almost had a heart attack. He forbade me to play with my new friend, but Mom stepped in. "Stacey will be friends with anyone she chooses, and you will accept it," she declared. She put her hand on her hip to reinforce her point. He was once again in Deborah trouble, and he knew when to back down. He wouldn't win this one. Deep down, even he knew he was wrong.

He tried to get in the last word, saying, "I'll be damned if those two girls walk through my front door."

But Mom told him, "They will as long as I am living here, and if you don't like it, you can leave."

I decided then and there that as much as I loved my father, I would not let a person's race or religion affect how I saw them. I didn't tell him that; I didn't want to fight. I didn't say anything when he told me not to date anyone outside of my race. I just didn't buy into his prejudiced philosophies. It was the first time I knew—most definitely—that he was wrong about something. This was one of the only issues my mom and I could agree on.

Otherwise, I thought she was constantly nagging Dad. He told me he came home late because he didn't want to listen to her badgering him about this or that. She was on his case constantly; I heard it most nights. I took his side because he spent more time with me. He sat down and cuddled with me. Also, he simply said that he was right, and Mom was wrong. I believed him with all my heart.

Christy didn't take his side like I did. He yelled at her more often, even when Mom told him to stop. I didn't understand why he got so irritated with her. He was never like that with me.

He'd snap at Christy at the dinner table and tell her to stop acting up when she asked for the salt or laughed at something on TV. He'd be so cross about it, Mom would say, "Why don't you yell at Stacey? Why is Stacey your favorite?"

He'd answer in a gruff voice: "Because Christy always starts it, and she isn't innocent like everyone thinks she is."

I felt funny when they had these conversations. I didn't want Christy to feel bad. I didn't like when he yelled at her. But at age eight, my thought process was not very complicated. I was—in spite of everything else—his Tiger. And everyone in the family knew it.

———

We were supposed to get a fresh start in Kansas City, but after less than a year, my dad moved out. Christy and I thought it was because his job assignment there had ended. We believed he went back to St. Louis to work. He lived five hours away from us. I was in the second grade, and I didn't know what was happening when we put our house on the market. I assumed we were going back to St. Louis to be with Daddy, but I found out twenty years later that my mom had spent $250 of her own money to file for divorce. The alcoholic rages had become too unpredictable for her. She didn't know if she'd see Good Tom or Bad Tom on any given night—and Bad Tom had become just too frightening for her.

Daddy visited some weekends, and I looked forward to seeing him all week long. I was mad at Mom because I felt like something was fishy, and it was all her fault. She had become so distant that it was easy to blame her. During the week, she spent a lot of time alone in her room. She was tired, or she was talking on the phone. Christy and I were alone more often. We'd play by ourselves or run around outside with kids in the neighborhood.

My heart was shattered without Daddy. He loved me the most, and I felt lonely without him around. One weekend visit, he brought me a dinosaur book. He'd sit down and read it to me every time we saw each other. I carried that book with me everywhere I went. Christy and I had no idea our parents were separated at that time. Sometimes when Daddy was home with us, we would all walk as a family to the neighborhood pizza place and then to the ice cream parlor. It was fun; things didn't seem that bad.

Around that time Grandma Paulson and Aunt Deanna came to visit for two weeks. Aunt Deanna was Mom's youngest sister, and she was only eight years older than me. I didn't know at the time that Grandma was there to help Mom make a tough decision—I found out much later. I just knew that Mom, Grandma, Christy, Deanna, and I went to the pool a lot. Aunt Deanna flirted with the boys. My mother said that Grandma Paulson gave her advice. She wanted Mom to give Dad another chance.

"That's all I'm asking you to do, Debbie," Grandma Paulson said.

"I would want him to do the same thing for you." She reminded my mom that families should stay together—that every household needs a man.

Shortly after they left, my mom took a short trip with my dad. I don't know where they went, and I don't remember whom we stayed with. I do know that when they returned, Mom and Dad were a team again. As soon as we sold the house, we would pack up the bananamobile again.

Apples in Alhambra

To keep the family together, Dad agreed to all of Mom's requests. He told her she was the one woman who could drive him out of his mind. She alone could bring out the best—or the beast—in him. If he was going to change, she was the only person he'd do it for. She made a list of her demands. At the top of the list, he had to drink less. Second, she wanted to move back home—to the slow, gentle countryside where she'd grown up. Also, she hoped he'd respect her more. He told her he wasn't fooling around this time. He'd really try. He desperately wanted another chance to make it work with my mother.

It's hard to imagine why my mother would want to go back home after the abuse she endured as a child. But her parents, especially her mother, were the only support system she had. Debbie didn't have anyone to help her but her family. And at that point in her life, she was still pretending that her childhood abuse had never happened. While she wasn't close to her dad, she knew he would protect her from anyone who might harm her—anyone except him. In this case the known—which was living the country life—was better than the unknown.

This move was supposed to be the answer to our problems, as if we could magically erase our worries with new walls, a new yard, and new neighbors. I wasn't skeptical then. I was all for it. This move felt different and exciting. Everyone walked around smiling for a while. Daddy came back from St. Louis more often to help us get the Kansas City house ready for sale. In the end, it sat on the market so long that we sold it to the real estate company at a loss. We just wanted to get to Alhambra before the new school year began.

Our parents told us Alhambra would finally be the end of packing boxes, wrapping dishes, and loading up the bananamobile. We were going to stay put for a nice long while. I'd never had the chance to get comfortable in my classrooms, so I was thrilled. As soon as I'd settle in with teachers and classmates, it was time to uproot and start over again. I was on my fifth move, and I was only eight.

We all needed to slow down. The country sounded like the perfect place to take a break and make things right. It was our new adventure—together. We bought a one-story brick house with an attic in Alhambra, Illinois, just forty-five minutes from St. Louis and ten minutes from Grandpa and Grandma Paulson's farm. Aunt Deanna was sixteen and still lived with them, and so did Uncle Derek. We heard so many promises; we really hoped Mom and Dad would get along better this time.

We had a red brick raised ranch with a big picture window to the right of the front door. Mom had a large kitchen with sparkly golden wallpaper. We had an attic I could use as my bedroom and a finished basement where I could hang out with my dad. We got a dog named Barron that I loved. We even got our own cats—my Bandit was black with a white stripe, and Buttercup was Christy's orange tabby. Animals were truly gifts to us. Christy and I had all kinds of room outside to play with them. This house sat on three acres of dreamlike property. I loved to be outdoors, especially there, where we had a stream and real apple trees. Our new yard was a treasure trove; it was my own private play world.

It didn't occur to me to be nervous about the wilderness—our Wild West. I didn't yet realize that I was a suburban girl who enjoyed neighborhood streets and big schools filled with different types of kids. At that time, I just knew the country was different. I saw trucks and tractors everywhere in Alhambra, way more than I'd seen in Creve Coeur, Missouri (where I was born), Cedar Rapids, Manchester, or Kansas City. The fields were big and sprawling, and not just near the interstate roadways. People actually farmed here. Some had barns instead of garages. They lived on vast properties, and you couldn't just walk to your neighbor's house to play. Mom was right; it all seemed so slow and gentle.

The day we arrived at our house with all of our stuff, Daddy walked me outside to the fruit trees. Apples dangled from every branch. He plucked one off and gave it to me. He'd read my mind, and I smiled. The move, the house, the yard—it was all surreal, like the magical village on *The Smurfs*. I mean, we had snacks right there in the front yard, and all we had to do was look up.

"We can grow whatever we want now," Daddy said. "And anytime you want an apple, we'll just go and get you one." I couldn't pick apples by myself. They were out of my reach. While I waited for my parents to move furniture and boxes, I sat under that tree for an hour eating my piece of fruit. I still remember the way it tasted, kind of tart.

Later that day, out in the front lawn, I told Daddy, "Promise me I can stay here until I go to college. Promise me we'll never leave."

His cutoff jean shorts were dusty, and he was tired but happy. He said, "I promise." Then he held me, and everything was great.

My father and I started becoming even closer then. He worked out in the yard all the time. He came home earlier from work, and he hung around the house more. So I'd help him whenever I could. We cut the sprawling fields of grass together. He put me in his lap on the tractor, and I'd get to drive. I helped him in the garage with his tools when he needed to fix stuff. This was special bonding time for us. I felt grounded, like I belonged in the world, and like I had a real home.

We had Barron, a little beagle-collie mix, for only about a week. I adored him. One summer morning, Christy and I were waiting at the bus stop in front of our house. We squealed happily when Barron ran through the front yard to tell us good-bye before we left for school. He was so excited to see us. But our house sat up on a hill—one of those steep, fast inclines that thrill-seeking drivers raced over so their stomachs lurched up into their throats. That morning, a young guy about twenty-four years old crashed into my cheerful, innocent dog. In an instant, Barron was killed—his body spread all over the road. I couldn't even find his tail. Christy and I screamed and cried. The driver stopped his car and tried to apologize. Mom had been at the bus stop with us, and she was as shocked as we were. She told us to stay back.

Dad hadn't gone to work yet, so he heard the commotion and came running out of the house. He told us to look the other way while he found a trash bag. The bus came, and he made us get on it. We were still crying, but it was probably better for us to get out of the way. Daddy and the young dog killer cleaned up the mess and buried Barron in the yard.

Later that night, Daddy told us, "These things happen."

Mom tried to comfort us, too. "We know you're hurt right now, but you will feel better soon."

I know they felt bad for us. Mom took us to the pound a few months later, and we picked out two dogs, nice-looking mutts, one for each of us. I chose Prince, and Christy got Benji. We were both overjoyed. I fell madly in love with Prince, and he was my constant companion while I tried to find my way in Alhambra.

I don't remember playing with Christy that much after we got to Alhambra. She definitely didn't hang out with me and Dad. She always went off to do her own thing or went on errands with Mom. She liked to play outside with Buttercup, the cat, and catch bugs. She captured lightning bugs, caterpillars, and ladybugs and housed them in jars. She liked to take care of her "pets" in her room. Sometimes she accidentally killed the little creatures, and other times, she set them free. She was quirky and sweet. We were just different people with individual interests.

When we did put our heads together, we could cause some trouble. That winter, we were waiting for the school bus while it snowed outside. We dared each other to lick the black metal mailbox. We stuck our tongues out, and they froze to the metal at exactly the same moment. All of a sudden, the winter weather wasn't so beautiful, and the idea wasn't so brilliant. Together, we were in a painful, frozen jail, hanging by our tongues. We screamed our earmuffs off, and without full use of our tongues, we sounded like howling beagles. Mom ran out when she heard us. She was kind of mad, but she was also laughing. She knew how to set us free—she brought out a bowl of warm water. We went off to school as usual. We were thankful that no one on the bus had seen what happened. Being the new girl—again—was hard enough without more embarrassment on top of it.

Around that same time, Christy and I went sledding for the first time by ourselves. There was a six-foot ditch way out in front of the house, and Mom finally decided we were old enough to go sledding alone. We could start at the top of the hill and get a short ride. She put me in charge. We were bundled up with hats, mittens, scarves, and layers of thermal underwear topped off with red snowsuits. We couldn't even bend our arms. We wore snow boots—actually they were more like moon boots. Mine were blue with rainbows, and Christy's were lilac. We loved them and begged to wear them. We didn't care that we could hardly walk. Our sled was orange plastic and had room for two people. It was huge and difficult for me to drag through the snow. It had a black brake in the center column, like the Ferrari of sleds. I could not wait to take it down that ditch for its maiden voyage with Christy. I felt old and wise as I trekked out into the snow—just my sister and me. The walk was hard, though. Snow swirled around our bodies and every step was stiff because of all our clothing. As I dragged the sled, the wind would catch it every so often, and I'd have to hang on for dear life. I kept that thing on the ground with pure might. I loved the rush of air that hit my face as I headed toward that ditch. Christy, however, was not high on snow like I was. Along the walk, she started to cry. She wanted to go home. She was cold. She was tired. She was hungry. *What a baby*, I thought. She was big enough to brave the elements.

If she didn't want to, I'd just have to make her.

Her whining meant nothing to me. That moment was *my* moment, and my baby sister was not going to ruin it. I told her to just come on, and I would pull her in the sled so she wouldn't have to walk. She climbed into it, but then I couldn't get the thing to budge. I wasn't the superwoman I thought I was, so I had to tell her to get out.

She didn't want to get out. She just sat there and cried.

I got frustrated and lost my temper. To get her to move, I kicked her. She carried her little body, heavy with tears and gear and snow, away from the sled. She just wouldn't stop crying. Her screechy, sniffly sounds were awful. Still, I somehow got her to walk to that ditch. We arrived, and the moment wasn't as glorious as I'd hoped. I sat in front of the sled to steer while Christy moaned in the back. Her job was to operate the brake. I got a thrill when I whooshed down the hill. I wanted more.

I talked her into another run. Or maybe I threatened her into it; I don't remember. I do know we managed to go down that hill a second time, but we hit a bump as big as a tree trunk. Christy flew up in the air, landed hard on her tailbone, and hurt herself. She really revved up and cried, so I gave up at that point. I wasn't mad anymore, and I gently took her home. It turned out she had a bad bruise on her tailbone, and Mom said it might've been cracked.

My mom wasn't happy with me. Even worse, I wasn't happy with me. Christy got hurt on my watch, and even if she was going to be okay, I felt terrible. I thought maybe my kick had caused that bruise on her butt. Or maybe I was evil for making her go sledding against her will in the first place. I didn't want to be bad again. I vowed right then that I would never physically hurt her, and I would always protect her whenever possible. I never raised my hand to her again.

I even tried to get between her and Dad as much as I could. I could smell their fights brewing like I could smell a storm coming. I seemed to be the only one who could settle them. If Mom got involved, the fight just got worse. Eventually—and early on—Dad and Christy just stopped talking to each other except when they absolutely had to. If he wanted something from her, he would ask me to ask her. If she needed to ask him about things, I would do her bidding. I got tired of playing their carrier pigeon, but I did it. It was better than listening to them fight, and it was much better than watching her get hurt.

After the move to Alhambra, my parents had a brief honeymoon where they got along great. But the peace lasted only a few months. Things took a turn when Dad started drinking beer again at night. Soon afterward, he started coming home late from work more and more often. His moods were difficult to predict. Sometimes he was happy, but he could also be dark.

Mom and Dad stopped speaking so nicely to each other. The volume went up in the house. She nagged him about leaving his stuff around the rooms, and he told her she needed to keep things cleaner. They went their separate ways after dinner. My parents could be watching the same television show, but she'd be upstairs while Dad stayed downstairs. Following their lead, Christy headed upstairs while I gravitated to the basement.

On the nights he didn't show up for supper, we'd eat in front of the TV on trays. That's when Mom would really get mad. She'd beg him to stop drinking and to get help.

"You're tearing this family apart; just look at your daughters," she'd yell at him from down the hallway.

We'd pretend like we couldn't hear them as we sat silently in front of the TV. If we still had food in front of us, we'd stop eating it.

Sometimes he was mean, and yelled all kinds of nasty things at her. Other times he was gentle, and he'd try to rub her arm. She'd say, "Don't touch me."

More often than not, we heard the words, "I'm not really drunk."

I believed him. Getting drunk was something that bad people did. My daddy was not bad. He couldn't be.

I thought all parents got along about the same as mine. I thought all moms and dads chose their favorite children. I thought all daddies came home late smelling funny and making noise. I didn't have close friends, so I couldn't compare my family to anyone else's. We had moved too often for me to get close to people. I didn't have a clue what was normal—and what was not.

I only knew that when he came looking for me, he made things better.

"Come here, Tiger. Sit on my lap," he'd say, smelling tangy yet sweet. His lap was soft and warm. "Tell me how your day was."

My mom never asked me about my day. She didn't tell me everything was going to turn out all right. She didn't hug me all the time. I couldn't comprehend how she got so mad at him. When he was drinking, he seemed happy to me. He'd make jokes and slow down and spend more time with me. We'd talk about everything. I could listen to him for a hundred years; it didn't matter what he said. He hugged me as I sat on his lap.

The Real Alhambra

Alhambra wasn't the Camelot I had hoped it would be. The village—it wasn't even a town—had fewer than six hundred people. Residents held various blue-collar jobs after the steel mills closed in the '80s. Of course, farming was big. Corn and soybean fields bordered long stretches of country roads. Alhambra was all-white, rural Midwestern American farmland.

Kids at school were mean. They had all grown up together, and I was a newcomer, and not in a good way. They called me a weirdo. All of their parents were truck drivers or farmers, and my dad was an actuary. They'd look at me cockeyed and ask, "What's that?" I couldn't explain it to them—I barely knew what my dad did. Those kids called me a snob, not realizing that I liked to play outside during the rain as much as they did.

When they asked me what kind of stuff I liked to do, I talked about waterskiing. That was a mistake. These kids swung from a rope into the lake or went fishing for bluegill. They'd never even heard of waterskiing, my favorite summertime activity in the world. I couldn't find common ground with them, and there was just no place for me to fit in. The girls had their little tomboy cliques, and compared to them, I looked like Malibu Barbie. I couldn't be known as the new girl because there was already another more popular new girl. So, for the first time, I dreaded going to school. Christy, however, liked her new first-grade class, and she made friends. Not me. I thought all rural kids were brutal in a yee-haw kind of way.

I missed my old classmates—suburban kids who seemed to be more open-minded. They had to be more adaptable and less judgmental. For instance, my last school had four classes for each grade level. In Alhambra, the one third-grade class had fifteen kids. I also had trouble with my teacher, and I had no choice but to stay in his class. If the kids were tough on me, Mr. Richardson was even tougher. Alhambra students had learned cursive writing in second grade. At my old school, we didn't learn it until third. I couldn't do the loopy script any better than I could go frog-gigging. So Mr. Richardson put Fs on my writing assignments because I completed them in print. My mom had to teach me cursive at home with workbooks. Meanwhile, he kept telling her I was slow. She told him—and me—that I most certainly was not slow. She went to battle over it, insisting that I was smart. The year before in Kansas, I had been asked to go into an advanced class, and now in that rinky-dink town, everyone thought I was dumb.

I knew I wasn't. About the same time, my aunt Deanna was studying to get her GED. She had decided to drop out of school. I looked at the workbooks and explained some of the exercises to her when she had trouble. We both took the practice tests, and sometimes I scored higher. She got mad at me, but I didn't care. At least I had proof that I wasn't stupid.

I didn't have school friends, so I spent most of my time with my family. Aunt Deanna lived close by, and I thought she was cool. She was the baby out of five kids, and her parents and siblings spoiled her rotten. She was very pretty—she looked like my mother, petite and blond. Deanna wore lots of makeup, and she always fixed her hair. Her smile alone told the world that she was beautiful. She carried herself in an entitled way, and she acted entitled. When she was a teenager, she went to Branson, Missouri, with us and bought a T-shirt that said, "God's gift." She wore it immediately.

Christy and I followed her around like puppy dogs. We danced around in her room to Madonna songs when she let us. She fixed our hair and let us play with her clothes. She let me wear her clogs; then she made me take them off. Deanna could flip her moods like a lightswitch.

Aunt Deanna was an addictive mix of good and bad. She could be entertaining, so we always came back for more abuse from our cool aunt. I also hung around with her because I didn't have any other friends. She was just another wacky, weird part of my new life in Alhambra.

Grandpa Paulson's Influence

Dad didn't like Grandpa Paulson, and to be honest, neither did I. Dad knew what Grandpa had done to my mother. My father called him a lowlife and a hillbilly right in front of us. But my dad, like me, didn't have a lot of friends in Alhambra. When the tractor broke, he called my grandfather. When the faucet needed fixing, Grandpa Paulson worked on it with him. Slowly, the two of them became friends.

Together they bought a 1950s Ford that needed a lot of work. They restored it in a shed my dad built for their project. On weekends, they'd tinker while they drank Busch. I'd go in and help sometimes, but I tried not to stay for long. My grandfather was too country. I didn't like some of the things he said. He thought children should be quiet and women should stay in their place. A woman's place, of course, was in the kitchen, and that went against everything my mom had taught me. She always told me I could be the president of Harvard if I set my mind to it. Grandpa didn't think a woman needed much education—especially if she was only going to cook, clean, and have babies.

Men had a natural right to do what they wanted to their women—that's what I think Grandpa believed.

My aunts, including Deanna, told me to stay away from him. That was fine with me; I didn't feel safe around Grandpa Paulson.

But there was no keeping Daddy from working on that old Ford with Grandpa. I can only guess what ideas he got from my grandfather. This was at the same time Mom and Dad were starting to fight again, and I know my dad complained to Grandpa Paulson about their problems. He complained to all of us about my mom. Grandpa took my dad's side, as any good ole boy would. Both Grandpa and Grandma thought my dad was great, and they didn't support my mom during their fights. With everything they said and did, they seemed to show that they loved my father more than they loved their daughter. They'd tell Mom her marital problems were her fault.

I cringe to imagine the marital advice Richard Paulson could have given my dad. I overheard him complaining that Mom wasn't "giving him any." I didn't know what "any" was. Looking back, I can picture Grandpa Paulson telling him, "Who cares? You've got Stacey."

The more terrible an idea is, the easier it can be to fall into.

I wish I hadn't been on my father's side back then, but I very much was. To me, he was right, and Mom was wrong. My eight-year-old eyes saw her as weak. She never stood up to her own parents. She couldn't control arguments with my dad. She did what he said, and he never did what she asked him to do. When they fought, Dad would call her "a worthless piece of shit." His put-downs became nastier over time. It was confusing for me because I didn't like what he said, but I loved him. Maybe she caused him to behave that way—as he claimed. No matter what, I supported him, and I wanted to be his favorite daughter.

Now I realize that the cards were stacked against Mom no matter what she did. Her family was rife with alcoholism and sexual abuse, and she didn't stand a chance as long as she accepted the role of victim. A victim is someone who relives her abuse and continues to suffer from it long after it's over. She thought the abuse she suffered was her fault, not her parents'. Mom wasn't a victim forever, but she was then. She thought she could find peace and happiness in what was familiar.

Instead, she brought Christy and me to an unsafe world.

A Death in the Family

When I was eight, Grandpa Lannert died. My dad hadn't been that close to him for several years, but he was devastated nonetheless. I didn't understand the meaning of death yet, so his passing was easy for me to accept. Paw Paw had been very ill after having several strokes, and he went peacefully in his sleep.

My dad couldn't accept it. The finality of their troubled relationship seemed to push him over the edge.

He went on drinking binges, sometimes with my other grandfather. I do believe Grandpa Paulson may have been a bad influence during that upside-down time. Dad fought with my mom and Christy nonstop. He spent hours and hours with me in the basement playing Ping-Pong and watching TV, the only times he seemed to feel better. Downstairs with me, he calmed down. He would even smile sometimes. He'd loosen up and turn into Daddy again, telling stories and cracking jokes. I wanted to help him. I stayed with him as often as he'd have me.

My mom was wearing down. She wasn't home as much, and when she was, she stayed in her room more often. When she was around, she and Dad fought. They even argued about sex in front of us. Christy and I didn't know what sex was; we just knew my mom "was a bitch" for not "giving it up."

Shortly after the funeral, Dad and I were in our downstairs family room as usual.

I was lying on the floor, and my father was relaxing in his recliner. He asked me to sit on his lap, and of course, I did.

"Come on, Tiger," he said to me.

"Okay, Daddy." I was excited that he was in a good mood again. He'd been so nasty since Paw Paw died.

"Honey, you're going to be nine years old soon. Do you know what that means?" he asked. He held my arms tight like he was about to say something very important.

"It means I get a lot of presents!" I answered. I loved birthdays.

"Yes," he said, smiling. Then he added. "Being nine means you're a big girl now—and big girls do certain things." He waited a few seconds. "Give me a kiss."

I gave him a proper kiss on the cheek like I always did.

He shook his head no. "That's not how big girls kiss."

"How do they kiss, Daddy?" I was curious, I wanted to be big, and I wanted to please him.

"Open your mouth, and I'll show you." He turned his head so it faced mine, and he got really close.

The position was weird. But I was always willing to try what he said. I opened my mouth as widely as I could. He rubbed my back, and he encouraged me to just relax.

Then he started nibbling on my lips. It felt okay—nothing about it hurt; nothing about it was unpleasant. But the kiss was also strange and tickly, so I started laughing.

"Just relax," he said. He told me to soften my face and mouth as he started nibbling my lips once again. After a few long seconds, he stuck his tongue in my mouth. I giggled. It felt funny playing Touch Tongues with Daddy. Christy and I played it. We stuck our tongues out at each other, shut our eyes, and moved in closer until our tongues collided. We'd fall over laughing about it.

He let me laugh for a while. Then he said, "Let's play again."

So I opened my mouth—not too wide, not too hard—to play Touch Tongues with Daddy.

"Wiggle your tongue a little bit, Tiger," he requested.

Strangeness wrapped me like a wet blanket. His tongue was a ball of gum, chokingly large. It was hard to breathe with his mouth clamped over mine. I was not having fun anymore, but he was. He made noises, and he told me I was doing a good job. As long as he was happy, I kept playing.

There were more rules to this game. Daddy took my hand and moved it to his crotch area. It was hard, and I had never felt or imagined anything like it.

"What's that?" I asked. I felt around just a little bit, fumbling with my fingers. I was curious. But I also wasn't sure I wanted to know the answer to my question.

He told me he had a special friend, and he asked if I would like to see it.

I said yes because I didn't want to disappoint him. But I was scared of his friend. Something felt off to me, but I tried not to worry because Daddy was happy, and Daddy would always protect me from everything. Next, he opened his pants and underwear and pulled it out. I stared in amazement at the first penis I'd ever seen. I mean, I had caught him naked once when I barged in on him in the bathroom, but that was an accident. This time was completely different.

I told myself, *Okay, this isn't too weird. Really, it's not weird.*

He asked me to kiss his friend, and I didn't hesitate. I always did what he told me to do. I didn't feel scared or threatened because I was with the one person in the world I trusted. His friend looked like a snake or something. It changed sizes and moved around. I couldn't stop laughing. I told him his friend was alive.

I said, "It keeps growing!" Then I giggled some more.

"Open your mouth, Tiger, and let my friend in." I opened as wide as I could for the second time that night. He put his friend inside my mouth and told me to close my mouth. He jumped suddenly and said ouch. I guess I bit him. He wasn't mad at me. He just told me to not close all the way.

"Keep your mouth open a little bit. Let my friend just sit inside." He rubbed my back trying to get me to relax.

This position was very uncomfortable for me, and when he started to move his penis back and forth, I choked. Instinctively, I backed away from him, sat up straight, and clamped my mouth shut. I hadn't meant to react so definitively; it just happened.

"You don't like that?" he asked. He was calm, kind, and patient with me.

I shook my head no. "It hurts me when he moves."

"Well, Tiger, my friend also likes to be licked. Can you do that?"

Of course, I'd try it if he wanted me too, and licking his friend didn't hurt as much. But then I stopped because white stuff came out, and it tasted bitter.

"You don't like that?" he asked. "That's marshmallow cream."

"It tastes funny! Yuck!" I wanted to stop.

He told me not to give up yet and to hang on a second. He went into a back room where we stored extra groceries. He had a jar of marshmallow cream in his hands. I was a little less worried because I loved marshmallow cream. I watched as he put some on his friend.

"Okay, this will be better," he said. "Try it again."

When I finished licking off all the cream, he put more on. He told me to keep going and to pretend it was a popsicle. I did, and more white stuff—not marshmallow cream—squirted into my mouth almost instantly. The taste was disgusting, so I ran into the bathroom and spit it out. I was scared to come out of the bathroom again. I didn't want to play with his friend anymore.

"Come here, Tiger," he said calmly. "Sit on my lap."

"I don't want to play anymore," I said from the bathroom.

"We're not going to play. Let's talk."

I still trusted him, so I walked toward him again. If he said we weren't going to play, then we weren't. I climbed into his lap in the exact spot I'd been sitting before.

"You know that you're a big girl now?" he asked.

"Uh-huh."

"Big girls know how to keep a secret. Can you keep a secret, Tiger?" He looked into my eyes, but I kept looking down.

"Yes."

"Our little game is our secret. My friend is our secret, okay?" He gently nudged me to make sure that I got it.

"Why?"

"Because I usually only play this game with Mommy, and she may get mad that I'm playing it with you instead of her. We don't want her mad at us, do we?" He was very serious about this talk, so I listened carefully.

"No." The last thing I wanted to do was give them something else to fight about.

"Good. Then this means that you're my number one daughter," he said, smiling.

I was so excited. I hugged him.

"Now we have a father-daughter secret. Christy doesn't have a secret, so that makes you my favorite daughter." He started to look away and fiddle around in the chair.

"I love you, Daddy!" I yelled it. I was delighted. At that moment, I was the happiest little girl in the world.

I had no idea that my life had changed forever.

Moody and Blue

The special game continued, and I played it with Daddy whenever he asked me to. If it made him happy, then I was happy. I didn't really like it, but the marshmallow cream made it more okay, and he wasn't physically hurting me. Daddy was just having fun with me, and that made me the lucky daughter. I got more of his love and attention than anyone else in our house. Our time together was a break from all of the other problems. School was still a drag, and if he and Mom weren't fighting, they were staying away from each other as much as possible. Sometimes they'd get along, but we just never knew what we'd get from one day to the next. The ups and downs in our house in Alhambra were unpredictable.

I wanted everything to be okay. I thought it was normal to sit on my daddy's lap until 3 a.m. watching TV and talking about what happened at school. I loved listening to him talk; it didn't even matter what he said. He'd hug me and hold me, and he was all I needed. I could pretend the family was as happy as we were supposed to be when we were together.

Mom was chasing her own happiness. She wanted to work. As long as he was the sole breadwinner, she said she felt weak and powerless. He didn't support the idea, but he didn't fight her. As much as they argued, he still loved her and wanted her to be happy. He just didn't know how to make that happen—or wasn't able to make it happen. So she decided to enroll in classes at the local college, Southern Illinois University Edwardsville. Even though she had never considered herself smart, she studied full time to be a secretary in a

certificate program. She was gone while we were at school, and sometimes when we got home. She made sure we stayed on top of our
schoolwork and had healthy food to eat, but her priorities were scat-
tered. She was way busier than she had ever been before.

She didn't just want to work; she needed to. We didn't have much
money in Alhambra. My classmates acted like we were the rich city
folks, but in reality, we lived just like everyone else there, struggling
from paycheck to paycheck. My dad was a partner in an actuarial
firm, but I don't think his business was going well. That's another
reason my mom wanted to chip in. She was tired of Grandma Lannert buying her daughters' clothes and toys.

I didn't understand the financial problems. They didn't affect
Christy and me because we still had everything we needed. Grandma
Lannert bought us anything we asked for. That's not why I loved her,
though. She was a special person to me. Happiness was a trip to her
house—every year, we'd go there for a week or two in the summer.
Sometimes we'd make it out there on a weekend, too, especially when
we lived closer. She'd take us to fancy lunches so we'd feel grown up.
She also let us just be kids—kids without arguments and troubles.
At her house, we could run around and scream—and eat sugar. The
basement and attic were packed with her clothes and scarves, and we
were allowed to play dress-up. It was a happy and predictable place,
and, best of all, no one raised her voice at Mee Maw's house. Nothing
bad ever happened there.

At home, we had our share of good times, too—surprisingly. Saturday barbecues were the best. Dad would gear up for one all week
long, saying things like, "Guess what we're going to do on Saturday."
He'd be so happy about it, just like a little kid.

The night before, he laid out pork steaks and chicken for him and
Mom and chicken legs for Christy and me. Mom went to the grocery
store with her list, usually with us in tow. On the day of the cookout,
he woke up early and prepared his special sauce with secret ingredi-
ents like beer and spices. Then he prepared the grill, layering charcoal

briquettes and hunks of hickory that produced the flavor he wanted. When he felt he had the perfect pyre, he lit his creation with lighter fluid. Christy and I ooohed and ahhhed at the big flames.

Mom worked inside preparing potato salad, baked beans, and corn on the cob. We "helped" her until eventually, she sent us back outside to "check on the meat." When everything was ready, we would sit down like a family. We would eat until our mouths were covered in barbecue sauce. No matter how destructive our family got, the barbecues pulled us back together, filling us with a sense of belonging while cooling our tempers. We reminded ourselves that we loved each other. No matter how bad our storms got, we were all we had to get through them.

Buttercup

One of the first times I saw Daddy in an all-out rage, we were in Mom's car. He was loose, loud, and mean. All four of us were coming back from the store or some other mundane afternoon errand. He was nastier than rotten garbage. He cursed all the way to our house, mostly about nothing. I tried not to look at his face; his blue eyes had turned to daggers. We pulled into our long driveway, and my sister's cat, Buttercup, was lying there waiting for Christy to get home. The cat did that all the time; it loved Christy and wanted to be with her whenever possible. She and I both adored our cats.

He stopped the car about a foot from the animal's purring body. Buttercup, a typical ridiculous feline, didn't move. She just flipped her tail.

"That goddamned cat better get outta my way." My dad was yelling at Christy like it was her fault. She started to cry in the back seat. I felt like crying, too, but I was too scared to say or do anything. Dad barely seemed human at that moment. He stopped and started the car, inching closer to the cat. Even if we had dared to, Christy and I couldn't get out to help Buttercup. We were stuck in the backseat of Mom's two-door car. Mom or Dad would have to open the door for us, and they were both sitting dead still.

Dad revved the car engine.

Buttercup just laid there looking hopeful—looking for Christy.

"Stop it, Tom," Mom yelled. She kept yelling at him. Then I couldn't hold it back. I started crying, too—loudly.

He raised his voice to all of us. He said, "That fucking cat. I'll just have to take care of it."

With those words, we felt a hard, sickening thump underneath the tires. Then he got out of the car and picked up the writhing, dying animal in slow motion. We couldn't do anything but watch and cry and feel sick to our stomachs. Barron had just died similarly, but this was much worse. Barron was an accident. Our sweet cat hadn't deserved to go like that. Buttercup bled everywhere as her contorted body writhed uncontrollably. It wasn't real; it was a horror movie. We could hardly believe it. Our daddy had caused all of this suffering.

He wasn't any daddy that I knew. This was him in his evil form. This was Tom.

Our mom screamed at him. "How could you do this?" she asked. "What is the matter with you?"

Once she got over her own shock, she ushered us inside and told us everything would be okay. She comforted us the best she could. I don't know what happened to poor Buttercup, but Tom took care of the mess himself. He disappeared for a few hours. Then around our bedtime, he found us. He hung his head low, and his eyes were bloodshot. He seemed miserable. He apologized for killing Christy's cat. He wasn't scary; he was just sorry.

He was Daddy again. Almost.

Scarred

When I think back on my childhood, I don't picture fuzzy memories filled with little girls' rainbows and hearts and jump ropes. Not that I would remember those things anyway. I was more likely to scrape my knees running through the backyard and riding down the driveway than I was to twirl around in skirts. I liked dollies too, but I was happier when I was playing with my pets, bicycle, and books. Nothing was better than hugging my baby sister and sitting on my daddy's lap. But almost always, the things that caused me the most joy in my life also caused me the most pain. I never knew any differently, and I survived by alternating my realities. I glossed over every bad thing that happened with thoughts of what was still good. I focused on the positives until the bad stuff stopped existing.

That's how I live with the scar on my left wrist. I used to be ashamed of the bumpy, reddish white line on my left wrist. I was sure everyone could see it, and I thought if someone really looked at it, they would know what had happened to me. They would know it and blame me and hate me for everything. Just a glance would get me antsy. In middle school volleyball, I'd freeze if a girl stared at my wrist for too long. Then I'd realize that she probably didn't notice my scar at all, and was just keeping her eye on the ball. My scar is in a place that you cannot cover with clothing. The mark is on my wrist but well before you get to my thumb. Clothes don't cover it. Makeup won't work on skin branded by heat and fire. If I could've hidden it; I would have.

I started wearing a watch on my left hand shortly after I got that scar, kind of covering it but not really. People asked me about the scar—but not nearly as often as I feared. I said I burned myself on a wood-burning stove. Since that time, the scar has transformed itself into a completely different mark. It's not glaringly obvious like it was years ago. It's not puffy anymore, and I can get through several days in a row without noticing it. I still know why it's there. I still know how I got it. I still feel bad when I let my mind linger in the shadows of that basement. But the scar, like the memory, fades. I wouldn't get rid of it now if I could. It's part of who I am. It's a reminder that there is much good in this world, but there is also much to be feared.

On a Saturday afternoon, when I was nine and a half years old, Dad and I met in the basement as usual. I went into the bathroom to spit out the "marshmallow cream." My father came up behind me as I was bending over the toilet to spit. He grabbed me by the back of my hair and pulled me straight up. Then he pulled my head back.

"Swallow it, you fucking bitch," he yelled. "Do you think that you are too good to swallow? Swallow it. Now!"

He held his hand over my mouth because I was crying and still trying to spit. He pinched my nose closed. I had no control over my mouth or my nose, and I was struggling to breathe. I swallowed.

"Open your mouth. Show me that it's gone." I did as he said except when my mouth opened, I also screamed. I desperately wanted my mother to hear. I needed someone to save me from this sick and crazy mess.

"You little bitch. You're going to pay for that. You're a little girl now, but I'm about to make you a woman." He rushed toward me. He was not a dad I had ever met before. The look in his eyes seared through me, and they told me all I needed to know. Yes, those were Daddy's eyes, but Daddy was no longer in the basement with me.

I loved Daddy. I didn't feel anything for this evil man who bullied me. The hatred and disgust in his eyes frightened me. I bolted to my feet and ran.

He caught me in an instant, so I kicked him in his shin and ran to the other door. He recovered quickly and caught me again. He threw me to the ground in front of our wood-burning stove and started to pull off my jeans. I tried to get away, but instead, I burned my left wrist on the stove while flailing my arms. After he got my pants off, he pinned me to the ground. He held me down with one arm and clasped his other hand over my mouth with the other. I couldn't breathe. My chest was hot and tight. I became dizzy. I couldn't move, even though my life depended on it.

He jabbed his fingers into me. I was in so much pain. I wriggled. My eyes bugged out.

He smiled.

He smiled again, this time jabbing "his friend" into me. I thought my body was ripping in half. The pain kept getting worse. The feeling of my flesh ripping to shreds went all the way up to my brain. I started going numb in my mind and body. I couldn't think; I couldn't feel; he was killing a part of me.

With every jab of his penis, he called me a whore. I experienced pain from the thrusting, heartache from the nasty words in my ear, and suffocation from the strength of his hand that stayed over my mouth. By the grace of God, I passed out. I wouldn't remember anything while I was unconscious, and that was a blessing.

I woke up a few minutes later. He was zipping his pants and laughing at me. I was lying in blood. It was on my bottom, and I got it on my hands. I started screaming again and scrambled to my feet.

He went into the bathroom, and I ran upstairs to find Momma. I had to get help. I needed to go to the hospital or the doctor or something. I was bleeding, and the pain made walking difficult. How could I make the burning go away? How could I make his voice stop ringing in my ears? Mom was nowhere in the house. I ran to the garage to see if her car was there. It wasn't. Christy was also gone.

I had no one. No one was going to help me. He had defeated me. I was alone, and he knew I knew it. The only person in the house was a monster. He was not my daddy. I was truly afraid because he was still downstairs.

I hid in the upstairs bathroom, locking the door. I ran the bathwater as hot as I could stand it. I tried to burn his germs off me. I scrubbed and scrubbed until I was raw, but I still felt filthy dirty. I positioned myself under the faucet trying to heal the parts of myself that he had just defiled. Eventually, I realized that I was burning myself down there and turned on the cold water. No matter what I did, it burned and burned.

After an hour, I'd had enough. I walked out of the bathroom, still terrified. He was standing there waiting. He was dressed, looking like nothing had happened. I clutched my towel for dear life, not wanting him to see my body. He was a stranger; he was the devil.

"You are mine; you will do what I want; and you will never tell anyone what happened today." I didn't recognize his voice; its depth was alarming. "I'll kill you. Do you understand? Do you?!" He spat at me with his nasty words.

I just looked at him. My knuckles were white from holding my towel.

"Your mom doesn't care," he said. "She wasn't here to help you, was she? *Was she?*"

I shook my head no. He was breathing heavily. My heart was racing; I was scared of what he'd do next if I didn't answer. I uttered the word *no*.

"That's because she doesn't love you. She never did, and she never will." He was yelling, but not as loudly. "If you tell her, she won't believe you. You're only a kid, and she'll hate you for lying."

Then he bent down to my eye level and added, "If you ever tell *anyone*, I will find out about it. And then I will kill you." Then he snapped his fingers in my ear as he added, "Just like that."

He walked away, and I went into my room. I lay down. I cried. I couldn't figure out exactly what I had done to deserve such a harsh punishment. I didn't know why this man hated me so much, and I wondered if he would ever love me again. I couldn't understand why my mother didn't love me either. What had I done? I was bad. I had been real, real bad. I didn't want to be bad anymore. I didn't want to be good either. I didn't want to be anything.

I went outside to find my dog, Prince. I held on to him. He licked the tears from my face while I talked to him. He knew what happened, and he wouldn't tell anyone. He would never leave me when I needed him most. He would love me no matter how terrible a daughter I had been.

That night, I slept with an ice-cold washcloth between my legs. It quickly became stained with blood. I fell asleep as I prayed to God. The next day, my prayers had not been answered because I was still breathing.

On Deck

I was in the school play that year. *The Wizard of Oz* sounded incredibly cool, and just like every other little girl, I was hoping to be Dorothy. No matter how much I clicked my heels, I didn't get my wish. Mr. Robinson told me I had to be the Wicked Witch. No one liked the witch. She was mean. I even had to wear green goo.

Tired of drama, I decided to try baseball that summer. Mom came to all of my games. She even made Dad attend sometimes. I thought joining the team would be lots of fun. But mostly, I hoped I would finally make some friends in Alhambra. I was still batting zero with my country peers.

I was young, and I didn't take all the factors into consideration. For one, Alhambra had a boys' baseball team. All the athletic teams were male because the school was so small. If girls wanted to play, they had to be tough enough to go against the boys. So different teams—soccer, track, and basketball—sometimes had one girl. The boys usually liked that girl as much as they liked striking out.

As it turned out, I wasn't the only girl on the team—I had to go and be the second. The boys didn't take too kindly to Kyla, but they accepted her because she'd been hanging around since T-ball days. Thanks to me, their team had two girls.

I don't know what I was thinking. During one of the games, I almost threw in the towel. I was at bat, getting ready to hit. I wound up and immediately dropped my Louisville Slugger. The pitcher had clocked me in the hand with the baseball. Meanwhile, the umpire called it a strike.

At least our coach was on my side. "Are you blind?" he yelled. I was playing it tough. I blinked. I made an angry face. If I really wanted baseball suicide, all I needed to do was cry.

"I heard a clink," the umpire said.

My mom ran over to make sure I was okay. At that point, my toughness melted along with my pride. I cried hard because my hand hurt like hell. Mom brought me ice while the coach argued with the umpire. The umpire won, and I was still out.

Mom said I could sit out the rest of the game if I wanted to, but I went back in and played till the end. That's the only way I could regain my reputation. I had started the game, and I was going to finish it. My parents didn't raise a quitter.

They always taught me persistence—to just keep getting along any way I could.

I was out in left field and at least I could move my fingers a little bit. If I had given up at that moment, then the boys who hated me would've won. So I finished the rest of the season with my chin up and my batting helmet—and gloves—on. I was careful not to get in the way of any more balls. I was glad when baseball was over.

I hadn't endeared myself to the boys in my school, and the girls were so "country" that I had a hard time adjusting. At least I had track. I could always run. I could jump, too. I was excited for our school's track and field days at the end of the year. The grandiose titles of Mr. and Miss Peanut would go to the two children who earned the most first-place ribbons in a series of competitions. I was good at sports, but I never dreamed I'd win the coveted title. I just know that this arrogant snob of a fifth grader named Keith was hot when I beat him in the short-distance run. I don't know why it bothered him so much; he could still beat me in the long run. I creamed him in the dashes, though, and he hated me for that. He always got Mr. Peanut, and that year was no different. There was one change, though: I stood next to him in the winner's spot. I was the underdog, and the surprise Miss Peanut winner. I had overthrown the reigning queen, Carla. I was proud of myself on the inside, but I couldn't be truly happy because everything I did made those kids hate me more. I felt so alone in Alhambra. My daddy—when he was Daddy, not when he was Tom—and my dog were the only two things I really had. I felt accepted only when I was at home with them.

It didn't matter how much, or how little, my mom did for me. I resented her, though I didn't yet hate her. Sure, she might come to my baseball games, but she hadn't come to my rescue. She was just starting secretarial school and sliding into her own world. She was building a life of her own that didn't include any of us—me, Christy, or Daddy. She was in her early thirties, and she acted like everyone else could just be damned. The change showed in the way she started speaking to Dad, and in the way she spoke a lot less to all of us. Her daughters came second to her own freedom. I could tell by the quick dinners and leaner lunches. I could tell by how much she was gone from the house. She had realized there was a way out of her unhappiness. School and education were her exit signs.

Meanwhile, my best friend Prince was misbehaving. He was an outdoor dog, and I never got to bring him inside. If I could've convinced my parents to let him be an indoor dog, maybe this wouldn't have happened. But they wouldn't have him shedding and getting into dog mischief in the house. Regardless, I needed Prince as badly as I needed air. Unfortunately, Prince had an addiction to chickens. He raided the neighbor's coop and killed some birds. The owner was upset and said my parents needed to keep Prince off his property.

So we bought a heavy chain for Prince, but that determined little dog broke through it. When we locked Prince up in the shed, he dug or scratched his way out. Then Dad would be mad because Prince messed up the shed.

He was such a strong little dog. He could carry the weight of my problems, but he wouldn't listen when I told him to stay out of the chicken coop. I begged my dog to leave those dumb birds alone.

Mom told me if he killed one more chicken, we'd have to get rid of him. I was terrified. The only time I felt protected and safe was when I was with that dog. I had another stern conversation with Prince that night. He couldn't do this to me; he had to stay with me. He had to stop with the chickens.

I whined about the situation to Daddy, too. He said I had to talk to my mom about it. So I bugged her again, and she told me we didn't have any other choice. She asked her parents for advice about Prince. They were the kind of country folks who knew how to hunt and skin their own food. So to them, an animal was just an animal—totally disposable. They told my mom to shoot Prince; that would be the end of it.

The next day, Prince had gnawed his way out of his doghouse again. More chickens were dead. When I got home from school, Prince wasn't there. I looked everywhere for him. My heart raced until Mom got home.

"Where is he?" I screamed and cried in the kitchen. I shook all over.

Mom said, "I'm sorry, honey, we had to get rid of him." I don't know which was worse—my inconsolable crying, or the rage I had toward her. She had taken him away from me. From then on I believed she was heartless. That was the end of our relationship as far as I was concerned. I had nothing left but Daddy—Daddy in his good mood. He was all I had to cling to in Alhambra.

I slept with Prince's collar. After the rapes that went on and on, I would hide outside and pretend to talk to my dog. Every time I missed Prince, I blamed my mother. I missed him all the time.

Not even a year later, Aunt Deanna babysat us, and I was still dragging his collar around.

"What's wrong with you? Why are you doing that?" she asked me, popping her gum. "Why are you talking to a stupid dog collar?"

"Maybe Prince will come back one day." I held myself together—crying would give Deanna way too much ammunition.

"Oh, he's not coming back." She was matter-of-fact. Christy was there, too, and she listened intently.

"You don't know anything," I said as I stared at the worn leather collar that still smelled of dog food and fur.

"I know they got rid of him, all right." As Deanna spoke, my stomach made its way to my barf reflex. She was almost laughing at me at this point. "Uncle Derek came and shot him a while back. He's buried in your backyard." Uncle Derek was Mom and Deanna's quiet, smart brother. I hated him with all my might.

Christy ran off, and I sat there with my head down.

"Wake up," Deanna said to me. "They shot him. He's not alive."

I ran outside. I couldn't take Deanna another second. I couldn't breathe either. I ran as hard as I could around our property. I ran until my sweat soaked my shirt. I didn't know what to do or who could help me. I knew where we had buried Buttercup and Bandit, so I figured Prince was buried there, too. I don't think I ever found the exact spot, but I pretended he was under my feet, right next to them. I went out often and talked to him. I felt like I had lost Prince twice, and both times messed me up.

As if I needed more to mess me up.

Mom found bloody underwear beneath the stairs. The incidents were happening in the basement. Afterward, I had a ritual of hiding the clothes, bathing, and then going outside to talk to Prince. I'd just shove my panties up under the wooden staircase because no one messed around in there. I was afraid someone might find the panties in the garbage can, and I didn't know what a nine-year-old was supposed to do with filthy, dirty clothes. I didn't know how to use the washing machine; I couldn't even reach it.

One weekend morning, Mom lined up Christy and me downstairs and stood across from us pointing her finger. Christy and I were pretty much the same size, and we grabbed our underwear out of the same drawer. We'd put on whatever panties were clean.

"Whose are these?!" she yelled at us. I didn't know how to deal with it. I was so scared. I couldn't tell her they were mine. If I did, I was afraid she'd hate me, and Dad would kill me.

"What happened?! Somebody better tell me something right now!" It was Saturday, and she was home doing the laundry in the basement.

Christy started crying, too. Mom didn't yell that much, and she rarely got that mad. Christy said absolutely nothing. She was seven, and she was confused.

"If you girls don't tell me whose these are, I'll take you to the doctor," Mom said, threatening us. "The doctor will know the answer. I'll take you both right now."

I knew I was never supposed to lie to the doctor. I was trapped. Through tears and sniffles, I told Mom that the panties were mine. She walked away. About an hour later, she found me and gave me a lecture about when a girl starts her period.

A few days later, Mom brought me to Grandma Paulson's house and said, "Stacey's become a woman." She told Aunt Deanna and Grandma. I even think one of my uncles overheard the conversation. I turned red, which just added embarrassment on top of embarrassment. I couldn't believe it. I didn't know what I could do.

For all I knew, I *was* getting my period. I'd seen a movie at school on this topic. I knew girls menstruated every month once they got to a certain age. So maybe what he was doing to me caused my period because after each time, I bled. I tried to put it all together, but nothing made sense. If I got my period, did that mean I would get pregnant? I did have a little belly. So was I pregnant? What exactly made me a woman? What he did to me, or getting my period? Had I really started my period?

I stopped sleeping well at night. My breath became shallow sometimes for no reason, and I struggled to stay calm. I woke up with nightmares. There was no woman in my body. I felt like a scared little girl.

Adding It Up

In the fifth grade, one thing—just one thing—started going right. I loved school again. This happened even though the man who had seemed so out to get me, Mr. Richardson, was again my teacher. He had been my dreaded third-grade teacher, too, the one who had tried to fail me for not knowing cursive. As time went on, he was nicer, thankfully. He was also my volleyball coach. Volleyball was great, too. My mom didn't go to many games, and my dad even fewer, but that was okay. I scored points and got comfortable with my teammates. We were the Alhambra Tigers, and while the girls weren't my best friends, they were much better than the boys, who gave me evil looks while holding their baseball bats.

At the end of that school year, I also scored high on the achievement tests. My scores put me in the gifted category, and I could finally relax. For the last year, I'd been worried that maybe I was slow at school. These tests gave me proof that I wasn't. Moreover, I was asked to go into a gifted program called the Think Tank. We came out of our regular class for a few hours on Tuesdays and Thursdays, and we got separate homework.

Because my dad was such an intelligent person, I thought he'd be proud of me. So I'd bring my Think Tank math problems home to him, hoping we'd work on them together. Turned out, my idea added up to nothing. While my dad was one of those people who got math and understood the way numbers flow, he wasn't the type who could explain those complicated equations. He was quickly frustrated with me and told me he didn't want to help me with my homework any-more. He got mad, huffing around the room and ignoring me.

Still, I'd strive for his approval even though he never gave it. I'd see glimpses of his satisfaction every once in a while in his sober smiles. I always hoped for those moments when things clicked with him. Once I made him happy, I wanted to make him happy again and again. I just wanted to see the daddy who picked that first apple for me in Alhambra. I wanted the daddy who put me on the tractor with him. Once I'd had Good Daddy, I wanted him back. I was hopeful, always.

Sometimes, when he was happy drunk, I'd get close to getting into his good graces. He'd give me these long lectures that I enjoyed. They were about school and boys. His advice was protective: "Never let a guy treat you badly" and "Study hard in school, so you can be-come anything." If I caught the happy drunk talk, he'd use the words, "I'm proud of you." I basked in those moments.

That year, my mom continued to have trouble with my father. Each day was one challenge after another. There were late dinners, late nights, and late fights. Why my mother wanted to memorialize that moment in time is beyond me, but when the time for school pictures came around, she signed us up. Christy and I got ours taken dur-ing the day, and they offered family portraits in the evening. Mom planned for it well in advance. She wanted us to have a proper family photo, and I still don't know why she cared. She was either fighting with my dad or away at school. She was not home enough. And she was never home when the incidents happened in the basement.

But we all tried for her sake. The whole week beforehand, Christy and I got our dresses together. Dad needed to have his nicest suit cleaned. We figured out how we would do our hair. I had a new short haircut that didn't require much fuss. Mom reminded us we had to be there at such and such a time. The family photo was a big deal to everyone—everyone except for Dad. That night, he came home two hours late and drunk. We were about ready to walk out the door without him.

The four of us headed to the school in case they could still squeeze in our appointment. Mom screamed at him the whole way. "I told you all week to get home in time. I can't believe you!" she yelled.

"Oh, Debbie, it's going to be all right," he said, driving the car way too fast. He was happy drunk that night. You can see it in how the picture turned out. His eyes were droopy, and his smile was easy. Meanwhile, our smiles were stiff, like we had something to hide.

When we arrived at our school, he tried to hug her, and she brushed him off. He had let her down one more time. She was upset, but Christy and I were just glad he was there. He was happy, so what was the problem? We wanted to get on with it. He did, too. He joked with the photographer and the assistants. He was having a good old time.

At that time, my parents had stopped sleeping together, though they still shared a bedroom. They didn't tell us this information; Christy and I picked it up during their fights. What he did to me happened mostly on the weekends when Mom went shopping, or right after school. He'd be home early, and Mom would still be out studying. She took Jazzercise classes afterward, so she'd come home late.

He didn't rape me more after their fights. He didn't rape me more when he was rip-roaring drunk, though he did rape me often when he was intoxicated. The incidents were steady, unpredictably predictable, and mind numbing. At about six o'clock in the afternoon, he and I were alone. Sometimes, he would come find me three times in one week, and sometimes he would leave me alone for a month. I never knew when to prepare, so my anxiety levels stayed high at all times just in case. I have trouble picturing Christy in my mind during those times. She must've been outside. I know she never came into the basement. It wasn't her territory, and she didn't dare trespass.

The basement was our special place. The more my parents pulled away from each other, the more often Dad and I went down there. He turned to me, and I felt horribly weak for letting him. I fought with him a few times in the beginning, and those were painful mistakes. I couldn't beat him no matter what. I couldn't win. So I became too quiet and too compliant. It didn't hurt so badly if I closed off my mind and shut down my body. I'd lie there while my thoughts took me other places.

Even then, he had different rules for his moods. He wasn't always hurtful. There were still times when he'd sit me on his lap and talk about nothing for hours. He'd keep me awake until one in the morning. Those were the times when I got what I needed from him. I got that he loved me and felt that I was special. We bonded during the good times, and I blocked out the bad.

I didn't think I had any other choice.

Miss Peanut

Junior high was much better than elementary school. The area towns of Alhambra, Grantfork, and Highland came together to form a bigger campus. So instead of having fifteen kids in the class, there were one hundred—like in Kansas City. I knew how to function in a larger, noisier, and more diverse social setting. At last, I found people to talk to. And even more than that, I was the tiniest bit popular because I was good in sports. The Alhambra kids had trouble adapting to the bigger school, and they faded into the background. Some of them still hated me. But at least there were other girls and boys who thought differently.

The boy from the Mr. and Miss Peanut competition, Keith, continued to despise me. We couldn't get away from each other because we both ran track. My feet were on fire when I ran, and I could outrace him completely by the seventh grade. He was not happy. Despite the bigger size of our junior high, it still had only a boys' track team. The coaches left a few slots open for girls. They usually accepted four—enough to make a relay team—and those girls were often eighth graders. I had to try out for two whole weeks for that team, and I made cut after cut. With one final cut left, we were doing heats. The team already had four girls, so I figured my chances were slim to none. My only hope was sprinting. The team didn't have a good sprinter, and I could run like lightning.

The coach was picking kids to compete against each other. He paired me and Keith in the 110-yard dash. I whupped his behind. Because of that one race, I got the spot on the team, and he didn't. I never had a better feeling in my life. I beat Mr. Peanut, the boy who had made grades three through six pure hell for me.

In that moment, I felt completely free. I'd held on to so much hurt from elementary school, and just like that, it was gone.

That night, I couldn't wait to tell Dad I'd made the track team. He'd been a track star at his high school. I was sure he'd be proud of me. I ran outside when I saw his bananamobile. He got out, dressed in his brown suit and wing-tip shoes.

"Guess what!" I told him everything about the tryouts, beating Keith, and most important, about the team.

He put down his briefcase. His look was stern and cold—and anything but pleased. He said, "There's no way a girl can be on the track team."

"But I did!" The lump in my chest dropped down to my stomach. Mom was happy for me; why wasn't he?

"Prove it," Dad said, loosening his tie. He drew an invisible starting line at the top of the driveway. He said we'd finish down where it ended. I stalled for a few minutes, wondering if he was serious.

My mom must've wondered what was going on. She came outside and told him, "Tom, this is ridiculous. She's on the track team."

"I'm not racing you," I said. I wasn't sure whether to cry or get fired up. Either reaction would get me into trouble, so I tried to stay steady. Life was always easier when I did what he said. He kept going on about how he could beat me. My mom told him more than once that he was a crazy man in a business suit.

But Dad laid down the law in our house. So he and I raced in the driveway. I beat him.

"Let's race again," he said.

I beat him twice.

"Again."

We raced over and over and over until my mom turned up the volume.

"Tom, you're drunk, and this has to stop." She was near tears, and by this time, I was full-out crying. I had a 220-pound drunk man practically spitting at me with his last breaths.

"I could still win," he said, even though he could barely speak, "if I didn't have this suit on." He headed toward the house, looking more angry than defeated. Before he got inside, he gruffly added, "A girl can never be on the track team."

My mind raced back to Grandma Lannert's house. In her living room, there were pictures of him in his track uniform, posing next to trophies. I wanted him to love me, and that's why I had sought out track in the first place. If he could do it, I could do it. Then we'd have more in common. Then we'd have something worthwhile to bond over. I needed reasons for him to want me for a daughter. Plus, I thought maybe if he loved me more, he would hurt me less.

Mom wasn't getting along great with her parents. She was starting to talk about the abuse she suffered as a child. Though my grandfather didn't rape her, he sexually abused her nonetheless. She went to the university's rape crisis center for help. Mom was taking care of herself first and foremost. Distancing herself from her daughters may not have been good, but at least working out her problems was a step in the right direction. She went to a counselor and even did some volunteering. I was a little resentful because she spent even more time away from us. She was trying to pull herself out of her world, a world that I lived in with her. She started worrying about the other girls in our family. She had a niece she thought might be suffering from sexual abuse, and she thought Christy might be, too. Apparently, Christy was acting out at that time, not listening to Mom and fighting with her about everything. Christy was just like that; she seemed fine to me.

All I know is that a chain of several strange events happened. I have a fuzzy memory of being alone in the backseat of a car. Grandma Paulson and Mom were in the front seat talking about me. I couldn't tell what they were saying; I just knew it wasn't good. Then Grandma looked at me.

"Stacey, does your daddy touch you?" Grandma yelled back at me.

I was shocked. I felt imaginary pins pricking my skin, and my back was nailed to a corner. If anything happened to me, it was my own fault, and what on earth was Grandma Paulson going to do about it anyway?

"Are you listening, child?" she asked again, her arm stretched across the front seat so she could turn her head to stare me down. "Is anybody touching you where they shouldn't be touching you?"

"Ewww. No! My daddy would never do that!" I yelled back at her. I didn't have words for this topic, not out loud and not even in my head. Ask any child this question point blank, and she will deny it.

She put her arm back into her lap in the front seat.

"See, Debbie, nobody's touching Stacey."

Shortly after that conversation, Mom loaded Christy, my cousin Candice, and me into her two-door car. She headed back to the rape crisis center. Christy, then eight, and Candice, five, were getting tested for possible sexual abuse. I remember waiting in the lobby—I spent the whole time coloring. They each went into a room where a young woman asked them a million questions. I didn't even know what a rape crisis center was, but I knew I was bored there. Christy's and Candice's tests were negative. Mom didn't have me tested because I'd already told Grandma that nothing had happened to me. Later, it came out that Candice *had* been abused, but she lied to the counselors that day because her mother had just left home, and she didn't want to lose her father, too. But at the time, I believe the negative results made Mom feel more secure, like all of the girls must be safe.

Around the same time, my mother also confronted Dad. I overheard it.

"Do you ever do anything with Stacey?" she asked during a heated conversation.

"You're crazy!" he yelled back at her. "You're paranoid, too. Just because your dad abused you doesn't mean I abuse my daughter."

"You're right, you're right," she'd say, almost shamefully.

"I'd never do that to a child, and I'd kill anyone who did," Dad told her.

"I'm probably reading too much into it." With that, she'd end the conversation. To her, she was just projecting—what happened to her as a girl couldn't possibly be happening to me. She blamed her suspicions on her work at the rape crisis center, and on her own silly head for playing tricks on her.

I'd die inside during these conversations. If I spoke up, God only knew what my dad would do to me. Besides, silence was strong; telling was weak. Telling meant everyone would know my shame, so I might as well keep it quiet. Another part of me wanted to protect my mom from what was really happening. She'd be torn up if she found out the truth. She was already upset most of the time—what would she do if she knew? Family dinners were strained enough. If Mom and Dad were going at it, our food might as well have been sawdust, because we couldn't eat it. Keeping my mouth shut was a way to keep the status quo. I didn't want to be the one who made things worse.

Also, I saw Mom as fragile. I've heard that some women are warriors; Mom was definitely not one of them. She wasn't strong enough to stand up for herself. She didn't think she was good at anything. She was mostly fair and kind, but those are different qualities altogether. She didn't have that certain umph some women have. She didn't have the inner determination to stand alone. She was the type of mild-mannered woman who could only stand beside someone else who is strong.

On the other hand, my nickname was Tiger. I was supposed to be a fighter. I believed I could handle everything myself, and I didn't assume that anyone was supposed to help me. There was no real help for me, only brief escapes when I ran track, or when I talked to Prince at his makeshift grave. Besides, if there was help for me, I didn't deserve it. I was a bad, dirty daughter.

When I'd ask myself, *Who's gonna help me? Who is supposed to?*

The only answer was: *Daddy.*

He was my only choice. He was supposed to help me. He was supposed to protect me.

Busted

The divorce happened on June 7, 1985. By that time, I was in seventh grade, and Mom had finished school and started working as a secretary. She had a little more feistiness in her after going to the rape crisis center and after graduating with an associate's degree. I remember her teaching me to drive a car out on those old country roads around that time. It was something really fun that she and I did together. Her parents had taught her when she was eleven or so, too. She told me she wanted me to know how to take care of myself—how to get away—if I ever needed to. She also stood up to Dad more and more often. And he would call her terrible names, from stupid whore to worthless bitch. He did that only when he was drunk. She used to just take it; the new Mom would tell him to shut up.

Dad had started his own actuary business with another man, and it wasn't working out. We were relying on Grandma Lannert more and more, and I felt kind of poor because they were always talking about watching their money. That was the main reason Mom went to work as quickly as she did. We needed her income.

One day, Dad came home and told my mom that he wanted to quit his job with his partner. He had a job offer that would mean moving to Omaha, Nebraska. Another guy named Marvin McCandless had offered him a great job in the city, and he was going to take it.

"That means you can quit working, Debbie," he told her, standing in the dining room.

"I like my job," she said, her hand on her hip. "I like working. Why should I quit?"

They went back and forth for a while. Christy and I ran in and out of the backyard as their fight escalated. We didn't want to hear it, but when a train's about to wreck, it's hard to look away.

He thought a woman should stay home and take care of her kids. Mom said she felt powerless when he was the sole breadwinner. She lit into him about his drinking, as usual. Then she ended her tirade with words that drove a stake through his heart.

"Not only do I want to keep my job," she said, lowering her voice, "I want a separation."

He cornered her in the room and drew his fist back.

She said, "Hit me if it makes you feel better. Go ahead." She had been hit so many times by her father that she didn't think one more pop from my dad was going to make any difference.

He didn't hit her.

Instead, he picked up a dining room chair and threw it at the chandelier. Glass flew all over the floor, the table, even into the other rooms. The chair landed upside down on the TV. Mom bent down to start picking up the sharp shards. With each piece, she got madder and madder.

Christy and I ran into the room, and Dad yelled at us, too. He said, "Get your asses back outside." We bawled and bawled. We knew this fight was one of their worst. We thought for sure one of those crashes was Mom getting thrown against the wall, but she looked okay. She was just shaking and crying. But she was also furious.

Her hands were filled with glass, and she threw the shards onto the floor. "You made this mess, you clean it up," she told my father. "I'm leaving."

He said back to her, "Don't let the door hit you in the ass."

She raced upstairs and started packing. The next day, Aunt Deanna was getting married for the second time. Mom was rushing to get all of our dresses and shoes plus the other things we'd need. He followed her throughout the house, muttering all kinds of drunken mad words.

We stayed at Grandma and Grandpa Paulson's for a few nights, maybe a week. Dad went to stay with his mother. We stayed with Mom at the house after that. When she was working, we stayed with our babysitter, Wendy.

Mom couldn't afford the house by herself, so she started to look for an apartment in nearby Highland. Dad was going to take over the house. Meanwhile, Christy and I were sent to Grandma Lannert's for the rest of the summer. It was a lot to keep up with.

I loved our babysitter Wendy. She was warm and kind, and she never yelled or screamed at us. On my final day with her before we were to move, she sat me down at the kitchen table. She told me she had been sexually abused when she was a kid, and she asked if the same thing was happening to me.

I said, "Yes." I drew invisible circles on her Formica table. "Yes, it's happening to me." I knew I could trust her.

Wendy said she was sorry this was happening. She offered the advice, "Stand up for yourself, and don't let anyone hurt you."

I felt like crying. I tried to explain to her how I loved my daddy so much; I absolutely adored him. But he hurt me, and he hurt me badly. I couldn't understand why. I couldn't make sense of what I should be doing, or how I should be feeling.

Wendy shook her head. She said, "I know, honey. I know."

Mom came to pick up Christy and me in the afternoon. Wendy walked out of her house with her arm around me. We stood outside when Wendy told my mother, "Tom is hurting Stacey."

I looked down at the ground. I didn't want to see Mom's face.

"I will take care of it, and I will not let it happen again," my mother said.

I was silent in the car and for the rest of the night. I was waiting for her to say something. I felt ashamed and sorry for what I had done—for the trouble I was causing. Mom didn't mention the matter. The next day, we went to Grandma Lannert's to stay. Mom and Dad passed each other briefly to exchange us. Mom didn't say anything to Dad as they stood alone outside. I felt like she could have; she had the opportunity.

Instead, she just left.

How could she do that? I look back and try to understand. To this day, she says she didn't know. She didn't equate "Tom is hurting Stacey" with rape. She thought if something so terrible was happening to me, I would've told her. I believe she was dealing with her own past. She didn't know how to confront what was going on in the present—and she just didn't have the strength.

That night, Dad stayed at Grandma Lannert's with us before he headed back to Alhambra.

He came after me at the one place where I had always felt safe. At Grandma's house, it happened again.

I was heartbroken.

Not only did my mom abandon me, she was also a big liar.

My mother was working and finding her own place to live. Dad was living in Alhambra and working in St. Louis. Christy and I just laid low and enjoyed the summer with Grandma as much as we could. It was hard because we felt abandoned, confused, and angry. Why didn't anyone want us that summer?

When school started again, they had divided their stuff, and Mom had her own place in Highland, Illinois, not far from our old house in Alhambra. Dad was living in Alhambra alone. Christy and I went to live with Mom.

Her apartment was right behind a Wal-Mart, and I started walking in and taking whatever I wanted. I wasn't even slick about it. I was in the eighth grade, and I was untouchable. I'd steal hair barrettes and makeup. I'd slip them into my purse right in the middle of the aisle. I didn't get caught. One of my aunts worked there, though, and she knew I was on Wal-Mart's watch list. Mom never found out.

What got me into trouble was breaking and entering. I had been babysitting for a family nearby, and I had their house key. So one night when I knew they weren't home, I walked in and took a shirt. They noticed immediately and called my mom.

I took stuff that wasn't mine because I didn't want to ask permission from anyone for anything—especially Mom. I believed deep in my heart that I was bad; so this was my way of playing the part. I also wanted attention from Dad, who loved me only half the time, and from Mom, who cared only about dating and work. I wanted Mom to step in and fix what was happening to me on the weekends I had to spend at Dad's.

Even better, maybe I would get sent away—far away.

I did not get the reaction I had hoped for. Instead, I got yelled at.

"Why are you doing this?" Mom asked me in the car, her quiet voice fierce.

"I don't know." I don't know was my standard answer.

"You know stealing is wrong; what is wrong with you?" she yelled.

"I don't know," I told her quietly, unable to feel anything.

On that same day, she woke me up in the middle of the night and told me to pack my bags.

"You're going to your Dad's, and you're going to a psychologist."

I wanted to go to the counselor and talk to her. But sometimes Dad would take me to the appointments, and he'd try to manipulate what I might say.

In the car outside her office, he would tell me, "Tell her how happy you are. Tell her you went to the ballgame. Don't tell her I was drunk. Don't tell her I yell at your sister."

He never said the words *Don't tell her what I do to you* because he was sober at the dropoff. He never, ever mentioned that topic unless he was drunk. But I knew what he meant.

So I never told my counselor the one thing she needed to know. I told her how hard it was for me to sleep, though. I told her about my anxiety.

After one of the sessions, my mom picked me up, and my psychologist asked to speak with her right in front of me. She told Mom that she believed I was being sexually abused.

"What? By who?" my mom asked, horrified.

"I'm not sure; someone's boyfriend, an uncle, or her father," the counselor said.

"But we asked her if she was being abused, and she said she wasn't," my mom replied.

The counselor said, "Stacey shows all of the signs of sexual abuse. All fourteen of the signs to be exact."

Mom was quiet in the car. It took her ten minutes to find the courage to ask me, "Is someone touching you?"

I knew what she wanted to hear. My answer was, "No."

After that conversation, I didn't go back to that psychologist.

She kept Christy, and I went back to our old house. He didn't have a choice but to take me. I didn't want to live with Dad, but I didn't want to be with her either. She didn't love me. At that time, he might've hurt me, but at least he loved me. She didn't care if I was alive or dead—she just wanted me out of her way. I wanted her to fight for me, but she didn't even want me. That's how I saw my mother at age thirteen.

My father abused me freely while they were getting divorced. I never knew when it was coming. The anticipation was unbearable, and the rapes were inevitable. Rather than sitting around waiting, I stayed inside the house not trying to hide from him. I hoped to control an uncontrollable situation by being available. I felt dirty and wrong. My plan would backfire when he'd wake me up in the middle of the night anyway.

Making the incidents even more unpleasant, he had ballooned up to three hundred pounds during their marriage. I didn't even register one hundred pounds at age thirteen. The extra weight made the sex hurt even more. I'd completely leave my small body when it happened. Either I had to pretend I wasn't there, or I had to find a way to die. The guilt I felt afterward—my shame and my belief that I had caused it—hurt me deeply all over again.

This whole time I was hateful to my mother. *Where was she?* She had moved into an apartment in Highland and was on the phone every time I stayed with her and Christy. Eventually, I moved back

in with them because Dad was getting ready to move out of Alhambra, to a townhouse in Soulard, another part of St. Louis. She had a
boyfriend, too, a man named Frank. He just happened to be my dad's
best friend from college. The drama was ridiculous. Dad called Mom
a whore every time he'd catch her on the phone or when he dropped
me off. Everything was falling apart, including me. I was a nervous
wreck, and I stopped being able to sleep more than a few hours at a
time. Danger was everywhere.

When Dad wasn't bad-mouthing Mom to me, he was trying to get
her back. He would call her at work and start talking about me and
Christy. She'd tell him she couldn't discuss anything with him at the
office. So he'd call her at home. Most of their conversations ended
with her refusing to make amends and his screaming at her. He'd tell
her that only she brought out the beast in him. All of his problems
were her fault, and she was just making them worse.

There were times when she felt like she should go back to Dad—
for our sake. That's exactly what her mother and father advised her
to do. Dad had always put on his best act in front of his in-laws. They
never saw him throw a dish or call my mom a bitch. Plus, Grandpa
loved when Dad would get drunk with him at our house. When I was
little, I used to look forward to going to Grandma's with Dad because
he'd act like such a gentleman there, and he'd become the perfect
daddy I'd created in my dreams. Maybe that's why they liked him so
much—or either their old-fashioned patriarchal beliefs simply made
them think Mom was wrong for leaving her man.

They went out on a date once during their separation, and my
dad told Mom that he had stopped drinking for good. They had a
nice dinner, but he was drunk by the end of it. She made sure the
divorce proceeded, and it was official in November of 1985. She had
turned her attentions to Frank, and that was that. Dad was nothing
but pissed.

That's why I was so relieved when he met Rosa, when I was in the
eighth grade. I found out late one night. I was at his house that weekend. I waited in the upstairs family room for him to come home. I was

worried because it was 11 p.m., and he wasn't home from work. I was used to his being late—but never that late. You'd think I wouldn't have cared what happened to him, but I did. Christy was at Mom's.

For better or worse, it was just the two of us.

I finally saw his headlights beaming through the big picture window. When he walked in, he was smiling. He was the good dad, if a little boozy. I could smile because Daddy was home, with no darkness in those ocean-blue eyes. Even though I was getting big, he asked me to sit on his lap. He told me about the most beautiful woman he'd ever met.

He said she was walking across a parking lot, and he walked up to her. He asked, "You're so beautiful, may I just know your name?" She smiled at him, and they spent the entire evening together having dinner and drinks. Dad was like a teenager in love.

My burden was lighter when he smiled like that.

Rosa looked Mexican. That surprised me, because my dad could be such a bigot. She was slightly heavy around her bosom and her butt, and she was about the same height as my mom, five feet four. But he was right: she was very pretty. She was in her early forties, and she had a daughter who was a few years older than me. I think Rosa worked in the sales department at the St. Louis branch of the *Wall Street Journal*. Whenever she was around, Dad was in a good mood. I liked her because she made the most amazing nachos, and she was nice to me.

Rosa gave him something to focus on besides his bitter divorce. When she was around, he didn't come to me as much in the middle of the night.

What Was Killing Me

In the seventh grade, I started having abdominal pain, so my parents—who were still together at that point—took me to a gastroenterologist. No one thought to take me to a gynecologist. I would double over from the lower-gut pain during school. Sometimes, I'd have to lie down in bed. The doctor diagnosed me with lactose intolerance, but I knew for sure that milk wasn't causing my problem. I drank the funky milk they gave me anyway, but I'd sneak regular when Mom and Dad weren't looking. Christy saw what I did, but she didn't tell on me. Yogurt was not causing this issue either, so I ate that, too. I knew this intuitively, but no one believed me. A few years later, they found out that I was right.

During the eighth grade, I lived with Mom in a house she rented. I had to spend every other weekend with my dad. He was now in his townhouse in Soulard, which was then a bad part of downtown St. Louis. I didn't like going there. He kept the place filthy, and he was always drunk. Christy and I shared a bedroom there, so he would wake me up and tell me to come downstairs, where he could get me alone. Then he would take me to his bedroom.

At least I had school. It was an escape, and I loved learning. It was the one place I could focus on what I wanted and not on all the problems and complaints. I didn't have good friends, because I couldn't let anyone get too close to me. I had a secret I had to keep. I was always afraid someone would find out, read into the scar on my wrist, or know how bad I really was, inside and out. I could talk to all different groups of kids at school, in the lunchroom and on sports teams, but friendships couldn't make their way over my wall. Besides, I couldn't have invited anyone over if I had wanted to—I had two very broken homes.

Mom was wrapped up in her work and her boyfriend. She was still dealing with her own healing, too.

I thought it was strange the day that she confronted Grandma Paulson about her own abuse right in front of me. For the first time, out of the blue, Mom told her mother that her father had abused her. The memory is fuzzy, but I know I heard it, and I've always wondered if Mom was trying to send me some sort of secret message. Since she couldn't speak up for me, maybe she wanted me to say something. Or maybe she wanted me to see that her mother knew, too.

Grandma wasn't having anything to do with the conversation. She didn't say anything at first; she just huffed. Then she said my mother's allegations were ridiculous.

"Nothing bad ever happened to you, Debbie." Grandma started to downplay the talk they were having. She changed the subject, like it was no big deal. My mom was nearly shaking, and we headed back home.

Grandma was in deep denial. But so were a lot of people I knew.

We spent a lot of time—too much—at Grandma Paulson's. One night, I was staying there after my first real date. I was in the eighth grade, and I fluttered with happiness. I was thirteen, and Steve and I had walked to the movies together, holding hands. Afterward, Grandma picked me up and brought me to her house. We were in the kitchen when Grandpa told me to come sit next to him in the living room. I did, and then he put his hands down my shirt.

"My hands are cold," the wrinkly old man said. He wasn't as tall as he used to be, and he was thin.

I went stiff, and then I ran. My only thought was: *I'm not going through this shit again.*

As I calmed down, my body shook. I really didn't know how I'd survive someone else touching me. And besides, who did Grandpa think he was to ruin my first date? He was ruining my whole night. I went to Grandma.

She was still in the kitchen cleaning up dishes. She said, "Honey, he just does that when he's drunk. You stay by me."

I didn't leave her side the rest of the night. I didn't sleep either. It was a really old farmhouse, and it creaked if someone sneezed. If I heard even the tiniest creak coming up those stairs toward my bedroom, then I was out the window. I had my escape all planned out. I'd just as soon kill myself jumping two stories than let another man touch me. I was ready; I left the window up.

The next morning, I was exhausted. I crept into the kitchen, scared of what might be waiting for me. Would he try it again? Would Grandma get mad? As it turned out, everything was normal. Neither one of them said a word at the kitchen table. They just went on eating their biscuits.

The next morning, I was headed to Dad's for the weekend. I couldn't believe I had to be there again—how could my mom let this happen to me? I didn't want to be there, or anywhere else for that matter. The second I heard his beer can pop open—before noon—I ran upstairs to my room. It was on the third floor, and there had to be some way to escape when he walked up at night to get me. My window led to a roof with a sharp slope—jumping would be too dangerous. I tried to figure out if I could get out through the skylight, but it was too high.

I realized, *Oh shit. I'm not getting out of here.*

That's when I started looking through his house for prescription drugs. He had nothing but bottles of beer and vodka. I did find a packet of adult-strength Dimetapp. In desperation—I wanted the abuse and my parents' problems to end—I took the whole pack of pills over the course of several hours. There were twelve yellow tablets—add them to a glass of water, and suicide was a few sips away.

I was so wrong. TV shows didn't show the part about pills making a person violently ill. About thirty minutes after I swallowed the handful, I started retching every five minutes. Vomit was coming out of my nose uncontrollably. Honestly, I would've let it go on. I could handle suffering, and I wanted something really bad to happen. But I couldn't go through with it because Christy was with me.

She cried and asked what was wrong with me. "Please don't let anything happen to you," she said.

I didn't want her freaking out, and I couldn't die like that with her right there. So I gave in and called Poison Control. I told them I had accidentally taken four Dimetapp Extentabs. They told me to get my dad on the phone. Christy went and got him off the couch downstairs. Poison Control instructed him to take me straight to the emergency room. I got sicker and sicker the whole way there.

Everyone thought it was an accident, and I never confessed to taking the whole packet. The nurses were nice to me, and they gave me a plastic bag to hold next to my face. I had to force myself to swallow this foul-smelling black charcoal gunk. But that didn't do any good; I threw it up instantly. Next, they pumped my stomach. It was very painful.

A psychologist did visit me in the ER, but I lied to him. I said I just got confused.

I explained, "The Dimetapp directions said to take two tablets, and they didn't work. So I took two more." Eventually, I upped the lie and told the doctors I had taken a total of eight.

"I didn't read the label carefully enough," I said, trying to hold my head up straight. "I understand now. I definitely won't make that mistake again."

They were convinced, and the hospital staff left me alone.

Dad was worried and very sympathetic. He'd rub my back and ask if I was okay. Back home the next day, he realized something wasn't adding up. He sat down on my bed.

"That wasn't an accident, was it?" He asked. "You lied to us all about it, didn't you?"

"I guess I lied."

He hugged me, and he said, "It's going to get better."

After that, he left me alone for a while. The incidents stopped, and he treated me like a daughter instead of his wife or slave. This went on for a blissful couple of months—the longest he ever went without bothering me. I was at my breaking point, and he understood that he couldn't push me anymore. Not at that time, anyway. He also quit drinking when I was around. But I visited only every other week, so who knows if he really slowed down.

Mom never asked me a thing about it, though I think Dad told her. The Dimetapp ordeal was swept under the rug.

Once I became a preteen, my mother didn't teach me things I should have known. The days when she'd spend hours reading books to me were long gone. As a result, she didn't show me how to curl my hair. I learned by myself while Christy watched and gave me tips. She didn't show me how to pluck my eyebrows or cook a chicken breast. Christy and I had to figure stuff out. She just wasn't that kind of mom anymore.

Oddly enough, she had taught me to drive. At thirteen, I was pretty good behind the wheel. I thought it was fun to steal her Cutlass Ciera. I did it because I didn't like her boyfriend Frank. She was getting set to move to Arizona with him, and Christy and I were supposed to come with her. At that time, Christy was living with Aunt Deanna, and I was still with Mom. We were living in our old house in Alhambra for the rest of the summer because the renters had moved out.

"It's going to be great!" Mom said to me while I rolled my eyes. Christy hated the idea, too. In fact, I wasn't even sure she'd actually come.

Frank called up one afternoon while Mom was out, and I picked up the phone.

He made small talk. I told him I didn't know where Mom was. Then he said, "I can't wait until you turn sixteen."

I was excited at first. I thought he was going to buy me a car. "Why?" I asked.

"Your mom says I'm the best sex she's ever had, and I can't wait to tickle your womb." He was slurring, and I knew that hazy male voice all too well. Frank was hitting on me—totally wasted. I was disgusted. He was nothing more than a desert rat. He was lanky with dark hair and a creepy mustache. He wasn't old, but he was very wrinkled.

I hung up on him, and he called right back to say more dirty sex stuff. I hung up again. I slid down the wall and cried.

Another drunk bastard, I thought. I *hated* Frank.

I took Mom's car while she was on the phone with him. He lived in Arizona, and they blabbed constantly. Almost all the time, she was working, shopping, or talking with him. I didn't feel big and grown up for stealing her car—it was more like, *Ha-ha, take that.* She would literally stay on the phone with him for two hours or more. She shut herself off from me. If I asked for supper, she'd just wave her hand, signaling me to get lost. I fended for myself—eating sandwiches for dinner—because she had to talk on the phone. And to whom? To a pig like Frank.

I'd steal the car to buy a can of soda even if we had a six-pack in the refrigerator.

Christy was with me one weekend—I liked weekends when she was around—and she caught me fixing to take Mom's boxy silver car for a drive. By this time, I'd known how to drive for almost two years.

"Let me drive it," Christy said. She was a beautiful little girl with white blond hair and big blue eyes. She could be very convincing—but not this particular time.

"Absolutely not. You'll kill us both." As usual, I was in charge of her. If anything happened on my watch, I'd get it.

"You have to let me drive it, or I'm telling Mom," she said, her neck moving back and forth. I didn't like to fight with Christy. She usually won.

I let Christy get behind the wheel of the car, even though Mom hadn't spent as much time teaching her as she had me. After all, Christy was only eleven. I just tried to keep her off the main drag. Christy pulled the Cutlass down an old road, and then up to this farmhouse that had a semicircular driveway. The path was so open and wide, I figured she couldn't possibly mess up.

But somehow, she really messed up.

She pulled into the huge driveway, didn't turn the wheel hard enough, and tapped into a barn. I screamed at her to stop the car and let me drive, but she backed up and hit a different barn. I screamed again, and that just made her hit the first barn a second time. I was beyond confused at how she'd managed to hit two barns three times.

We screamed and squealed. We were probably going four miles per hour, but we might as well have been clocking sixty. We got out of Mom's car, and there was no damage. The barns had small dents, though. I did not notice that Mom's front license plate was lying on the ground in front of one of the barns.

I forced Christy out of the car and drove us home.

"Let's get out of here!" I told her, and this time, she listened.

Once we got home, we agreed that we weren't doing that again.

Then we heard a knock at the door.

It turns out that all the neighbors knew I'd been sneaking out with the car. The policeman didn't have a tough time putting the pieces together.

The state cop arrived with the license plate in hand and asked me, "So have you been driving your mom's car?"

Christy was shaking behind me, holding my leg. She muttered, "Nuh-uh."

I decided right then and there that telling the truth might be the best option. "Uh-huh," I answered.

I was a nervous wreck. Christy and I had to go to juvenile court. Dad thought it was funny, but he wasn't there with us. Mom was, and she was not one bit amused.

When the judge was considering my punishment, Mom spoke up.

"If anyone should be punished, it should be Stacey," she said, bitterness in her voice. "Stacey was the one who was driving, and she knew better. Christy was too little to know any better."

I was shocked to hear those words. I would've been less hurt if she'd taken a steak knife and cut me up with it.

I didn't speak to her for a long time after that. Mom knew what had happened. She knew I hadn't handed Christy the key. She knew

Christy had blackmailed me into driving her car. She knew Christy had caused the wreckage. I knew I hadn't done the right thing, but I couldn't understand how my own mother could stand up in front of a judge and make matters worse for me. Or maybe I could, considering everything else.

The judge had a surprised look on his face. I don't think he believed what he had heard either. At least his punishment was pretty light. Both of us had to go to a juvenile detention facility for a tour. They left us in a cell for a couple of hours to scare us, and then they let us go. Mom was fined $1,000 in court fees that Dad ended up paying. He called me Crash and Burn for a long time after that.

Meanwhile, Mom grounded me. I thought, *Big deal.* We were living out in the middle of nowhere in Highland, so there wasn't much to do anyway. The worst part of the whole ordeal was the spanking she gave me.

Then she moved to Arizona with Frank, and I obviously wasn't going anywhere with that sorry sack of crap. I went back to Dad's (Rosa was staying there) while Christy went to live with Grandma and Grandpa Paulson. Mom thought her dad had changed his ways. She wasn't worried about him molesting Christy because, according to family rumor, Grandpa had never touched Aunt Deanna. I don't know whether he did touch Christy; she never said he did. But I do know she hated living with them. They were stern and strict, and she was about as carefree as they come. Before long, she moved in with Aunt Deanna.

Dad became only more pissed about Frank. *Pissed.* He talked about how much he hated Mom and Frank all the time. If Dad picked up the phone when Mom called for me, he'd yell, "Stacey, the slut's on the phone for you."

She didn't argue with him anymore at that point. She just let him insult her. What could she say? Nothing would make him stop. Plus, she'd run off with his best friend from college. Even I knew that people weren't supposed to do things like that to each other. Something just seemed wrong with her.

Our parents kept moving us back and forth, and we felt like nobody wanted us. The truth was, nobody did. They always told us we could choose where we wanted to live, but neither of them lobbied to get us. Christy had to do the merry-go-round more than I did. She never knew where she'd be sleeping. I always got sent back to Dad. I didn't want to go, but at least he showed an interest in me when no one else did. So I lived with Dad and Rosa down in Soulard for about six months. I wasn't scared of living with him because I'd done it before. I knew how to be compliant, and I knew how to make the situation work. The rules were simple: if you fought with Dad, you wouldn't win. So I didn't fight. Besides, I was happy that Rosa was going to be there to sleep with him.

Rosa didn't know how to be compliant with Dad. She yelled back when he went into his alcoholic rages. She didn't know that the best thing to do was to run away and hide. So they'd get into screaming matches, and he punched holes in the walls. But even those times eased my worries. At least he was flying off the handle at her and not at me. I was thankful for the break.

Rosa didn't know how to get along with me either because I was still a klepto, getting into her jewelry and other belongings.

We had a big blow-up. I defended myself and lied until my face turned blue. She told me I needed to act right, but I didn't know what right was anymore. She started to resent me because I caused problems.

She also resented me because Dad said things to me in front of her. Things like, "Rosa will leave us just like your mother did." He often sided with me in arguments, and she'd tell him to choose between her and me. He told her no one would ever tell him what to do.

Dad did listen to her on one point. She insisted Dad take me to another psychologist. But I thought, *The first one didn't fix me, so what's the second one going to do?*

I felt like I lived alone—and in a terrible neighborhood. We rented a three-story red brick townhouse, and some of the nearby homes were boarded up. I was scared. People outside on the streets looked hungry, like they might use a pocketknife to steal my lunch. This part of town was so bad that I couldn't attend the public school safely, so Dad enrolled me in a private Catholic school called St. Elizabeth's Academy. That was the expensive school that Rosa's daughter attended.

I got on the city bus every day by myself wearing my plaid school uniform. I was the youngest rider by far, and I couldn't have looked more out of place. As the faces became more familiar, though, I started to feel safer. People on that bus route were very nice to me. Maybe they had sympathy for the lone thirteen-year-old. I rode the same bus home on my bus pass. I didn't ask Dad for a ride anywhere.

He wasn't home to give me a ride anyway. He was always at work, at the bar, or out with Rosa into the late hours of the night. There were bars on every corner—Soulard was one big drinking hole—and he and Rosa frequented all of them. When I wasn't hiding out on the third floor of our place, I was out walking around. I used to go to the farmer's market to see the live chickens they sold there. For dinner, I'd head to the gas station on the corner for a packaged sandwich, or just go to McDonald's. I strolled all over Soulard, safe or not, because there was nothing else to do.

All of the nothingness got to me.

One night, Rosa accused me of drinking a glass of beer that was left on the table. She was steamed about it. This was my last straw. I wasn't into drinking, and I hadn't touched any damn beer. I told her so. I was just really unhappy. I hated the all-girls school. I had no friends. I couldn't keep track of where my sister was living. My mom had taken off with some slimeball who hit on me. Life sucked.

And my dad was still coming for me sometimes.

A fight with Rosa was all I needed that night to send me over yet another ledge.

I went upstairs, as usual, to eat in my room alone. I had an orange and a paring knife.

This is it, I thought. *I can do something now. I can end this.* No one was there to bother me. Rosa never came up to the third floor, and who knew where Dad was or when he would be coming home.

I intended to slit my wrists. I had no idea that committing suicide required an actual razor blade; that it was very hard to do with a dull kitchen knife. I just believed what I'd seen on dramatic shows like *Dallas*, where women killed themselves often, and made dying look easy. Dying seemed way better than living my life, so I tried to cut across the width of my flesh, across the blue veins. It hurt, and I didn't even break the skin. I sawed some more. Still not a drop of blood, just more red, raw, inflamed skin. I wasn't sadistic or anything—the paring knife clearly wasn't going to work. After fifteen minutes, I stopped trying because it hurt too much.

I felt disappointed. I'd have to keep on living, and I didn't know if I could. Overwhelmingly, I also felt stupid. I wasn't even smart enough to commit suicide right.

While I was miserable with Dad in Soulard, Mom had been miserable in Arizona. She had finally opened her eyes to see that Frank was just another alcoholic asshole. She was living in Highland again—alone.

The next day, I ran into Dad in the kitchen, and he immediately noticed my wrists. He told me he knew this was the second time I'd tried to commit suicide in six months. He seemed concerned.

"This isn't working," he told me. He wasn't mad or anything. He was worried and sad. He was being my daddy, not Tom. I needed a daddy, but I was slowly coming to the realization that I didn't have one. Still, I clung to the slightest bit of hope that the good side of Dad would come back. Maybe it would one day. Maybe he would walk through the door and be the daddy I had loved so much back in Cedar Rapids. That could happen, but I couldn't wait any longer.

"I want you safe," he added. "So I'm going to send you to your mom's. I don't know what to do for you, and I don't think I'm the right thing."

The right thing didn't exist, but I didn't dare say that. Instead, I went upstairs to pack what little stuff I had. I was at Mom's later that day.

My disappointment mounted. Sure, Mom's apartment was safer than Dad's, but it was every bit as toxic. I had only one thing to look forward to: I'd get to live with Christy again. I just hoped she wasn't too messed up. Aunt Deanna hadn't been the greatest parent while Mom was gone. Christy had been slacking in her schoolwork, and sometimes she just skipped it altogether. She was eleven years old.

Christy was feisty and mouthy. She mouthed off to me like it was her job, and I really couldn't blame her. When she had to visit Dad, for example, he'd always leave and put me in charge. So I'd take care of her and discipline her. It was weird to relate to her like a parent when we were only two years apart. But Mom had the same expectations. Christy felt like I bossed her around and made her do too much housework.

When Mom wasn't around, Christy had no problem telling me, "Fuck off and leave me alone."

I didn't fight with her that much because I understood where her attitude came from. I tried to smooth things out and make the best of our situation. Christy had a lot of fight in her that I didn't have. She wasn't scared of other kids or people or our parents. I wanted to keep the peace at all times, and she was hell-bent on disrupting it.

I always thought she was strong because she would take risks. She had spirit, and I felt like mine had been beaten down. Even though we had it out often, I loved her, and I loved living with her again during my freshman and sophomore years.

Last Laugh

Frank was madly in love with my mother, and he was enraged when she broke up with him. His mother owned a successful rental company, and she had been supporting them financially in Arizona. I don't know all of the details; I just know Frank called begging for Mom to come back to him. She wanted no part of him. Frank's mother was in contact with us, too. I opened a letter that she wrote to Mom. Basically, it said:

I'm wondering why you left Frank, and I want to know if it was because of his drinking.

I had her name and return address, so I looked her up in the phone book and called her. I needed someone to listen—someone to believe in me. I had told Mom what Frank said to me, but she brushed it off.

"Frank didn't mean it, he only said that to hurt me," Mom told me. I wasn't surprised when she didn't take me seriously. I was used to being disappointed.

I called Frank's mother, told her who I was, and I said, "I am thirteen years old, and my mother would never tell you this, but Frank hit on me. He said he couldn't wait to tickle my womb."

"Are you sure that's what he said?" the old lady asked me.

"Yes."

"Thank you for telling me," she replied, hanging up. After that, Frank's mother cut him off financially.

A few weeks later, Frank was so mad that he came looking for me with a gun. I couldn't go out of the apartment because he had called. He told me he was going to kill me.

I was scared. But more than that, I was secretly validated. Finally, someone—a person who didn't even know me—believed what had happened to me. Someone had done something on my behalf.

On the other hand, it also seemed that telling the truth can get you killed.

Grandpa Paulson came over and sat on Mom's porch with a shotgun in his hand to protect me. Grandpa would've blown Frank's head off if he had set foot near our property. Grandpa was like that. Nobody hurt his flock without suffering the consequences. He could hurt his family all day long, but by God, no one else could.

I heard Grandpa say, "If anyone hurts you, I'm taking him down." He waited all day, and he got ruffled up only one time when Frank came around the block in his car. Frank saw my grandfather, took note of the shotgun, and my mother's ex boyfriend never showed his face again.

One weekend, Christy and I were staying at Dad's. Rosa had moved out, but they had decided to continue dating. I literally couldn't get out of bed because of what felt like knives stabbing me in the abdomen. Dad was attentive to me this time, maybe because deep in his heart, he knew my medical problems might be the result of something he had done. He lifted me out of bed to his car and drove me to the children's hospital. In the emergency room, a doctor told me I had cysts on my ovaries, and my specific problem was cystic ovarian pain. The words terrified me—I dreamed of getting married and having kids one day. I didn't know what it all meant. The doctor just gave me medicine and referred me to a gynecologist.

Dad took me to my appointment; Mom didn't come. I told the gynecologist that I was sexually active, which nearly killed me. In my mind, I was still a virgin because what happened with my father couldn't possibly count. But it was what it was, and I couldn't hide. I chose to say I'd had sex because the pain was awful, and I figured she'd be able to tell anyway. She didn't ask for any more information than that.

She sent me home with prescriptions, and Dad told me to take them. He took care of me when I was sick this time. It was my mom who seemed to know nothing about it.

Mom lived in an apartment over the town square in Highland, near Alhambra. Most of the burnout kids hung out at the pavilion right in front of our apartment, which was over the music store. I would go outside and hang around, tentatively at first. I wasn't in their social circle, but then again, I wasn't in any social group yet since I'd just switched schools again, to Highland High School. I was reconnecting with old friends while trying to make some new ones. This new crew smoked a lot of cigarettes, and I started doing it sometimes, too. Aunt Deanna had taught me how when I was eight years old. She would make me light up with her, so I couldn't tattle on her.

A boy named Jake seemed to be the leader of the burnouts. He was tall, lanky, and beautiful in a first-crush kind of way. I'd gone to grade school with him in Alhambra, and we had ridden the same country bus home from school every day. We didn't really speak then because he was two years older.

By this time, I was fourteen, and he was sixteen. The group of kids were freshmen like me, but he was a junior with a car. Everyone, myself included, looked up to him with reverence. We hoped to be as cool as he was in a few years. Jake was godlike in that he gave us freedom. He would load us up in his turquoise 1960 Chevy Bel Air and take us wherever we wanted to go. We could stuff up to eight teenagers in that thing.

He started coming around the square more often. One of the other guys I was kind of friends with, Chris, told me Jake liked me. My heart beat faster.

"Really?" I asked. I thought maybe Chris was making a mistake. Surely he meant another Stacey.

Chris told me not to be scared. Jake said he knew I was younger, and he wouldn't have any expectations. Jake would be gentle with me. He just wanted to go out and make me feel safe.

I asked my mom if I could go on a date with Jake. I was not allowed to ride in cars with boys, not when she knew about it anyway, but I could walk to the movie theater with him. She finally agreed to let him pick me up in his car on the way to school, and that was cool. He'd come into the apartment and spend time with Mom, slowly winning her over.

He'd already won me over. I was in love for the first time. Jake was my world.

Mom didn't approve of my crush, and she said she didn't want us to become serious. She told me I was too young, he was too old, and there was too much trouble we could get into. That's exactly the kind of adult talk that makes teenagers want to kiss in dark alleyways.

Jake gave me his aquamarine class ring, and my infatuation reached new highs. So it would fit my finger, I wrapped it in embroidery floss instead of yarn with a glossy coat of clear nail polish. I'd get fancy with it, sometimes wrapping two or three colors of floss in an alternating pattern. I had plenty of time to do this while Jake was working as a busboy at a nearby restaurant. I was careful to hide his ring from my mother.

Mom was also dating a guy who worked at a local resort. His name was Bear, and he was big and sweet. I liked him. He invited us to go swimming at the resort with him. I was so excited about our fun day that I got sloppy—when Christy and I got in her car, Mom saw the ring I had accidentally left on.

"Are you and Jake going steady?" she asked, looking cute in her romper with a swimming suit underneath. She still drove the Cutlass we had crashed into the barns.

I wasn't backing down on this one. My mom's string of boyfriends gave her no right to rag on mine. I looked her square in the eye and said, "Yes." I was all geared up.

"Give it back," she said. "You're not even supposed to see him that much."

"No way," I replied, turning up the attitude. "If you want me to take off the ring, quit your job, stay home, and follow me around." I talked to her like that all the time, trying to give her a hard time.

She didn't have anything to say back to me. She could ground and spank me all she wanted, but she knew I'd sneak out the windows if that's what it took to see Jake. Usually, though, I could just use the door because Mom was hardly ever home, and she knew it. Instead of putting up a fight, she conceded. She started letting me go out with Jake—even in his car.

I was too charmed to see Jake's faults. He wanted sex, but he had agreed to wait, so I didn't feel much pressure. He was also a drifter, hanging out with various social groups. That didn't strike me as strange at the time because I drifted, too. I just wasn't as popular as he was. I didn't know or care what made him so well liked.

Then one day, Mom asked me, "Does Jake sell drugs?"

"What? No!" I was appalled. I couldn't believe she'd accuse him of something awful like that. Sure, I'd seen him smoke a joint, but all the kids out in the pavilion did that. They didn't pressure me about it; they knew I wasn't into weed. I was the straight-edge girl on the track team, and I didn't want to screw that up.

I saw Jake later that night and asked him. He threw his head back and laughed at me. Then I had to decide whether to stay with a pot smoker. I chose to stay.

Our relationship stayed fun and easygoing for about three months. Then one day I was waiting for Jake with that group of teen-agers down by his car. He would park near the pavilion for work so I could kiss him hello and good-bye as he came and went.

One day, there was another girl waiting for Jake by his car. I asked her what was going on. She told me her name was Anita Green and that she and Jake were dating.

"That's impossible, I've got his ring," I said. Surely, this was all just a misunderstanding. Jake wouldn't do anything like that to me.

She saw the ring and became really upset. The pain on her face was proof enough that she wasn't lying. "He told me his mother wouldn't let him give it out," Anita said. She was taller than me, with acne and large hips, and probably a little older, too.

I asked her if she had slept with him. She said she had. I was crushed. I hadn't had sex with Jake yet. He told me he loved me enough to wait. He respected the fact that I was a good girl—or at least I was trying to be.

I asked Jake about Anita later that night, and he fessed up to seeing her. I was heartbroken. I hated him and loved him. But I did what I was supposed to do: I broke up with Jake. I cried for days. Finally, I asked Mom for advice.

I told her Jake had cheated on me with another girl, but he wanted me back. "What should I do?"

"If you love him, go back to him," she said on a weeknight when she was home from work. "You're old enough to make your own choices about what you want and what you don't want. So if you forgive him, go back to him."

We had study hall together, and I'd see him passing notes back and forth with this cute girl named Judy. That tore me up. That's when I told him I missed him and loved him. He said he missed me, too. We wound up getting back together, though things were never the same.

At that point in our relationship, I thought I had to have sex if I wanted to keep him. So I waited for a night when I had just started my period to sleep with Jake for the first time. I knew there was supposed to be blood when a girl lost her virginity, and I wanted him to believe he was my first. To me, he was. I was so afraid he'd be able to tell something was wrong with me. I was worrying for nothing, though. Jake did not care about anything technical—he was a seventeen-year-old boy, and he just wanted to get laid. We had a sexual relationship for a long time. It ended when we both cheated on each other. The breakup was long and painful. I never should have gotten back together with him.

I had a hard time getting over Jake, even when he was awful to me. One day, I came home from track practice to find my sister passed out in the bathroom. I shook her until she opened her eyes. She told me she had smoked pot, and Jake had given it to her. I had just turned fifteen, and she was only thirteen. I was furious.

Mom was going to be home in a few hours, and I had no idea what was happening to Christy. She kept laughing and noodling around the room. I was afraid I'd get in trouble because she was acting like a fool. Also, I didn't know if she was going to be okay. How was she feeling? I was pissed and nervous and scared all at the same time.

I ran down to the square and asked the kids if they had seen Jake. I found out he had left a while ago. I asked Chris if he had any weed.

He laughed and said, "You don't smoke, why do you want it?"

"If Christy is high, I need to get high, too." Then he really laughed. I was freaking out. But he found me some, and one of the kids showed me what to do with it. I found out exactly how Christy felt. I was scared at first because Mom once told me she'd seen white horses the first time she smoked. I guess I was lucky—I didn't see any wild animals. I just relaxed and stopped worrying about Jake and Christy and my mom and everything. It was great. I shed all of the anxiety, fear, and pain by breathing in deeply. Where had pot been all my life? I was loving it.

I went back upstairs to goof around with Christy. We were fine by the time Mom got home, and she didn't notice a thing. Not that she would have anyway; she didn't pay that much attention to us.

Eventually, I told Jake I was furious with him for preying on my sister, and I also told him something else: I thought I was pregnant. I hadn't had my period, and my belly was swollen. He wasn't nice to me; he wasn't even concerned. Instead, we broke up for good—no more messing around. Then he pretty much stabbed me in the back. I don't know why he did this, but he told the whole school I was having a baby. As if that weren't cruel enough, he also spread the rumor that I was a "dead fuck."

Maybe he was just being a stupid teenager. It was hard to think that this boy I had loved so much could obliterate me so easily. I knew too well that males could break my heart. But Jake's words and actions took me by surprise, devastating me. I cried and avoided all my old friends. I got my period shortly after that—thank God, because I wouldn't have known whether the baby was Jake's or my father's.

I didn't go around telling everyone I got my period, of course. I kept quiet while everyone talked about me. I was ashamed and embarrassed that people knew such intimate details about me. Maybe I did just lie there during sex. With my father, the less you moved, the less you got hurt. Anything I knew about sex was closely linked to surviving it. This time was no different.

As for my reputation, I was no longer a Goody Two-shoes—I became the school slut. I was mortified in that small town filled with kids I'd known for years. I didn't confirm or deny any rumors about me; I just focused on schoolwork. I spent more time with Christy. I lay low while the rumor went around that I'd had an abortion. Who knows where that started? I let them think whatever they wanted. What difference did it make?

Passing Out

Something was wrong with Christy. She was no longer the little doll I wanted to hug and hold. Instead, she was a strong and beautiful ball of trouble. Dad abused her, not sexually, but physically and emotionally. She spent as little time as possible with him because she was tired of getting hit and being called a "fucking little bitch." As far back as age seven or eight, he would tell her things like, "I'm going to break your fucking neck." She couldn't get along with Mom much better, so she lived with whoever would take her. She moved around constantly from our parents' houses to an aunt's and to our grandparents'.

Maybe that's how she became a twelve-year-old alcoholic. Starting at nine or ten, she'd raid whoever's liquor cabinet was the closest. She thought adults seemed to relax when they drank. She wanted to relax, too.

I tried to protect her as much as I could. But it's hard to protect a kid whose biggest enemy is herself. As much as she fought me—and everyone else who was supposedly taking care of her—she knew I was her fallback. I was the one who would truly do anything for her. The feeling was mutual.

Christy was feisty. She thought she could fight because I always let her beat me up. As a teenager, I rarely hit Christy, for two reasons. One, she could whip me. Two, I would have felt too guilty if I ever hurt her. Everyone else might try to harm my sister, but I sure wasn't going to.

Somehow, Christy got the idea that she was the destroyer. When she was twelve, she used to climb all the way to the top of a neighborhood swing set, right above the swings where nobody in their right mind would hang out. She liked to waste time there and spy on all the kids at the playground. One of the school's biggest bullies, Rosie, stood underneath Christy one day to talk to her.

"Where's your sister?" Rosie asked.

"What's it to you?" Christy asked, her long blond hair dancing below her shoulders. She wore it in a curly perm like everyone did back then.

"I hate her, that's all," Rosie said. "I can't stand that bitch."

It didn't occur to Christy to be scared of Rosie, a girl who beat up younger kids just for breathing. Instead she spit on Rosie's head.

Then Christy added, "Hey, it must be raining."

I'm just glad I wasn't there; Rosie would've whipped us both. Christy wasn't stupid; she stayed on top of the swing set until it got dark and Rosie got tired of waiting for her to come down. Rosie didn't bother Christy again.

Another time, Christy went to a pizza place with a bunch of friends. That was no big deal—we all used to go there after we went to the movie theater nearby. But that night, Christy came home with a big patch of hair missing. She'd gotten into a fight with some big country girl when she was only in the seventh grade. She was that feisty. Christy was proud of herself.

I always thought she was strong because she would take risks, and I wouldn't. I was outgoing enough, but I spent most of my time trying to keep the peace with Mom, Dad, kids at school, or whoever. Christy didn't care about peace. Our voices sounded the same—they still do—but somehow, our words came out quite differently.

At this point, we still lived with Mom, and Christy never gave her a break. Mom was seriously dating a man named John, and she was planning to marry him. She tried to get along with us sometimes, but we were holding on to too much anger to take Mom seriously. She'd tell us to make our beds, and we'd say, "Hell no." If she told us to make dinner, we'd tell her to go make it herself.

One day, we were going down the steps of our apartment building with Mom, heading out together somewhere. Christy, then age thirteen, said, "Mom, I wonder what would happen if I pushed you down."

Mom was used to this kind of talk—the kind of words Christy had learned at our dad's house. She had become numb to our nastiness. She didn't try to correct it; she gave up. Mom didn't raise an eyebrow when she answered, "You'd better not."

Our mother was working all day and romancing all night. In some ways, teenagers love freedom. But secretly, they also wish they had boundaries. Boundaries and rules would've shown Christy and me that someone cared about our existence. We retaliated in the only way we knew—we'd have friends over to the apartment at all hours to tear up the place. We didn't let Mom have any control; we didn't feel like she deserved it. She hadn't earned or demanded our respect, so we didn't give it to her.

It's a wonder our mother invited us to Arkansas at all.

Mom and John got married in Arkansas at a beautiful mill. Christy and I went with them, a mistake. The wedding was great, and then they took us to a place called Water World of Fun. They rented a cute two-bedroom house so we could test how the four of us got along. For a minute there, we were thinking things with John might turn out okay.

After spending a day with us, they started their honeymoon. They spent the next two days—and I mean they barely came out for fresh air—in their bedroom. Christy and I had never been so bored or uncomfortable in all our lives. They were too busy having sex to check on us. We didn't know anything about the area we were in, so we couldn't find any trouble to get into. We were fine—just restless. We watched the entire *North and South* miniseries while they celebrated their marriage. We couldn't wait to get back home to Highland. If living with them was going to mean watching TV while they did it all day, they could count us out.

Shortly afterward, Christy and I were at Dad's for the weekend in Soulard. Some visits with him were nightmares, and some were surprisingly nice. This one was in between. Dad sat us both down on the couch to tell us something.

"Your mom is moving to Arkansas with John," he said, sober and scratching his head. "She's leaving you."

We weren't exactly shocked. Ever since their marriage, we had known they wanted to live there eventually. We were just surprised they were going so soon. Later, Mom said she was sorry because she was supposed to be the one to tell us. Dad was always doing stuff like that to her when he could get away with it. We were used to getting stuck in the middle of their business.

He explained to us that we had options—we could move in with him or with them. It was our choice.

"I know we've had some problems," he said, rubbing his knees, "but I really want us to be a family."

I felt torn, but that was nothing new. I hated living with Mom. I didn't know John because he barely talked to me. And living with Dad was a mess, but there were moments of happiness when he was sober. Either way, we never experienced feelings of being settled or wanted. No matter where we turned, we ran into more isolation.

It was kind of scary to trust him, but he'd been gentle and kind for the last few months. He'd gone easier on me, and he'd stopped traumatizing Christy. He had straightened up because he'd been planning for this exact situation.

"I'm going to buy the house two doors down from Grandma's," he said, pacing in front of us. He was going to pay $71,000 for a decent-sized brick cottage much like Mee Maw's. I'm sure my grandmother was helping him with the down payment, just like she always did—she had money during her marriage and even more after my grandfather died. St. John was a great St. Louis suburb, and the house had two bedrooms—or more if you considered the space in the partly finished basement. It was an awesome little place, much better than his narrow, ratty Soulard apartment. But the house in St. John had a history. Because I had spent so much time in the neighborhood at Grandma Lannert's, I knew that two men had died there. The original owner had died of old age, and the current owner's father had lived there through an illness and passed away, too. I tried not to let silly superstitions influence my decision.

I thought about getting a new start at a new school. I needed a clean reputation. I'd get to attend Ritenour High School, same as my dad. Definitely, the biggest draw was Grandma Lannert. Living near her sounded fantastic. She was older by then, and we had to take care of her more. But she never stopped being the loving, doting woman who spoiled us rotten. She had been a consistent source of happiness and predictability through our family's rocky years.

I was old enough to understand that my father was an ass. But his actions and words led us to believe that he wanted us. We rarely felt that from either parent—so when we did, we clamored like kids at a cotton candy stand. Kids love to be loved, and we were no different. Meanwhile, Mom and John never tried to talk us into living with them.

That day, Dad told us, "I'll try. That's all I can do."

He promised he'd slow down on his drinking. "Things will be different," he said, reassuringly. He promised he would change—*really change*—this time. He promised Christy he'd do his best to get along with her. He smiled at me in that old way, in the good daddy way. He made me trust him in that moment.

He kept talking, but I stopped listening. It didn't really matter what he said. I was going to live with him in St. John because my grandmother was the best. I had hoped to live with her before, but she wasn't healthy enough to take care of me. In fact, she needed me to take care of her. She had diabetes, and she couldn't drive much anymore. I wanted to be there for her.

Sometimes, if my father acted really bad, and I didn't know what else to say, I'd tell him, "If you do that, I'm telling Grandma Lannert." Threatening to spill everything to her was the only consequence I could hang over his head. Usually when I used it, he would rein himself in. He truly loved her and cared about her opinion.

The choice was easy for Christy, too. We had faith in Dad. We clung to the hope that everything might get back to the way it used to be—back when we lived in Cedar Rapids and Kansas City. Faith and hope were all we had.

We packed up our things while he finalized the purchase of the house in St. John. And on my sixteenth birthday, Mom moved to Arkansas for good. When I complained—couldn't she choose any other day?—she lectured me that she had celebrated my birthday with me the year before. She and John moved to a different state on May 28, 1988.

I got the chance to take one long, deep breath—maybe even two. That's how long Tom stayed Daddy. While he slowed down on his drinking, he still popped open cans of Busch or Bud every night. He did it at home, taking a hiatus from the bars and the martinis for a few weeks. It was a break when I needed one.

From the beginning, I had a lot of responsibility. I was constantly helping Grandma Lannert monitor her blood sugar levels. I also had to monitor Christy. By the time she was fourteen, getting her to stay sober and go to school was a full-time job.

I also felt responsible for Dad. He was trying to cut down on his drinking, and he told me he needed my help. I stayed up worrying when he didn't come home at night. He'd be out at some bar, and I didn't want him to die behind the wheel. He'd had too many drunk driving accidents already. I'd be so worried that I couldn't go to sleep. I knew his favorite spots, mostly a place called The Edge. I had my license, so I'd drive around until I found him. He'd let me bring him home without much fuss. The first few times, he'd be the happy drunk dad that I could love—keeping me up past 1 a.m. talking about school and life and stuff.

Then one night after I found him and drove him home, he attacked me. I wasn't going to bring him home just so he could rape me. After that, I started to feel like he should go ahead and die out there on the road; he wasn't even worth my gas money. That was the end for me. I stopped worrying about him. I didn't try to help with the drinking. I no longer felt responsible for making our living arrangement work.

His alcoholism got worse. He threw up a lot. Christy and I lost it the first few times we saw him pass out. He would come home late, unable even to change his clothes. We'd find him in a heap near his bedroom door, half-dressed and in a pool of vomit. When we spoke to him, he couldn't hear us. He wouldn't move. He would smell awful, and we'd lean down to check his breathing.

We'd say to each other, "Yep, he's still alive."

In the morning, he'd wake up like nothing had happened. He'd be all confused. "What's this mess in here?"

I'd tell him, "You passed out. You need to stop that."

He didn't believe anything strange had happened. He surely hadn't done anything stupid or reckless, like driving after nearly drinking himself to death. The truth was, he couldn't remember any of it.

"I'm not cleaning it up," I'd say. Most times, he wouldn't make me.

Seeing him that drunk was nightmarish at first. But after a while, the vomiting and passing out happened so often that we stopped noticing. Dad's drinking was a normal part of our life in St. John.

Another Terrifying Scene

I liked taking care of my grandmother. She took care of me, too. I had someone to eat dinner with sometimes, and she had me to help her monitor her blood sugar levels. My dad was supposed to help her, but he'd forget. She relied on me. I liked being the one who took her to her hair appointments. Even as an elderly woman, she always wore fashionable clothes and kept herself up. She didn't leave the house much by then, but that didn't matter when it came to looking nice.

Her diabetes had grown worse. I had the job of filling her needles with insulin and placing them on her kitchen table in the butter dish. I wanted her medication to be ready when she needed it throughout the day. I'd write the date and the dosage in big letters on a piece of tape attached to each needle so she wouldn't get confused. My dad was supposed to take turns with me on this task, but just to be safe; I'd leave her several days' worth at a time.

I was responsible for Christy, too. I was sixteen and had a car, so if she needed to go somewhere, it was my job to take her. I had taken buses and walked everywhere when I was fourteen, but Christy had a chauffeur. I didn't mind so much; that was just how it was. And of course, I taught her how to drive in case of an emergency. I was supposed to help Christy with her homework—if she bothered to bring it home. And I even made sure there was food in the refrigerator for us. She and I ate simple things like Hamburger Helper and sandwiches. Dad usually made his own meals—he had lost weight so he mostly ate lean chicken breasts. We all fended for ourselves. Often, I just drove to McDonald's or White Castle where I could get a cheeseburger for thirty-three cents. I lived on burgers, fries, and Dr. Pepper. So did Christy.

Christy wasn't easy to watch. She was a drinker, and Dad didn't care if she popped open a beer right in front of him. If he did say something, she'd cuss him. Then he'd smack her. She'd keep right on drinking, though. She figured he was going to smack her anyway, so she might as well give him a reason. Their fights made my jaw drop. They kept at it all the time.

I never drank with him. He knew I drank once in a while with my friends. He also knew I smoked pot occasionally. He didn't care. Sometimes, he'd smoke with me—or more likely, he'd make me find him some weed.

Dad wasn't that responsible, even though he thought he was. So I helped him manage the money. He was cheap, and he didn't want to be bothered with the needs of two teenage girls. If I wanted $5 for shampoo, he'd get mad when I asked him for it. He wanted me to leave him alone and take money for Christy and me out of his checking account. I also took checks and forged his name; he didn't care. We had an unspoken agreement that he paid the mortgage, and I bought the incidentals like toiletries, groceries, and whatever else my sister and I had to have for school. He always looked at the monthly bank statements, and he okayed the checks I wrote. He knew I was thrifty, even though he complained about how much we spent at the drugstore. He knew I wasn't a mall girl. I liked picking through the racks for cool clothes at the Salvation Army. If I splurged and bought clothes for myself and Christy from a sale rack at a department store, I used my cash from waitressing at a local restaurant called Indian Delights.

We seemed to have enough money, but it was tight sometimes. Dad jumped around from company to company, his jobs changing faster than my boyfriends. He'd buy in to an actuarial consulting firm and become a partner; then he'd get bought out. It seemed like he was home a lot during the day when other dads were working. But then again, he created jobs that gave him a lot of leeway. He had a computer, so he could work from home. He always made a case for showing up late for work—or not going in at all. We never knew if he'd be home after school or even later that night.

We just knew he probably wouldn't be sober.

I felt tremendous pressure. One way I handled it was to date a lot of guys. I just made sure I didn't play around with high school boys, especially not ones from my new school, Ritenour High. I'd learned my lesson: one bad romance can ruin your whole life. But I did become promiscuous with guys I met through work—or wherever. My father called me a slut when he was drunk, and I was tired of it. I figured if I was a whore, I might as well act like one. My father had made me hate everything about myself.

I thought all guys expected sex from me, so I put out. Then I'd be disappointed because neither the sex nor the guy ever lived up to my expectations. I would become resentful and tell them, "How dare you touch me like that!" I'd make up fights with my boyfriends so I could walk away whenever I wanted.

I didn't know why I slept around. It's not like I wanted to have sex. The men I dated couldn't possibly love me because I didn't let them know me. I thought if they did know me, they'd just see how bad I was. They'd see something terrible inside me, someone my dad liked to hurt. Yet I slept with them anyway.

The guilt I felt was unbearable.

I felt guilty for everything. Sex with random boys was my fault. Plus, I was a shameful, horrible person who let her father do what he wanted to her. Even worse, there was pleasure that went along with the pain my dad caused me. That guilt was worse than all the rest combined. I couldn't figure out what kind of sick girl would have a positive physical reaction to a rape she didn't want.

When I was asleep, he'd perform oral sex on me. I would wake up right in the middle of having an orgasm.

The first time it happened was an absolute nightmare.

I had no idea what was going on inside my body. Time stood still while everything shook. My toes curled, and I started screaming. I thought maybe I was dying. I wasn't even sure whether I was feeling pleasure or pain at first. Slowly, it felt a little bit good.

When it was over, he sat beside me and held my hand, stroking it gently. "Felt nice, didn't it, Tiger? I did it for you because I love you."

I said, "Get away from me. Don't touch me again!"

He said, "Silly child, didn't that feel good? That's the way you make me feel. We love one another, and when you love someone, you do certain things. We are just expressing it. Now it's my turn, so open your mouth."

"I don't feel good, can't I just go back to sleep?" I asked. I saw the familiar, scary anger flash in his eyes. He pulled the hair on the back of my head so hard I thought my neck would snap.

"There you go, acting just like a woman," he said, not yelling, but mean as a rattlesnake. "You've had yours, now I want mine! Get down on the floor and open your fucking mouth. Now."

I hated it. I hated it. I hated it. I opened my mouth and did what he told me to. He was still grabbing my hair, making me go faster. He kept ramming his penis down my throat, and eventually, I threw up.

He was mad as hell. He told me I was a disgusting bitch, and to lick it up. This went on for a while until he finally left, and I was too afraid and too weak to move. I lay there in my own vomit for more than an hour. My father had humiliated me—it wasn't the first time, and it wouldn't be the last.

My body and my mind were beat up. I gathered the strength to clean up the mess. I realized I needed help.

Who could help me? Who would believe me? I asked myself.

My mom was in Arkansas—not that she even cared. The Paulson grandparents barely spoke to me after I told Grandma that Grandpa had touched me. Grandma Lannert was my only hope, but she was too sick to worry about something so serious. Plus, my father was her baby, and in her eyes, he could do no wrong.

Why should anyone believe me? My father said I was an "ungrateful little bitch."

Completely exhausted, I fell asleep for a few brief hours. Then I woke up and went to school. I pushed the memory into the crawl-space of my mind and pretended that I was just a normal kid. That's what I always did.

All of a sudden, I felt surrounded by filth. I knew what had just happened was wrong, and I cried.

My reaction sickened me; I didn't want to feel anything with my father. The act was dirty and shameful, and I was sure it was my fault. I don't know who I hated more—him or me.

Christmas Eve

I met guys older than me around town. I was always hanging out with someone. If Dad caught on, he approved at first. He was okay with a guy who called or stopped by once or twice. But soon, he'd say I was spending too much time with so-and-so and tell me I wasn't allowed to date anymore. He'd try to ground me or keep me home with some rule. Then I'd start sneaking around.

I don't think he was jealous; I think he wanted to keep me isolated from others. The fewer people I talked to, the less he had to worry about. He didn't want me to spend too much time with boyfriends, other friends, and sometimes even my cousins. I could be close to someone for just a moment. That was fine. But Dad wouldn't let me stick with anyone for long. He'd complain about who I hung around with. Then he'd visit me in the middle of the night to remind me of all I had to hide. He had his ways of making me feel unworthy of real relationships.

I didn't really know what other people were like. I didn't go to their houses; I didn't spend the night with anyone. Instead of hanging out with one person, I hung out with different groups from school. I fit in well with the kids at Ritenour, but I never had a best friend. I shifted in and out of all the cliques—jocks, popular kids, geeks, and burnouts. I never found out what their families were like, or if they were different from mine. I didn't want to know. I realized something was off with my parents, but I didn't think they were completely twisted until later.

I did have one girlfriend—the principal's daughter, Inga. She was taller than most of the girls in the class. She had gorgeous, thick, honey-blond hair and beautiful brown eyes. She wore braces and was very friendly. We were on the tennis team together and would meet each other at school events. She had the same sense of responsibility that I had, and, just like me, she couldn't let go because of how others might see her. She was proper and respectable, but also funny and smart. She became the class valedictorian.

If I wanted to party, I'd run off with a different crowd. But I was always careful about what I did. I never wanted to give my classmates a reason to bad-mouth me again—not like I had in Highland. The guys I dated were far removed from school; I met most of them through my job at Indian Delights. No one knew anything about anyone I was seeing, sometimes not even Christy.

At school, I tried to be quiet and unassuming. If I needed to stand up for Christy or for anything else, I spoke up, but I did it diplomatically. I didn't argue with teachers or catfight with girls. I wanted no problems, and I didn't get into any trouble at school. I was a B-plus student who rarely got Cs. I got As in English and physical education. I loved everything about school at Ritenour: classes, sports, and the kids. The only subject I hated was math—precisely because my dad loved it.

Early on, I did meet one high school boy who was special to me. He was in my Spanish class. Tom Wilson, a junior like me, was hot. He was tall and slim with dark brown hair and these amazing brown eyes. He had chiseled cheeks and the most perfect upturned nose. But I was drawn to more than his looks. When he smiled, he was gentle. When he looked my way, it was with kindness. He was clearly shy; he hardly spoke at all in class. I had to get to know him. I could tell he wasn't the type of guy who would approach me—or anyone for that matter.

So I picked him up.

I passed him a note that read, *Hi, my name is Stacey. Do you have a girlfriend?* At first, he thought it was from another girl with the same name. Then he realized it was from me, the new girl. He waved. We were having group discussions in Spanish at that time, so he walked right over to me. I was pleasantly surprised.

He called me as soon as I got home that day, and we went on a date over the weekend. He was too good to be true—a Christian minister's son. We had a wonderful two-week romance, and then I called it off. We didn't have a big breakup or even a fight. I told him I loved him dearly as a friend, and I didn't want to mess that up. I pushed him away because he was someone I could've been close to, and I couldn't let that happen. I couldn't let my guard down. I had three reasons. First, he might find out that I wasn't the good girl he thought I was. Second, he was in my high school. Third, I wasn't willing to let my heart get broken again. I was scared.

Tom W. said he didn't want to lose me. If I only wanted to be friends, he'd learn to live with it. That's just the kind of guy he was—rarely thinking about himself first. He became one of the best friends I've ever had, more reliable and trustworthy than almost anyone I've ever met. We sat next to each other in Spanish for the rest of the school year.

I hung out with Tom W. and his friends the most. I became more involved and comfortable in their clique than I had in any other group. They were just nice guys—not popular or unpopular—and very cool.

Mike, Ricky, and Tom W. were the core of the group. Sometimes Eddie, Terry, and Jason would come around for a while, then gravitate back to their own circles. Mike, Ricky, and Tom W. always talked fondly about one friend in particular: Rob. Rob was supposedly the coolest. He had already graduated and gone into the military.

We'd all talk after school and go cruising in Creve Coeur Park, a popular hangout. They even dragged me to *The Rocky Horror Picture Show*. When we went go-cart racing, I won. I loved having boys as friends. They didn't ask questions, and they never wanted to get mushy or too close.

I was a mature teenager; at least that's what Tom W. told me. I don't know if I believed that since I was the only one of us who had a car, a '76 Chevy Impala. I drove him and our friends around all the time, and he appreciated that. They liked to drink on the weekends. I had been tipsy a few times, and I hated the taste of alcohol. I also hated losing my self-control. So I preferred to drink soda, which made me a natural choice for designated driver. I didn't tell them this, but I'd grown up watching Dad drink and drive. I knew how dangerous it could be.

During those two weeks when I was dating Tom W., I called him on Christmas Eve to see if he wanted to hang out with me and Christy. He couldn't do anything with me because he was a deacon at his church, and he had to attend the Christmas Eve service.

He stopped by my house at 9:30 that night, taking me by surprise. He knocked on the door along with his friend Ricky, who was dating Christy at the time. I was afraid Dad would be mad for a lot of reasons—but mainly because Ricky was half Mexican.

"It's open!" yelled a gruff voice. Our living room was right inside the front door. To the left was a TV that was always on. To the right was a long beige couch. My dad was usually sitting—or sleeping—on it. That night was no different.

Our friends opened the door, and my dad was lying there drunk. Tom W. tried to introduce himself and ask for me. Tom W. held out his hand to my dad, who didn't move a muscle to shake it—or even get up. Ricky tried to say hello, too.

Without looking, my father waved his hand and said, "They're downstairs." Some dads would bother to find out if these guys were dating their daughters. Some might wonder why two high school boys would show up on Christmas Eve. Not mine.

I didn't know how I felt about Tom W. visiting me at home. His house was filled with Christmas music, lights, and decorations. He had a happy mom and stepdad who were loving and kind. The only thing buzzing at my house was my father. He made me keep our house clean, but it was ugly inside. We had awful shag carpets he wouldn't let me replace. Just past the living room was a small dining room that we never ate in. My father kept his computer and stacks of books and papers in there. A ledge separated the dining room from the kitchen. The kitchen was yellow and tiny and old. It didn't have a dishwasher. My father liked to play a game when he was mad at us. When Christy or I did the dishes, he'd place the utensil holder on the counter to the left of the sink with the fork prongs and knife blades facing upward. When our arms passed over the top of the fork prongs, he'd push them down so we'd scrape our skin.

Christy and I spent most of our time in the half-finished basement while Dad stayed on the couch upstairs. My room, painted a bright green, was in the back of the finished area. The last owner's father had died there, which was creepy. The other finished room was a little living area with dark wood paneling and a fireplace. The unfinished part of the basement, just next to my room, had a washer and dryer in it.

I didn't want Tom W. and Ricky in our depressing house or in our private little basement. It was too weird.

Mae

I was worried about Grandma Lannert. She hadn't been as active or talkative for the last few months. I knew she was getting old. I just wished I could've kept her young forever. I loved the way she smelled, like Avon, and she still wore rouge and red lipstick. I would sit with her for hours, and our time together was peaceful. She would tell me how much she loved me, and we would daydream about what kind of life I might have in the future. She always said she wanted to live long enough to watch me graduate from Ritenour and then Mizzou.

She used to tell me, "You'd make a great lawyer because you're so smart. Or maybe you should be a journalist because you write so well. Or I know . . . You should be a doctor because you take such great care of me."

I was at her house almost every day. I'd go over in the mornings before school just to make sure she was getting along okay and to drop off those insulin needles. One morning, I headed to Mee Maw's house as usual when Dad told me to stop—he was going to check on her and drop off the needles.

"Go on to school," he said, totally confusing me. But my mind was occupied with other things. It was prom night: May 6, 1989.

I got in my car and went to Ritenour like he said. But I didn't feel right all day. I was very worried about Mee Maw, and I didn't know why. I had a friend pretend to call the school to say I had a doctor's appointment so I could get an absence pass. Right before lunch, I walked through the school doors.

I drove home and found Mee Maw's little Chrysler LeBaron in her driveway like it was supposed to be. She rarely drove it, and I would've worried if she had. I thought I was being silly, so I walked into our house. I felt stupid for worrying so much. Dad had said he was going to check on her, so surely he did. I needed to get over myself. I started cleaning up our house.

At 3 p.m., one of my grandmother's friends called while I was doing dishes. She told me she'd been trying to reach Mae all day. This alarmed me, but I was in the middle of cleaning up a big mess in the kitchen. Dad wasn't home, so I sent Christy over there.

She came running back. Grandma was passed out on the floor with the TV on, and she had urinated all over herself. I called 911 and bolted out the door to be with her. Christy waited outside until the ambulance came. I called Dad and told him to meet us at the hospital. He said he was coming home first. So I left Christy there to go with Dad, and I followed the ambulance in my car.

When Grandma arrived at the hospital, she seemed much better. She was talking to me and asking for things. She was cussing out the nurses, saying, "I'm cold, damn it!" and "My husband died in this place!"

Her feistiness was one of her best attributes. These were good signs as far as I could tell. The doctor said she had hypoglycemia and needed fluids. He was going to keep her overnight, but she would be fine.

Dad said, "Go ahead and get to the prom. I'll see you tomorrow." He'd told me I was allowed to stay out all night.

At that point, I was shaken up, but I wasn't worried about her anymore. I was looking forward to going to the prom dateless with a girlfriend, but she canceled on me at the last minute. I was dating some guy at the time, but it was nothing serious and I didn't want to go with him. I decided I didn't want to go at all. I had a dress, shoes, and everything, and I never wore them. I only went to the after-prom parties.

This was one of the rare nights that I drank. I'd had a rough day, and I pounded my liquor. By pounding, I mean I had one beer and one vodka shot. I was wasted. I waited several hours until I sobered up, then drove home. I felt nauseous, so I went to bed.

At 6 a.m., Dad came into my room. "If you want to see your grandma alive, you better get to the hospital right now." He was not worried or upset; he was just blank. He seemed annoyed at me for my obvious hangover, and I didn't understand why. He'd seen me drink before.

I threw on some jeans and a button-down shirt and drove to the hospital. I was shocked to find out that Mee Maw was in intensive care. She was hooked up to several tubes and machines. I wasn't eighteen yet, and I wasn't supposed to go in the ICU. But I had to be with her. I couldn't understand how this had happened. Just like that, she was lying in a bed looking like she was about to die.

I thought, *Did someone do something to her?*

I even wondered what could've happened the previous morning when Dad had been in charge of her needles. He had been asking her for $20,000 to start a new company, and she'd been telling him no. Ever since we moved to her street, she had wised up about his drinking. She could finally see some of his wrongdoings. As a result, Dad and Grandma had been arguing recently. She was shortening her purse strings, and he knew it. I worried that our house might have to go on the market because Dad couldn't afford it along with his drinking habit.

All of that aside, I was devastated to see her like that. I busted into her room; I got as close to her as I could. She still smelled nice, like my Mee Maw. Then, in all of my seventeen-year-old wisdom, I started flipping out. The rest of the family was in the waiting room when I yelled, "What happened to you? You can't leave us! I can't do this without you! I can't handle it!"

She couldn't speak to me because she had a tube down her throat, but she was conscious. Her eyes went wide, and her chest rose. My outburst upset her, and her heart rate monitor went berserk. The nurses pulled me out of the room, and I got into trouble. I decided to walk down to the hospital chapel, where I lost it. I cried and cried and cried.

I prayed to God: *It's selfish for me to want her to stay when she's suffering so much, but I can't keep this family together if she leaves.*

I knew something terrible would happen without Grandma Lannert around to talk sense into all of us. She was dependable and reliable. She was the only person who really loved us. She was strong. She was the only consequence I could hold over my dad's head. In the entire world, he cared only about one person's opinion: Mae Lannert's.

I took a deep breath. I thought about right and wrong. I left the chapel and bypassed the nurses and the rest of the family. I grabbed her hand. I had prayed to God about this moment, and I understood that she needed peace. Her comfort was more important than mine. I would have to learn to live with whatever God had planned for us.

It hurt me to say the words to her: "Okay, if you want to go, go." I kissed her forehead. She sighed deeply with a tear in her eye.

I was holding her hand, and just like that, Grandma Lannert died quietly.

By the time the nurses got there, I was still holding her hand, sobbing. Christy was there, and she cried hard, too. Eventually, we hugged each other. Dad wasn't there.

I drove home and told him, "You need to go to the hospital. Grandma died."

He seemed surprised. He wanted to know how I knew.

"I was there."

Then he panicked, even though he must've known this was coming. "What do you mean she's dead!? How do you know?" He put his hands on my shoulders, and he shook me back and forth hard. "How do you know?!!!"

"Go to the hospital," I repeated as I walked out our door and went inside Grandma's house. I needed to be with her there. I wanted to be in the one place in the world where I'd had so many happy memories. I lay on her floor, and I didn't try to stop my tears.

———

A piece of my heart died with my grandmother, and once again my mom was not there for me. A few months earlier, she had moved halfway around the world to Guam, where John, who was in the air force, had an assignment. We didn't want to go; being with her was a lonely option. With Dad there was yelling and screaming, but at least there was something. His displays at least showed some level of involvement in our lives. Her silence toward us was nothing, and there wasn't anything worse than nothing. I couldn't blame her for wanting to run away from her family. She had two rowdy, troubled teenage girls who didn't fit into her dreams of happily-ever-after with her new husband. Mom saw leaving as a way to finally find peace and happiness. We saw it as more abandonment. Right before she left, she took Christy and me to a St. Louis Cardinals game and then to lunch. There is a picture of the two of us standing in front of a downtown fountain with our arms outstretched wide. We were showing off, like *nana-nana-boo-boo; we'll be fine without you.* We were mean to her—ignoring her the whole time, making awful comments, and acting like we didn't care what she did. We were kids, and we didn't know how to tell her we needed her. We didn't know how to beg her to stay and please take better care of us. So we pushed her away. We were nasty to her, but we were going to miss her more than she would ever know.

Mom called me from Guam to tell me how sorry she was that Grandma had died.

I didn't want to hear from her. I said, "I bet you're glad she's dead." Then I hung up.

Dad was still on and off with Rosa. He'd had a married girlfriend named Deborah Jean for a while and had begged her to marry him, but she wouldn't leave her husband. Her husband came to Dad's workplace and created a huge scene, so that relationship ended. Dad always made his way back to Rosa. She was a good person. When he fell apart after Grandma died, Rosa helped him plan her funeral. She took care of Dad during those dark days.

Despite Rosa's best efforts, Dad's downward spiral took a nosedive. Without Grandma Lannert in the world, he was volatile. He was never at peace.

I told him that Christy and I needed dresses and shoes for the funeral, and he gave us his credit card. He often gave it to me. He told me to spend only $50 on everything for both of us. He barely looked me in the eye; he was being mean and cheap. I worried myself sick when I spent $75, buying the least expensive outfits I could find anywhere. It turned out he didn't even notice or care. It was like he enjoyed giving me a hard time.

At the funeral, he was beside himself. He knew I smoked pot, and he asked me if I had any. I didn't, so he got pissed off. He actually made me leave my grandmother's funeral to get weed from the dealer I knew. I felt I had to because he acted like he might create a scene. On my way back to the funeral, I stopped at White Castle. I put the weed in the white sack so I could pass the drugs to him discreetly.

Directly in front of the funeral home, I was pulled over by the cops for running a red light. That's when I lost it emotionally. I was a crying mess, and the cop took pity on me. All I got was a warning, and the officer didn't even glance at my White Castle bag.

When I pulled into the parking lot, a crowd of people stood there watching.

Dad marched up to me and said, "How dare you get in trouble like that at your grandmother's funeral!"

I couldn't believe him. I never would have been on the road if he hadn't made me buy him weed. I said, "How dare you ask for this." I shoved the white paper bag into his hands.

Christy

Two days later, Dad took off on a fishing trip. He would be gone for my seventeenth birthday, so he gave me my present early—my grandma's Chrysler LeBaron. I wasn't sorry to see him go, but I was terrified of what he'd be like when he returned. It would be just the two of us living in St. John—Christy had told me she had to get away. She was moving back to Aunt Deanna's.

I hated to lose Christy, too. I didn't want to be alone. But as awful as Aunt Deanna was, she was better than Dad. I encouraged her to go. Shortly after Christy moved, I wouldn't even speak to my aunt. She had a husband named Randy at the time, and she was cheating on him. Randy had come home one day and found a used condom on the floor. Randy thought that was strange because he'd had a vasectomy. So Aunt Deanna used me as her scapegoat.

She called me and said, "Stacey, I'm putting Randy on the phone so you can tell him that this condom is yours." She breathed heavily, clearly in the middle of a fight.

I covered for her skankiness. I told Randy that I had been over there with my boyfriend. I lied and said the condom must've been mine. Then I asked to speak to Deanna.

"Don't you ever do that to me again," I said, fuming. "I like Randy, and what you're doing is wrong."

I hung up and took a deep breath. I wasn't surprised, really. I had so much to worry about that I told myself to leave this one alone. Aunt Deanna wasn't worth getting worked up over.

Aunt Deanna was hardly the good influence that Christy needed. Not that I expected her to be. Christy was already skipping school when she lived at Dad's house, but at least he'd give her a hard time about it—and sometimes a smack in the head. Deanna, on the other hand, encouraged Christy to become a delinquent. Christy was smart. Like me, she was capable of higher-than-average grades. But by age fourteen, she no longer cared. We were lucky if she brought home Cs. Aunt Deanna had three kids when Christy lived there. She would ask my sister to stay home all day and babysit while she went out and had affairs behind Randy's back.

When Christy blossomed into a teenager, she became only more beautiful. She had thick blond hair with gold and red highlights. Aunt Deanna taught Christy all about makeup, and Christy's blue eyes just seemed to glow. She was gorgeous. Christy—taking after Deanna— was aware of how boys and men stared at her, and she flaunted it sometimes. Other times, she seemed self-conscious and almost ashamed about her perfectly shaped body. In that way, she was just like me. We'd heard our dad call us worthless enough times to believe it. And anytime he called our mother plain or ugly, he might as well have said those words to us.

With Deanna, though, Christy could be completely self-absorbed. Deanna cared only about herself, and her attitude rubbed off on Christy. My sister turned into an out-of-control fourteen-year-old; she didn't need much prodding to go over the edge. Still, I tried to do what I could for her, and I visited Christy often. Once, she called me begging me to see her. I thought something was wrong—maybe she was feeling bad about Grandma or maybe Aunt Deanna had done something.

I dropped my homework and drove over, thinking I was going to take her to the pizza parlor for some one-on-one time. But on the way to the restaurant, she had me pick up one of her friends. Then she had me pick up another. Once we arrived, the girls huddled together and ignored me the whole time. I was huffy, but I tried to give her some slack. Christy didn't have it easy.

A few days later, she called and asked me to take her to the pizza parlor again. As much as I loved her, I wasn't a sucker. I told her no.

She didn't fault me for it. I knew that no matter what, she still had my back. And if I ever needed someone to defend me, I could call on my strong, courageous little sister. I remembered when we lived on the square in Highland with Mom; Christy once came home with a big bruise on her tanned face. She seemed kind of proud of how she got it: an older girl's boyfriend had been hanging out with my boyfriend. One day for no reason this girl—who was twenty-one—assumed her man was after me. She had the audacity to come knocking on our front door. Christy was home when the girl told her, "You tell your bitch of a sister I'm looking for her."

Christy stood up straighter and stuck her chest out. She looked this stranger in the eye and said, "Tell her yourself, you fat bitch."

The woman clocked Christy in the face, and Christy clocked her back. Luckily, neither of them got hurt too badly. Mom was livid about the situation and pressed charges against the twenty-one-year-old. Then she blamed me for the whole mess. I got yelled at because Christy got punched for me. Mom was mad because I had put Christy in a dangerous situation.

Hot and Cold

I still had dreams of going to college, but that college was in the state of Missouri and part of me wanted to go farther away—as far away as possible. I had taken the ASVAB (Armed Services Vocational Aptitude Battery) test at school and done well. My scores were high enough to merit a good bonus if I signed up. I saw the military as a way out. I could leave my mom and dad in the dust, and then I wouldn't have to depend on them for anything. I could still go to college if I signed up, but I would be able to pay for it myself with the GI Bill. It seemed like a smart plan.

I talked to an air force recruiter who had spoken at school. My stepdad, John, was in the air force, and I liked that branch the best. I hoped to do something with psychology, maybe something that could help heal people. I would have signed on the dotted line right away, but I was under eighteen. I needed a parent's signature for permission. I knew I wasn't going to get that, so I planned to keep this idea secret. I could always make a final decision about the military after my eighteenth birthday.

I never expected the recruiter to show up at my house. He knocked on the door one day about 3 or 4 p.m. Dad would leave work whenever he felt like it, so I never knew when to expect him. He was home.

Dad was cordial and shook the officer's hand. He was in a uniform, and I think that scared my father. Dad had just started drinking, so he didn't say much.

At least he waited until the officer left.

"You're fucking some man in our house!" he yelled at me that afternoon. "How dare you let that man come onto my property."

I knew better than to get upset. I just stayed calm and explained to him what was going on. I convinced him that I wasn't dating the officer, but was planning to join the air force. He cooled off for a second and then got hot again.

"You will *never* go into the military," Dad said, pacing around our living room. "All you do in the air force is clean up shit. You'd never make it. You'll never make anything of yourself."

His words hurt me, but I was used to them. They didn't make me crazy with fury, though I did cry a little bit. Mostly, I was prickly inside—going numb. I would start fantasizing that I was on a plane headed to a beautiful beach in France—anywhere. I would pretend I was as far away from St. John as possible.

My dad wasn't finished with me. His words brought me back down to earth. "If you do go into the military, I'll pull you out."

"You can't," I said, trying to show as little emotion as possible—trying to be there with him without really being there.

"My parents did it to me, and I can do it to you." He was settling down, moving toward the couch. His voice became sharp and cold.

"How are you going to do that? This isn't the same." I knew how his parents used the only surviving child rule to get him out of the Marines after his brother Bill died.

"Sole surviving son works for daughters as well." His eyes were full of hate and brutality. "Don't you think I won't use it."

It took me a second, but I caught his drift. He was telling me that Christy was expendable. He would kill her in an instant to pull me out of the air force. All I had to do was push him. My shoulders shivered. I looked into his eyes, and I believed him.

Sex, Pain, and Love

I don't know what got into me. One night, I went to a party with Tom W., Ricky, and our friends. A guy who was five years older, Rob, came along with us. He had been the much-loved leader of the group when he was in high school. He was cool, and I liked him. But I wasn't as interested in him as he seemed to be in me. He was a bit heavyset and not my usual type. That particular night, I decided I wasn't going to be the designated driver. I might drink, but just a little. Once we got to our friends' party, peer pressure got the best of me. Everyone was shoving alcohol down my throat, and I didn't stop them. I wound up having ten to fifteen vodka shots. Being that dumb got me more wasted than I had ever been in my life. Of course, I don't remember much of it. I know I ended up puking—a lot. Someone drove my car home for me, and my misery continued.

I slowly started to feel better the next morning—until I freaked out. I found an unexplained hickey on my neck. I had no idea where it had come from. Nothing gave me more anxiety than when I lost control. I was very mad—at myself and at whoever had put it there. Unfortunately, things like this happened to me sometimes. I would wake up in the morning with little bruises on my arms or legs. I'd just know my dad had been there—I'd smell him, or see some other sign of his presence. But my dad never left marks that were in visible places, and he never left a hickey. How could I have let another man do the same thing to me? I also worried that my dad would see it and punish me. If that happened, I would never hear the end of it from him. I could already hear the word *whore* burning in my ears.

I called Tom W., and I was pissed. I didn't know whether to cry or tear my hair out. Then I called Rob and really chewed him out because I was fairly sure he was the hickey man. I told him he was a sick human being, and I never wanted to talk to him again.

A few weeks later, my stomach pains came back strong. These were the same ones I'd been having on and off since I was a preteen. By this time, everyone believed me. My cramps weren't due to lactose intolerance. Steadily, I had been feeling worse and worse. The upper part of my pelvis hurt terribly before, during, and after sex. I didn't think I had any option but to live with the stabbing, searing pain until one day, I doubled over. I couldn't stand up straight. The pain blasted through my body, and I couldn't even talk.

My dad took me to the hospital. Doctors did every test imaginable: STD tests, blood work, and white cell count. My white blood cells came out a little low, but that was no cause for concern. The pain was still unbearable, and I was moaning and writhing. Perplexed, my gynecologist scheduled exploratory surgery, a laparoscopy. The doctors cut me open to find out I was rife with infection. They were shocked. They cut out as much disease as they could from my uterus and fallopian tubes, but I still had more.

At that point, I had to stay in the hospital on intravenous antibiotics for at least one week. The pain from the infection and from being opened up was overwhelming. My dad visited me every day, but I wasn't excited to see him. Somehow, I just knew this problem would point back to him. My mom was in Guam, and she didn't even know. Christy didn't have a car, and no one brought her to see me. Grandma Lannert was dead; my other grandparents didn't know. At least my dad's girlfriend, Rosa, stopped by. But no one at school knew why I'd been absent—and I didn't exactly call Tom W. or anyone else to tell them what was happening to me. It was a lonely time.

That's why I didn't turn Rob away when he showed up at my bedside after I'd been there alone for a few days. When he heard I hadn't been at school, he called my house over and over trying to find out what was wrong. Finally, my dad told him where I was and advised him to go visit me.

Rob came to my bedside every day after that, though I didn't tell him exactly why I was there. He kept apologizing for the hickey, and he was so sweet that I had to forgive him. He brought flowers, balloons, and a card. But none of that mattered as much as having his company. His timing had been perfect, and I fell for him just like that. Homecoming was in a few days, and he asked me to go with him. I told him I would if I could get myself out of the hospital.

I begged the doctors and nurses to let me out in time for the dance. They told me I could go if I could hold food down. I did it. They were reluctant, but they discharged me. I was instructed to take it easy, and if I had any more pain, to come right back.

I didn't feel very good—I had been diagnosed with pelvic inflammatory disease (PID)—but I made it to that dance. I had a dress at home, but it barely fit because I'd lost so much weight in the hospital. While I had been out sick, Rosa had bought me a necklace, bracelet, and shoes to match my outfit. For a second, I got to be happy. Rob provided so much warmth. He turned out to be a solid, caring, honest guy. We started dating seriously after that. We went out together all the time, and I completely adored him. Even his face had a soft, teddy bear–like quality. He had rounded cheeks and chestnut eyes. He was big and strong, but every muscle in his body was gentle. Some of my favorite times were when we'd babysit his little brothers together. He would play with them so tenderly, I could watch him with those children all day. There was something special about Rob; he was the kind of guy who'd be a wonderful father when that time came. He cared about me with the same lovingness. I didn't think I was worthy of that kind of love, and every time I pulled away from Rob, he'd reel me back in. He made me feel safe.

We dated for a few months, which was a really long time for me. He knew a little bit about my female issues, but not too much. Dad wasn't concerned about Rob at first. With other recent boyfriends,

Dad had tried to make me stop dating them. He'd say I was grounded or tell them I wasn't there when they called me on the phone. When he met guys, he'd act nice to their faces, but when they left, he'd tell me, "He's a piece of shit and a loser. You're not dating him anymore."

Dad wasn't like that with Rob. Most of the time, he really liked him. Dad did tell me to break up with him once, and I refused. Dad didn't make me. He didn't know that Rob spent the night sometimes. The only reason I could get away with that was because Dad was dating Rosa again. On nights Rosa stayed, I knew he wouldn't come into my room. Besides, I had just been very sick. Dad went easy on me. He left me alone at night for a good long while. I went into the hospital in October and by December, he had bothered me only twice. I considered that a respite.

Dad felt really bad about my PID, and he could see how incredibly happy I was with Rob. I could see myself with Rob forever. Rob was the only guy who'd made me feel truly special. He was the only guy who ever got me to trust him enough to fall—and stay—in love. I also thought Rob could handle my dad if it ever came to that. Rob had already spent four years in the military, and he was big. Rob could protect me if I needed that.

But the pain from PID was still unbelievable. PID is an infection of the uterus, fallopian tubes, and other reproductive organs. It's often caused by STDs, such as gonorrhea or chlamydia. But I hadn't tested positive for any of these. The cause of PID is this: bacteria move upward from the vagina or cervix into the reproductive system. Then the infection invades the reproductive organs—especially the fallopian tubes—and inflammation causes normal tissue to turn into scar tissue. A small percentage of women get PID because they are sexually active very early—before the cervix is fully mature. The cervix is supposed to block bacteria from entering the body. It can't do its job when it's only nine years old.

Prompt treatment can prevent complications of PID, including the damage it did to my organs. Multiple episodes of PID cause more serious problems. I was seventeen, and I figured I'd had untreated PID since I was twelve.

I had to go back to my ob/gyn because of the pain. She told me there wasn't much else to do; she didn't even give me medication. She said I would have to learn to tolerate the discomfort because I had a lot of scar tissue, and that sex would probably be painful for most of my life, something I already knew. Then she told me I needed to be really careful when I had sex. While the chances of my getting pregnant were slim to none, I could have an ectopic pregnancy. That occurs when an egg gets fertilized and pregnancy begins and ends— painfully—in the fallopian tubes instead of the uterus. If not discovered and treated, the tube can rupture and cause a life-threatening hemorrhage.

The news—all of it—was devastating. My heart sank. My whole life, I had wanted to have kids. I loved children. I wanted to have them so I could love and protect them, so I could make up for some of the mistakes that my parents had made with Christy and me. I dreamed of having a happy family one day—one that had no ties to years of abuse and neglect.

At school each day I'd see all the teenage girls who were normal. Most of them would be able to have kids one day. Thinking about it, I would become physically sick, running into the bathroom to vomit. I cried all the time. I couldn't stand the sight of babies on the street. I had been stripped of the one basic hope I'd had for my life— to become a mother.

I called another gynecologist and brought him all my medical records. I told him that I couldn't have children. I said I'd heard about a surgery where doctors could open up the fallopian tube with a tiny balloon.

I said, "I want that. I want that done right now."

He shook his head. "You're seventeen years old, and there isn't anybody in the world who is going to do this operation on a teenager. It's unethical at your age."

He didn't understand. I told him I'd use condoms; I just needed to regain the *ability* to have children. I begged and pleaded, but he still said no.

Then he told me that on top of my PID, I'd probably need surgery every five years to remove the scar tissue that could keep growing. All he gave me was more bad news.

I was almost suicidal. But my grandmother had just died six months earlier, and I had new thoughts about life and death. I was a senior at this point, but my junior thesis had been on reincarnation. I wanted to know what happened after a person died. Could Mee Maw live again as a butterfly or a bird? Was I thinking wishfully, or was it a real possibility? Through my research, I began to believe in reincarnation like the Buddhists do. I read that if you kill yourself, your body becomes trapped in the place where you died. I hung on to the idea that the soul can only exist where life ended. I thought, *I can't get stuck in this hell forever.* I also remembered my sickening botched attempt with Dimetapp. Suicide wasn't the answer this time, but I sure thought about it.

I didn't tell Rob what I was going through. He knew a little bit about the health issue, but not too much. I would just see him and cry for no reason. I had been visiting doctors trying to get fixed. I thought, if I have a problem, well then, *fix it!* If I could get back the ability to have children, everything would be okay with me. Everything would be okay with Rob and me, too. But that wasn't happening. He didn't understand where all my crying was coming from. He was patient, though, because he knew I'd been in pain. When we had sex, I'd cry again. It hurt physically and emotionally. Sex was a reminder that I was barren. I had nothing to give him.

I couldn't look at my dad. I blamed him completely, and I was always mad at him. I hated him for what he had done and continued to do to me. I hated him for the things he'd made me do against my will. Before I'd been treated for PID, I could still bring myself to separate him into two people. I could see the traces of Daddy, the man on the tractor with me in Alhambra. But once I was told I would never have kids, he became just Tom. Something inside me changed. I stopped loving my father. I stopped making excuses for him. Everything just stopped. I felt numb when I thought of him. He knew it because for the first time, I started becoming aggressive toward him. Before I'd gone into the hospital, I'd given him two Rolling Stones tickets for his birthday. The show date was after I got out.

He asked me if I wanted to go. I told him, "No, and you're lucky you got those from me."

He didn't understand. He couldn't put my behavior in perspective. I was hurt emotionally and physically, but I'd always been hurt. Now I was damaged, but I was almost an adult. I was overcome with hate and anger, and he didn't know what to do about it. I became a daughter he didn't recognize.

Everything was bad all the time. I didn't know how to separate pain from pleasure anymore. Life was too terrible too suddenly. I couldn't function. I had to leave but I didn't know where to go. I thought about telling Rob, because I knew he would stand up for me. But his mother and young brothers happened to live in Highland, of all places. My dad would be able to find them easily, and he would threaten to harm them if that's what it took to get back at me.

I called my mother and told her that I was coming to live with her. She wasn't tickled pink, but she told me I was welcome. Arrangements had to be made. My dad had to be convinced to let me go.

In my mixed-up mental state, I went to my high school guidance counselor with the news that I was moving to Guam to be with my mother. She was confused because it was December of my senior year. She talked to me about finishing out the school year. I told her I absolutely wouldn't be graduating from Ritenour. Then she reminded me that I was a good student, and I should be applying to colleges no matter where I wound up going to school. I nodded my head yes and told her of course I would be going to college.

Out of the blue, I blurted out: "Someone who lives with us is raping me."

She was silent. She didn't even look at me; she just fumbled around with her papers. She obviously didn't know what to say, so she didn't say much. I stood there acting just as shocked as she was. I couldn't believe I had said that. I started sweating. Over the next weeks, I worried about what might happen. Turned out, I worried for nothing. She did not inform the authorities or even the principal. She had no more conversations about it with me. She must've figured I was on my way to Guam and was getting out of the situation. I would be eighteen soon, and I would be okay.

I guess she thought it wasn't her business, and she was better off staying out of it.

Miles Away

My father told me there was no way in hell I was going to Guam. He wasn't going to have it and even went as far as forbidding it. According to him, I needed to keep my ass in school and graduate.

I saw his temper tantrum coming. I had planned for it by cooking up a story.

I told him my friend Shannon was a narc. He knew Shannon well, even though she was a new friend of mine. She was like me—she lived with her dad and had limited contact with her mom. She was at our house a lot, and Dad commented on how pretty she was. After that, I made sure we always left when he came home drunk.

I told Dad that Shannon was a plant, someone who is older but poses as a high school student to bust drug rings. I told him the police had been investigating and had a huge case built against me. But they didn't want me; they wanted my dealer. I explained to Dad that the police had brought me in for questioning, and I told the police who the dealer was so they wouldn't press charges against me.

My dad, the alcoholic child abuser, took the bait.

Inspired by an episode of *21 Jump Street*, I embellished my story further. Because I had given up the drug dealer and told the cops everything they wanted to know, the drug dealer was after me. He wanted me dead, and his people were on the hunt for me. Of my two parents, Dad was the one who fixed things. He paid the fine when I hit the barn with Mom's car. He took me to the hospital when I had the worst pains of my life. This time was no different. Dad bought me a ticket to Guam that day. My flight was in two weeks.

But because I was in trouble for my life, I had to leave St. John. I packed everything and drove to Uncle Daniel's house in Illinois. I rushed away with Dad's blessing.

I had just one stop to make: Rob's house.

He wasn't there during the day, and I knew that. So I left him a Christmas present, a teddy bear. I wrote him a Dear John letter to say good-bye. All the PID pain combined was nothing compared to the pain of breaking up with Rob. I loved him more than I could ever convey in a silly love letter. I knew he'd be furious with me when he read it; that was even harder for me to deal with. My wonderful, kind boyfriend Rob would hate me forever because I upped and left without warning or good reason. No good reason he knew about anyway. In his eyes, I just vanished. He didn't know where I was going, and he had no way to reach me. I couldn't tell him those details without telling him all the other stuff. If only I could have opened up to him, but I didn't dare—I was scared. Every time I'd opened up—to my babysitter, my mom, my guidance counselor—nothing happened. I'd always felt more desperate, more stupid, and more alone.

After I was gone, Dad's lawyer called the police station to find out what was going on and to help me out. With that simple phone call, my jig was up. Dad unraveled my web of big fat lies—and he was pissed. He called Illinois to scream at me, to let me know my ass belonged back at home. But he knew I'd ignore him. It didn't matter what he said or did. I was already a few hours away in Illinois with a plane ticket in my hand. I would soon be traveling halfway around the world from the monster. I would be 7,396 miles away from Tom Lannert.

I had won.

Tom Lannert couldn't touch me.

Life in Guam

Mom was going to be my out. Whether she knew it or not, she was the answer to all of my problems. I thought things would be okay with her and John—how could they be worse than what I was coming from?

But from the moment I stepped into their small house, I was taken back to the days of their honeymoon. Even though we lived in a tight air force housing unit, I didn't see them much. The apartment was a flat duplex, and two noisy rottweilers lived next door. There was a huge cactus outside our front door. Geckos and island lizards crawled around the yard. You entered the apartment through a lanai, which is sort of like a front porch, but enclosed with walls. The living and dining rooms were nice, and my bedroom was on the right.

Mom and I didn't exactly hit it off. One of our first conversations was about my PID. I brought my medical records to show her. I needed her to really know about what I'd been through. I thought maybe, just this once, she could step up to the plate. Maybe she could do or say something to help me, to make me feel better. Maybe she would put two and two together and decode my secret. I didn't have anywhere else to turn, so it was worth a shot.

She was less than supportive. Even worse, she was mad at me.

She flipped through the papers in the folder. "Stacey, the most disturbing part of this report is that you're having sex!" she said in a high-pitched voice.

She didn't care about the pain I'd had. She didn't even mention that I would never bear her grandchild. Her only concern was that I'd had premarital intercourse.

She went on and on with her sex lecture, clearly unhappy with me. She was so confrontational that I backed down. I gave up.

She obviously didn't get it, and I obviously wasn't going to get the support I needed. To put out the fire and change the subject, I convinced her that I'd had sex only once. She still didn't approve, but she dropped the issue.

That conversation had gone completely wrong. A wet noodle could've given me more support than my mother did. I was furious at her insensitive reaction. I was also disappointed and heartbroken.

The whole time I was in Guam, I think I spent about four hours total with Mom. I saw John just a little more. He would get off work at 2 p.m. every day, come in the house, go directly to his bedroom, and lock himself in there. I liked him, I guess, but he wasn't warm to me.

I believe he felt that I was trying to seduce him. And maybe I was in a weird way. If so, it was because I expected to be defiled by every grown man who ever got close to me. All the guys I'd known—except for my friend Tom W.—had disappointed me in some way. Subconsciously, I wore a shirt that came just to my belly button and a little pair of boxer shorts around the apartment. The outfit wasn't sexy in my mind; it was light and comfortable in the boiling hot Guam weather. Later, I found out that John told Mom I should cover up when he was around. John didn't think my boxers were appropriate. All the while, I was leery of him though he gave me no reason to be. I acted hateful just because he was a man.

With my bad attitude, I tried to convey a message: back off, and don't bother me. At the same time, I expected him to want me sexually; I assumed he would act inappropriately. As it turned out, I had nothing to worry about. John was the only grown man from my childhood who wasn't a pedophile. He was a decent person. I just didn't realize it, and I didn't understand healthy sexual boundaries.

John was militaristic and very, very strict, so I can't say I liked living with him. I'd come from a house where I was basically in charge and could do anything I wanted 90 percent of the time. Then I landed at John's, where I had to be accountable. For example, he'd complain about how I used the iron. I'd leave it on—standing up, of course—for hours so I could come back and forth and do my laundry. He said that was dangerous. I kept forgetting to turn the iron off, so finally, he told me I wasn't allowed to use it at all.

I needed a car. I was stuck at home in tropical limbo. I had spent only four weeks in high school. In Guam, most of the American kids go to private school. I was at Simon Sanchez High, a public school, where I was considered a *haole* (pronounced "howly"). That was their racist term for a no-account white foreigner. The native kids stuck to their own cliques, never letting the *haoles* in. Some of them were mean. There was a culture of bullying in the Guam public schools that was condoned by the teachers. They thought kids should work things out themselves. As a result, it wasn't unusual for a white girl to get beat up repeatedly.

I looked for other American kids, but there weren't many. They were already into their tight group, and they made no room for me. It was already January of our senior year; why should they? I started to miss all my friends at Ritenour. I was sad that I wouldn't be walking down the aisle in my cap and gown with them. But there, I had missed a lot of school because of PID. I had fallen a semester—maybe even a year—behind. Plus, some days, my pain was still too unbearable to get out of bed. I was miserable at home and at school. The girls at Sanchez hated me so much they'd slam me up against my locker as they walked down the halls. They didn't want me there flirting with their boys. I didn't want to get involved in their dangerous nonsense. One day, I woke up and decided I wasn't going back to Simon Sanchez High.

My mom thought life would be easier for me if I just got my GED so I could start college. John took me to the GED office on the air force base. Instructors there gave me a pretest and invited me to take the real test the next day. I didn't even need to study. I remembered parts of it from when I was eight years old, helping Aunt Deanna prepare. I finished my GED test in half the time allotted with an above-average score. Just like that, I was done with high school.

I wanted to go to the University of Guam. It was supposed to be a good school. But I couldn't get there—or anywhere—without a car. Guam was a tiny island out in the middle of nowhere with terrible public transportation. Without a car, I was on an island on an island. Mom and John were not helpful. First, they worried about how I'd pay for car insurance. Then they said they didn't have extra money to help me with that or with gas. They explained over and over that they were struggling financially. In fact, I had to pay them $100 a month for rent. She took it out of the $300 per month I got for child support. I never understood that, but I didn't make a fuss. I reminded myself that I was still happy to be out of St. John.

I pushed the car issue, asking them to buy me one of those little Guam cars. Lots of people drove these rusty-framed beach cars that cost only $500. Mom wouldn't budge. She kept saying, "Ask Dad."

I didn't want to ask him for anything. But the car situation—or lack thereof—really sucked. I called him to explain everything, and he always took my calls. He was eager to have contact with me—to take any opportunity to try to change my mind. He was still furious about the way I had left, but even so, he obviously missed me.

"Sure, you can have a car," Dad said. "Actually, you have one right here in the driveway."

"Come on Dad, for real." I hated playing these games with him. "Just ship it to me."

"It doesn't have to be that difficult, Stacey," he said. "Just come home to get it."

With nothing better to do, I started acting up. The drinking age in Guam was eighteen, and I couldn't be the designated driver because I didn't have a car. So I went to the bars by myself, ordered fruity beach drinks, and stayed out late. I was almost eighteen, and to the bartenders there, that was good enough. Mom and John didn't approve of my new bar friends who drove me around. They hated to see me partying constantly. I was just trying to stay busy. They thought I was ungrateful and a handful. Mom and John saw me as a complication in their otherwise peaceful lives. Even I saw myself as a bother; I just didn't know what else to do with myself.

I wasn't happy or unhappy there. For all of its flaws, living in Guam was far less dramatic than living in St. John. I was bored, but I had three meals a day for the first time in a long time. When I left Missouri, I weighed barely 90 pounds and wore a size 0. In Guam, I could cook real food—Mom kept the kitchen well stocked—and I gained at least ten pounds. I was determined to cruise along just like I was until my birthday on May 28. Once I turned eighteen, I could make more decisions for myself. In the back of my head, I always thought I could fade away into the military if the college thing didn't work out for me. I just had to find a way to keep Christy away from Dad, in case he was serious about harming her so he could pull me out. I hoped she would eventually end up in Guam.

That's when the phone calls from Christy started. She was supposed to be at Aunt Deanna's, but instead, Dad forced her to move back in with him. He knew there was only one way to get to me, and he had her. Dad took Christy from Deanna's because Christy was partying around the clock and skipping school more than she went. He was going to bring her to St. John and whip her into shape. Literally.

She'd call me in the middle of the night crying—Guam is fifteen hours ahead of St. Louis. Wasted, she'd tell me she was sleeping with too many boys, and Dad was constantly threatening to beat her to a pulp. She was fifteen, and she looked up to me for advice. She was still partying and skipping school, but Dad yelled at her for it. Aunt Deanna could've cared less what Christy did as long as she babysat for her kids. Meanwhile, Dad expected Christy to do the cleaning and grocery shopping like I had done. She'd tell him to go fuck himself; he'd hit her and toss her down the basement stairs. Christy and Dad were a doomed pair. I was terrified for her. He had calculated a perfect storm, and he did it just for me.

Dad called Mom and said, "I'm putting Christy on a plane right now." I don't think he meant it. He knew Mom would say no. After Highland, she had made it clear that she didn't want us both at the same time.

"Christy can't come while Stacey's here." I begged her to let Christy share a bedroom with me, but she wouldn't budge. "It's too hard with you both at the same time."

Dad would call back and yell at me. "Get this fucking little bitch out of my house before I kill her."

I couldn't sleep at night. I had done absolutely everything in my power to keep him away from Christy for seventeen years. I knew he physically abused her, but he hadn't sexually abused her.

Not yet.

I knew this deep in my heart; I knew it as surely as I knew my birth date. But I was no longer there. If he became sexually violent, whom would he turn to? The thoughts began to haunt me every second of every day.

I was halfway around the world pleading with Christy to please go to Grandma and Grandpa Paulson's. She said no. I asked her to please go stay with her friends. She told me no. Run back to Deanna's, I told her.

Christy's answer was the same. "No, no, no. Fuck no."

She was wasted most of the time I spoke to her, and I knew there was no reasoning with an alcoholic. There's no predicting what an alcoholic will say or do, not even a baby one.

"Stacey, please come home," Christy said, crying to me.

It was April, and I was going to be eighteen in a month and a half. I could live with whatever shit he had to give me. But I couldn't live knowing he would most definitely rape Christy if I didn't go home to save her. Mom and John bought my plane ticket. I was on the next flight to the United States.

Unhappy Birthday

I had hoped to put Christy on a plane straight to Mom's when I got home. I would use Dad's credit card for the plane ticket if I had to, and pay him back. I'd find a way.

But that's not how things went down. Christy refused to go to Mom's. And anyway, Mom said she wasn't ready for Christy yet. Mom needed some time between daughters. Mom was so clueless then. The alcoholic she had divorced was a saint compared to the alcoholic we were stuck with.

Christy hated our father. She hoped everyone would die—Dad, Deanna, John, our grandparents, and most of all, our mother. Like me, she blamed Mom for things Mom didn't even know she'd done. She hated the world and everything in it.

I was the only person related to Christy that she didn't hate. She had friends, but they weren't going to make sure she ate breakfast and got home safely at night. She could count on me—and only me. I wanted to take care of her, and to help make things better for her. I took responsibility for my younger sister—God knows, no one else did.

Dad was a prick when I came back—not that I was surprised. He'd stayed on his steady path of decline since Grandma Lannert had died. He drank more—as if that were possible—and he was meaner. But his anger wasn't contingent on how much alcohol he consumed; he was volatile all the time. Moments of peace were rare. He seemed the worse for wear ever since I tricked him about Guam.

I don't know what he was so mad about because in the end, he had won the battle between us. I was back.

Grandma Lannert's house had sat vacant while I'd been gone. I kept telling Dad he needed to clean it out. I thought maybe we could move into it—it was nicer than ours. He'd grunt and shoo me away. Thoughts of that house obviously brought him pain. The house made me sad, but it was still a symbol of good times for me. I had a strong attachment to it.

One day, he decided he didn't want to ignore the issue any longer. Like a flipped switch, he woke up and decided to clean it out. He didn't even tell me what he was doing. He didn't let me help as he lined up trash bags by the curb. He saved a few things, gave other stuff away, and chucked most of Grandma's belongings. He went about it very harshly.

My heart was broken. I couldn't understand what he was doing or why. Christy felt the sting of it, too. That house wasn't just his; it was ours. Grandma told us many times: that house was for Christy and me. She wanted us to come back to it when we graduated from college. She wanted us to use it when we needed it. Of course, she didn't put her intentions in writing, so everything she had—about $150,000 plus her house—went straight to Dad.

He still didn't tell us what was going on when the For Sale sign went up. When we begged him to stop, he'd just tell us to shut up. He'd been raised there, and he was giving up a house his parents had built with their own hands. Meanwhile, my happy place—Mee Maw's house—was going to the highest bidder, meaningless to him. It was a place I could go to just sit quietly and recharge, and I ran over there often. For me and Christy, Grandma's house was our escape when things got too intense.

With the house on the market, we hit another dark turning point. Whatever safety was left in my world vanished. Where could we go to hide? Nowhere. No place was okay after that. Dad's decision took the wind out of me, and I crashed.

So did Dad.

Anger emanated from him all the time. The biggest and worst change was when he stopped sleeping in his bedroom. He took up permanent residence in the living room on that couch. It was the center of the household. It was right by the front door where we always came in and out. The back door off the kitchen had a metal storm door that went *thwack,* so we rarely used it. It woke him up, which would piss him off. No matter how we tried to leave his house, he'd know it if he was on the couch. It was a huge problem. We didn't want to stir him because if we did, he'd start something with us. He'd find anything to scream about; he'd yell at us for stuff we didn't even do.

For example, it might be 1 p.m., and he'd be passed out on that couch. If I tried to go out somewhere, he'd hear me fiddling with the front door and tell me to step back.

"Where do you think you're going?" he'd ask. "You need to stay home and clean the house." Drunks can speak surprisingly clearly sometimes—they become immune to their alcohol. He'd be wasted, and I wouldn't know it by his voice alone. Other times, he wouldn't be drunk at all, but his words would still be mean—for no good reason.

With my car keys in hand, I'd say, "We just cleaned the house yesterday."

"You're going to clean it again." Even when he didn't yell, his tone was terrifying. It was so scary that we did what he said, hoped he'd fall back to sleep soon, and then tried to scoot out again.

Sometimes, he would keep catching me at the front door, and I couldn't get out at all. He'd make me sit on the couch with him. He wouldn't even talk to me. He did this to Christy, too. He just wanted to dominate and control us. He'd act ignorant. If he knew I had to be somewhere, he'd tell me to take all the shirts out of his closet and make sure everything was lined up and facing the right way. He wasn't one of those organized types of people. He was just looking for stupid things to make me do. Or he'd pull out a drawer in the kitchen or his bedroom and dump the contents all over the floor.

"Pick it up," he said, standing over me as I knelt on the ground.

He'd cuss while I cleaned up his mess. His favorite thing to say was, "You're just like your mother. Ungrateful."

He knew he was hurting me. He was humiliating and insulting on purpose. He was aware of my relationship with Mom and how bad it was. He knew I hated being compared to her and that I didn't want to be anything like her. When he was drunk, he'd call me by her name. If he was drunk *and* hell-bent on being rotten, he would call me her name while he raped me.

I had moved Christy into the basement, so my room was right across from his and near the living room—very convenient for him.

He'd sneak in at night, scaring me. While on top of me, he'd ask, "Do you like that?"

Of course, I don't like that, I thought. *I hate this. I hate you.* I'd tune him out the best I could. My mind would go back to a beach on Guam. I would travel all over the world—anywhere to get out of the basement with him.

He'd speak into my ear, holding his mouth close to my head. To this day, I can't stand somebody whispering to me. I can't stand the feeling of weight on my chest.

Most of the time, I would hear his voice no matter how far away I tried to go in my head. Often, he'd call me a slut or a tramp. "How many men, Deborah?!" he'd yell as he jabbed. "How many men?"

He never called me Deb or Debbie, the casual names my mom used.

When he got cruel, he'd say, "De-BOR-ah."

It didn't matter which women he dated, he was still in love with her—as much as a man like him could be in love with anyone. He would pretend I was her. It wasn't much of a stretch. As I grew into an adult, I looked exactly like my mom.

"Deborah, Deborah, Deborah," he'd say. "You're a bitch and a whore."

He called me a lot of things, but he never called me Stacey.

Christy and I devised an escape plan so we could get out of the house without being harassed or harmed. We tried to create lives outside as much as we could. She hung around with a group of friends from high school. I never told any of my old friends—Tom W., Rob, or Inga—that I was back from Guam. I hadn't planned on sticking around St.

John long enough to fall back into old patterns. Plus, I had walked away from them all, and I felt like a failure for being back at square one. But I still knew people—just the wrong people. When you smoke pot, you fall into one of two groups. There are the upscale kids who just play around with it; those were my old friends. Then there's the downscale side of weed—the people who deal it and commit other minor crimes. After Guam, I fell into the downscale group. In fact, I ran into an old friend named Ron. He used to be Aunt Deanna's best friend, and the two of them babysat me when I was little. Ron had a girlfriend and two little kids. I'd hang out at their house and babysit. I'd loan him small amounts of money when he was hard up. Ron was a small-time criminal always looking to make money without actual effort. Aunt Deanna told me Ron was trouble and to stay away from him. So of course, he became my new regular buddy. At least I had somewhere to go when I needed to get out of the house.

Another friend, Jason, called my house because he knew we had extra cars after Grandma died. We had a 1976 Impala and the 1982 LeBaron. He was hoping my dad would sell him one cheap. I answered the phone, and our friendship was rekindled. Dad agreed to sell him one of the cars, but he didn't know Jason's had been im-pounded after a cop found pot in it. Jason thought my father was a cool, outgoing, boozy guy who had a little bit of money. Once, Jason was at my house when I found a receipt for a $100,000 withdrawal my dad had made from one of Grandma's accounts. I told Jason I was pissed at Dad for drinking away all of Grandma's money. Dad was nice to Jason's face, and he took Jason's money for the car. But privately, Dad told me I wasn't allowed to hang around with Jason—because he was half black.

To hang out with my friends, I started sneaking around. Christy had moved her bedroom into the basement living area, so the base-ment bedroom became our living room, complete with a couch, TV, and bookshelf—and a window with two panes. The outside pane had a latch that had to be unhooked from the outside. I had to unlatch it while he wasn't looking, or I wouldn't be able to get out later. The inside pane was easy to take on and off from either direction. If we didn't remember to fix the window, we would be stuck inside. He was always lying on the couch in a drunken stupor, monitoring the front door. Christy and I tried to remember to leave a chair underneath that window for reentering, to break our fall.

Even during broad daylight (Christy wasn't at school that often), we used that basement window to go in and out as often as we could. Or if we forgot to unlatch it beforehand, we'd wait downstairs, quiet as trees. When everything was silent upstairs for long stretches of time, we'd try to get out the front door.

I'd park on the perpendicular street, McNaulty Drive, in front of a neighbor's house so he wouldn't see my car. Then I'd run through other people's yards to sneak into the basement window that was in the back of our house. The less he knew where I was, the better.

With everything inside of me, I wanted to leave his house for good, and he could sense that. I reminded him that I was almost eighteen. I taunted him with the possibility of my saying good-bye forever. He countered by telling me he had control over me until I was twenty-one. He was becoming more desperate.

So was I.

On May 28, 1990, I turned eighteen. My birthday fell around Memorial Day weekend, and Jason asked if I wanted to go to Steelville, Missouri, with him to go three-wheeling and hang out in the country—just as friends. Christy was leaving for the long weekend, so I said yes. I took off without asking Dad. When we got there, we found that Jason's cousin had a litter of adorable beagle-mix puppies. The first thing I did for my birthday was get one. I thought, *I'm going to love it and cherish it.* I named her Caitlin.

I came home on Sunday around 4 p.m. wearing a bikini covered by jean shorts and my track team sweatshirt. I knew better than to walk into my house wearing a bikini top. I opened the front door with my duffel bag in one hand and my puppy in the other.

He was on the couch. "What are you doing with that fucking dog?"

"She's mine, and her name is Caitlin." I gently put the dog on the floor and let her sniff around.

"You have until the end of next week to get rid of that fucking dog," Tom said, slurring.

I felt more powerful than I'd ever felt before. He could tell it. I said, "I'm not going to. Fuck you. I'm eighteen now, and I'm moving out on my own. I'm taking Christy with me."

He laughed at me, disdainfully. "You're mine. You'll always be mine. There's no place you can go. Your car is in my name. I have your Social Security number. I'll track you down, and you'll always be connected to me." He got up from the couch.

I dropped my duffel as he flipped me around and pushed me up against the wall to the left of the front door. He shoved his hands into my pants and brought them back out. He said I smelled like a man. "Who have you been with?"

"No one." That was the truth. I wasn't into dating at that time. My focus was on getting out of his house. "You sick bastard."

"It's because you're so pretty," he said. "But I can fix that." I heard a familiar flick as he opened up his pocketknife with a rusty blade. He slid the knife down my cheek from my ear to my lip. "If you weren't so pretty, there'd be no men."

He had taken me by surprise, and I was pinned in the corner of the living room between the front door and the TV. I felt the heat from a drop of blood on my face. He yanked my head back by my ponytail. My neck ached, and I heard a sawing sound. He had to saw hard to cut my ponytail off with that dull blade. Once I realized what was happening, I was relieved that he wasn't cutting up my face.

After he let go, I dropped down on the floor into a little ball. I was freaking out. He reached down and flipped me over, yanking off my shorts. He raped me right there on the living room floor. A lot of times, I knew it was coming, and I could prepare myself by counting backward and going off to some other place. This time, it happened too quickly, and I felt everything. It was overwhelmingly painful, and I curled back into a little ball when he finished. I blacked out for a minute or two. I woke when he kicked me hard in the ribs.

He stood over me as he got $40 out of his wallet. He threw the money on my body and said, "Happy birthday. Go buy yourself something nice." He walked away, and then left the house.

I just lay there hurting and breaking. When I could, I got up and found my new puppy in one of the other rooms. I held her and cried. *What do I do now?* I thought over and over. I could hardly breathe, and my ribs hurt from his kick. His words, *You're mine,* were stuck in my head. I felt a new sense of hopelessness mixed with hate.

My blond hair was all over the place, and I had to clean it up before Christy returned the next day. I hid everything from her, as I had for years. She had enough of her own issues—he physically abused her nearly every day. So Monday morning, I went and got my hair fixed.

I also bought myself a $400 car stereo on his credit card—"something nice for my birthday."

I became obsessed with getting out of that house. I applied to Mizzou. I hoped I might be able to enroll in classes in the fall. I prayed that I would find a way to live on campus, away from him. He wouldn't let me work; he wanted me to be totally dependent on him. I had some time to plan. So I held on to the hope that I could get Christy out of Dad's, and then I would be able to leave, too. If I didn't cling to that hope, I had no reason to live.

I had started taking summer classes at Flo Valley, also known as St. Louis Community College—Florissant Valley. At least I had something worthwhile to do besides keep tabs on my sister and hang out with stoners. But Flo Valley was at home, and Mizzou was more than three hours away. I needed to get away. I filled out my application, which carried a $25 application fee. He saw me write the check and sign his name—something I often did. Then he watched as I tried to figure out how to fill out my application. It was supposed to be typed, and we didn't have a typewriter. In what I believed was a rare moment of sober kindness, he offered to take the application to his secretary's office to have her type it up. Despite his drinking, he was still working—I don't know how. He didn't keep jobs for long. Regardless, I wrote out all of the answers, attached the forms and the check, and sent him to work with everything he needed for my Missouri State University application.

He promised me that his secretary would send in everything from the office.

A few weeks later, he came home with an envelope with a Mizzou return address label. He waved it in the air and told me I had been denied admission for the fall semester.

"They don't want you," he said, standing by our dining room table, which was covered by his computer, books, and work papers. "Sorry to tell you this, but you're too stupid."

I wanted to read the letter, but he wouldn't let me. He held it up in the air where I couldn't reach it. He made fun of me. He said I was too dumb to even read it.

I didn't know what to do from there. I didn't cry or get mad. I didn't say anything. I let him walk off. I just couldn't believe it. From the time I was a little girl, my nickname was Tiger, and I was supposed to go to Mizzou. That's where he went; that's where my uncle and cousin went. My whole life, I had kept up my grades so I could attend that school. That was what I was going to do—study, choose a career, and finally have a life of my own. I'd work, get married, and have children.

Except that I couldn't have children because of him. At seventeen, that chance got taken away from me. Then I'm told I can't go to college. The military was out until Christy lived somewhere more safe and stable.

I was too consumed with self-pity to put it all together at the time. Of course, my father was lying to me about the admissions denial. Later, I went through his checking account stubs—he knew I had access to all of that stuff. I couldn't find the canceled check made out to Missouri State. I checked the statements, too. Then I confronted him.

He said he hadn't used the check I wrote but had paid the fee over the phone by credit card. I couldn't find the credit card statements to check for myself. He continued to try to convince me that the school just didn't want me.

For a long while, I doubted myself. I thought he was right. I was a stupid girl with a GED. Then I started to question him. Since I couldn't find proof of payment to Mizzou, maybe he had been lying the whole time. I didn't know how to find out. Was I even allowed to call the university? I had no clue. Either way, I was distraught. I started to believe I was stupid. I even dropped out of Flo Valley.

I was consumed with my own negative thoughts. *What's the point? Why should I go to school if I'm just an idiot? What good is school going to do if I can't even get out of this house?*

I became depressed. I was devastated; I felt like I would be trapped forever. Forever is a long time when you're living in hell.

In those moments, I lost all hope. He was never going to let me leave while there was still breath in his body.

Pushed

By this point, I was saying to him, "If you don't stop, I'll kill you." I had fantasies about what kind of life I could have if he weren't in it.

He'd say, "Yeah, right. You don't have the balls." We both used the word *kill* obsessively—him especially. He'd describe all of the ways he wanted to kill Christy—and me too, while he was at it.

We had one bathroom in the house, and I still took ritualistic long, hot baths after attacks that were happening constantly. I'd be in the tub, and he would barge right in. It was a small room. When you walked in, the white ceramic tub was on the left, and the small sink and mirrored medicine cabinet were directly across on the right. There was an electrical outlet next to the mirror, and I kept a radio plugged into it.

"I can come in and throw this radio in the tub and electrocute you," he said, snapping his fingers. "What would you do about it?"

The bathroom was very narrow. I bolted out of the tub to run from the room, but he blocked the door. Then he tossed me back into the water. As a strict rule, I stopped bathing when he was home. I was terrified. He'd say the same stuff to my sister, but he didn't barge in on her like he did me.

Rickety wooden steps led down to the basement. He said he could throw us down the steps and break our necks. That's another reason we used the basement window as much as possible. We didn't want to give him opportunities to go through with his threats.

He said to me, "I'll throw Christy down the steps and stab you and tell the police that you were trying to take my money to buy drugs." He made up all kinds of ridiculous stories to scare me. Only they weren't so ridiculous at the time; I believed him. His eyes were hardly blue any more; they had turned to pure fire and hate.

He started walking around the house holding his .22 caliber rifle down by his side to intimidate us. He was so out of control that no one could come to our house anymore. We were too scared to be there ourselves.

I started to wish he were dead in a way I hadn't before. There hadn't been as much urgency in the past. But now Christy and I were living in a nightmare with him. If things continued the way they were, one of us was going to lose our life. I didn't believe I could be the cause of his death, or that I was capable of killing him myself.

But I didn't want to die. I took his .22 to Ron's so he could show me how to use it. Then I taught Christy how to shoot out in an old field in Alhambra. We both needed to know how to defend ourselves, just in case.

I took his gun when he wasn't looking and slept with it under my bed. I thought, *Okay, if he walks through that door tonight, I'm just going to shoot him.* I tried to stay awake for a few nights, so when he arrived in the night (I never knew when), I'd be ready. I couldn't do it. I kept falling asleep. He'd wake me up, and it was too late. I couldn't reach the weapon that was right underneath me. How would I get my hands on it with him standing right there?

One night, he noticed that his loaded rifle was missing. He stumbled into my room at 3 a.m. and found it under my bed. He knew I wanted to kill him, and he laughed at me. He said I'd never be able to do it—I didn't have the balls. But he could kill me anytime he wanted.

To prove his point, I had woken up with my hands and feet bound to the four corners of the bed with an orange electrical cord. I couldn't move when he raped me with the very weapon I had taken to protect myself.

With the .22 rifle inside me, he pulled the trigger. I heard the soft click and welcomed death. I felt peace that he could kill me this way,

and people would finally find out. They would know him for the monster he had become. My sister would be saved from him. As I realized
that the gun had been unloaded before he terrorized me with it, I felt
cheated. I was still alive as he left.

A few days later, I was leaving the house to hang out with friends,
and sober Dad told me to call him if I couldn't drive home safely, and
he would pick me up. He gave me a lecture about drinking and driving, pointing out his many accidents. He'd had another near-death
car wreck right before I left for Guam. Miraculously, he walked away
from it.

I was headed to Ron's, and I had a ridiculous 10 p.m. curfew because I hadn't cleaned the house well enough. It wasn't a big deal,
and half the time, Dad wouldn't remember my punishments anyway.
But he had told me to call him if I drank or smoked too much. I was
thirty minutes away from home when I looked at the clock. It was
9:45 p.m.

I called Dad. I said, "I've been drinking, and I shouldn't drive. I
should wait a few hours." I'd had only one drink, but I could still feel
it. I was too terrified from all of Dad's wrecks to put myself in that
position behind the wheel.

"Get your fucking ass home right now," he yelled. Drunk Dad had
answered the phone. He could hear people in the background. Ron
wasn't having a party, but two or three of his guy friends were over.
Drunk Dad could hear them. "How many men are you fucking right
now?" he said, screaming. "You little slut. Fucking whore. You have
twenty minutes to get back home."

I started crying, and Ron walked over and stood next to me.
"I'll be home as soon as I can," I told my father before hanging up. I
wasn't going to drive, and I prayed he'd be passed out by the time I
made my way back to St. John.

Ron asked me what was wrong. He wore dark tinted eyeglasses all
the time. He had curly red hair and lots of freckles.

I said, "I just wish he were dead."

"That can be arranged," Ron replied.

I rolled my eyes. "Yeah, I wish." That was the end of the conversation.

There were four conversations like that, and Jason heard one of them. I never, ever brought it up to Ron. Instead, I'd be over at his house—I never should've kept going back there—and he would nudge me with his elbow.

"$2,500, and it's done," he said.

Every time, I played it down. I knew I couldn't say how I really felt. Instead, I said, "Yeah, I've thought about it. But I don't want to go there." It would've been so easy to say, *Yes, let's do it. Here you go. Here's $2,500.* But there was still a part of me that was sane.

Ron had run-ins with the law. For example, he had been in trouble for taking off with an underage girlfriend. I didn't know that until much later. Ron and his girlfriend, Theresa, were simply two of the only friends I had. They knew I had problems with my dad, but they didn't know the specifics.

The truth was, I did want him dead. I fantasized about it more and more often. *What if he did kill himself in one of those car crashes? What if I hadn't picked him up from The Edge that night he was so drunk he couldn't walk? What if I had let him lie there on his back, unconscious, while he vomited? What if I hadn't turned him over to his side? How many times have I saved him?*

Then my brain snapped back into reality. I'd think to myself, *Damn, I am so wrong. I make myself sick.*

I knew I should do no harm.

I never thought I could do harm.

Wishing for someone's death is wrong.

One of my father's friends from college was a man named Denny. He was the general manager of one of the Marriott hotels—I didn't know which one—in St. Louis. He was a well-known local business-man, and my dad always talked about him with reverence. Everything was so out of control, I needed someone—anyone—to talk to. I thought maybe this guy Denny could speak to Dad. Maybe Dad would listen to someone he respected. I knew I couldn't handle the situation by myself anymore. I had my speech planned out. I was going to tell him that my father's alcoholism had reached its breaking point, and he needed help. I was going to explain that we were living in a dangerous situation and ask for help.

I called the Marriott at the airport. It was a big Marriott, so maybe he worked at that one. Surely, the operator would just connect me.

The operator wanted to know who I was, and then she said she couldn't connect me or give out his information. So I drove to the hotel, went up to the front desk, and asked if he was there. I knew he had to be in one of those hotels somewhere. I was desperate. The receptionist finally agreed to take my message asking my father's friend to call me. For the next few days, I waited anxiously to hear from him.

He never called.

The Fourth of July

The morning of July 4 didn't start off badly. For the first time in over a year, Dad said we were going to barbecue. I was surprised—he grilled outside only when he was happy. He already had pork steaks marinating in the refrigerator. He had been to the grocery store, and it was the first time in a long while that I hadn't had to stock the kitchen.

I thought, *Okay!* I was looking forward to it. Maybe he'd had a change of heart. Maybe his sanity was coming back to him. He'd bought the baked beans, and we were actually going to cook and eat together for once. No one was coming over—not Rosa or anyone else. He was going to all of this trouble just for Christy and me. I was looking forward to the Fourth of July.

By 1 p.m. that day, I was no longer hopeful.

Dad was drunk, and he was fighting terribly with Christy. I used to give her my car keys in the evening when I knew he was drunk. I wanted her to be safe from him at night, and if that meant taking my car, so be it. A few days earlier, she had gotten caught driving without a license and been arrested. He had to bail her out, and he was pissed. He was also mad because I had taken her to get a haircut and a new inexpensive outfit the day before. He didn't want any of his money being spent on Christy.

He wanted to know how she was going to pay him back for the haircut. Oddly, he wasn't demanding the bail money.

"Fuck you. You're my father and you're supposed to provide for me, you drunk asshole," she yelled back at him.

I tried to calm Christy down so we could just leave. I told her we'd go to the big St. Louis Fair (it was called the VP Fair then) and forget about him. But I had to take my dog out first. Caitlin was still housebreaking, so she had to stay in the basement. Christy and I went downstairs to get her, then walked past dad in the living room, heading toward the door. We didn't make it outside—Caitlin stopped and peed on the carpet right in front of Dad.

He got up off the couch and started kicking the dog.

"Stop it!" I was screaming and grabbing for my little dog.

"This goddamned dog has to go!" he finally said.

The dog was my one love, my one piece of independence. I told him no. "The dog stays."

"I'll kill her then." Dad stood over me, glaring.

"If the dog goes, I go," I said. I was just numb from all of the fighting. At that moment, I didn't care if he hit or kicked me. He knew I didn't care, so he tried a different approach.

"Fine, go," Dad said, looking at Christy. "I have your replacement."

He grabbed her, and they started fighting. They were throwing things—pillows, cups, lights—at each other. She was kicking and screaming as he threw her around. Both of them hurled foul, disgusting insults. They were so physical that I couldn't get between them without getting hurt. They had torn down the blinds in the front room. They were heading toward the back of the house.

Christy and I were both crying hysterically.

I begged Dad to stop punishing her. Whatever she had done, it couldn't be that bad.

He said, "Shut up, bitch." I don't know which one of us he was talking to.

He took Christy into his bedroom, which he never used. It was the only bedroom with a lock. The other bedroom was across from his, and I used to sleep there. One night, he kicked in that lock when he came looking for me. He never had that lock repaired.

I screamed and yelled that he didn't need to do this. I begged for him to take me into that room instead. He held onto Christy tightly while she screamed.

"Do whatever you want to me, just please don't take her." I was sobbing uncontrollably.

He threw her across the room and slammed the door, nearly crushing my fingers. I heard everything. I knew what he was doing to her. I knew the sounds of zippers and struggle and clothes and submissive tears.

I could hardly breathe as I crumpled onto the floor outside of Dad's bedroom door. Christy's screams curdled my blood. Her voice still wakes me up in my worst dreams. I got up and ran outside to try to break into the bedroom window. The window was six feet off the ground, and there was no way I could reach it without a ladder. I didn't have that much time. I ran back inside.

I don't know how long he kept her in there. It felt like eighteen years. He finally threw her out. Her black mascara was all over her face, and her skin was red and bruised. I think he stayed in his room. I didn't see him again for a while.

I pulled Christy outside on the front lawn, and I put her into my car. I gave her my keys and told her to leave. She didn't have her license, but she could definitely drive. I had just experienced the biggest failure of my life—my failure to protect her. Christy had to get out of there, and I wouldn't let her come back in if I could help it. We tried to stop crying as she opened the car door. We barely breathed. We didn't say anything to each other. We didn't look at each other. I told her to pick me up in front of the neighbor's house, where he couldn't see us, in an hour.

I was going to argue with him some more. I was going to do something or say something to make him realize what he'd done. I was going to make him understand that he had become a despicable madman. But once she was gone, I couldn't fight with him. I didn't have anything left in me. All I could do was cry. I didn't talk to him. I just went downstairs to our living room where I fell onto the couch in a heap. He had decimated me years ago. Now he had decimated both of us.

I was face down on the couch when I heard a noise, a loud popping sound. On hearing the noise again—a gunshot—I looked up. He was standing in my doorway with the gun by his side.

He had fired the .22 caliber, hitting the wall a foot above my head. He leaned the gun against the bookshelf in the room.

He smiled.

He said, "See how easy an accident can be?"

I don't remember what else was said. I only remember his sinister smile. He went back up the steps, leaving the gun there to further terrorize me. I looked above my head, and there were two small bullet holes in the wall.

My whole body shook, but not from the gun he'd just waved at me. I wasn't scared for me; I couldn't care less what he did to me. I wished he had killed me because I couldn't stand the pain I felt. I was in shock that he had raped my sister.

I stopped feeling.

I stopped crying.

And I got real quiet.

I waited downstairs for a long time, until I didn't hear him moving around anymore. If he did come down those stairs, I had already planned to fly out the basement window. All I heard above me was silence. After twenty minutes, I knew he had passed out or left. I ran up the stairs, and I didn't see him. I didn't know where he had gone—I guessed he was in his bedroom. I grabbed my little red purse from the dining room ledge. I kept it there for inspection because he was always going through it anyway. I ran out the door to the pick-up spot in front of the neighbor's house. Christy was there waiting for me.

That afternoon, she and I had plans to go to the VP Fair with a group of friends. We went out all the time, not just on this day. We were accustomed to living with terror inside our house. Then we'd walk out of our hellhole and act like everything was okay. We'd put on our normal faces so we could have somewhat ordinary lives with our friends. We didn't want anyone to know about the monster we lived with.

We went to the fair and pretended that nothing was wrong. We drank, hoping it would dull our senses. It didn't. We passed the time by going to the Olive Garden and hanging out at a friend's house. Late that night, around 11 p.m., I was able to drive. I was exhausted but sober. I planned for us to stay at a hotel. But I realized I had to go back to St. John.

I'd left my new dog in the basement. I had to get Caitlin. If she were still alive, it wouldn't be for long.

The Scene of a Crime

I had told myself I wouldn't let Christy come back into that house. I made a huge mistake that night when I let her crawl through the basement window with me. We were only going to get my dog from the basement; she was fine.

But then Christy wanted to grab her things. I told her not to go upstairs. She said she had some things she had to get.

Everything was quiet, so I thought it would be okay. She took to the steps. I was right behind her. I had the gun in my hands. If Dad was there, he would only hurt us over my dead body.

We saw him sleeping on the couch. The sight of him made me so sick my head spun. I leaned the gun behind the dining room ledge in the corner against the wall where I usually kept my red purse. We both grabbed a few of our things.

And just like that, I snapped.

I couldn't take it.

I couldn't live with it.

Now was my chance to break out of the prison he had created for me.

I didn't think about right and wrong—obviously. I thought only about my life, my sister's life, and our chances for survival.

I walked slowly over to the dining room ledge and picked up the gun in the corner. My fingers felt the smooth wooden sides of the gun. My thumb and pointer finger slid onto the cold metal trigger. I didn't know whether or not the safety was on.

I didn't aim; I didn't even look at what I was doing. I just pulled the trigger with my eyes shut. I guess I hit him in the shoulder, in his collarbone. I wasn't thinking. I wasn't anything. I picked up the gun and leaned it on the ledge about eight feet from the couch. But the outcome was obvious. I picked up the rifle.

He woke up, bleeding, and bolted to his feet. He told me to call an ambulance right that fucking second. Instead, I pulled the trigger. I dropped the gun on the floor in between us. I felt terrible for what I'd done, and I wanted to help him. I handed him a pillow to soak up the blood.

I ran to the phone to dial 911. The upstairs phone wasn't in its usual spot. I ran downstairs, but I couldn't find one there either. Then I remembered that he had pulled all of the cords out of the wall in our cruel and gruesome fight earlier that day. He didn't want us to be able to call for help while he terrorized us and raped my sister. Now I couldn't call for help for him. He started cursing and screaming that he was going to kill us this time. We were fucking sorry-ass little bitches.

He passed out on the couch, probably from a combination of being shot and shit-faced drunk. I had done wrong. I knew that, and I was sorry for it. But there was a force rising inside me that was even stronger than remorse. Since the age of eight—most of my life—he had humiliated and terrorized me. I felt deeply, irrevocably damaged. Every part of my mind and body had been mangled and tortured by my father.

A very bad feeling swelled. Darkness coursed through my veins.

I could see the gun on the carpet. My intention had been to shoot him and scare him. I wanted him to finally understand that there would be consequences for raping his daughters. I just wanted to convince him that it was in his best interest to stop abusing us.

But whatever sanity I had left was gone in that instant. I stopped contemplating right and wrong. I stopped feeling. I still cannot recall exactly how I brought myself to the point of killing; I do not know exactly how I did it.

But the outcome was obvious. I put my fingers back on the trigger, cocked the gun, and fired it without thinking. I fired it without reason or compassion or sanity. I hit him in the head. He did not get up off the couch again. I could hear the choking, the gurgling.

Then everything went fuzzy. It is still dark.

If I felt anything at all, the feelings were numb and indescribable. Was I scared? Was I in denial? Was I horrified? Was I relieved? Did I cry? Did I throw up? I don't know. My mind floated into a fantasy world so I could try to walk out of the house and survive. Did I even deserve to survive? I had done an evil thing.

But I was alive.

I turned my back. I walked away.

I was a murderer.

Christy screamed. I cried. As fast as we could, we left that house. We took my dog with us.

I was safe.

Christy was safe.

Sealing My Fate

I flipped out.

I became stupid. I became despicable.

Wearing an old pair of my grandmother's gardening gloves, I threw the gun, used shells, and the gun case into the back of my LeBaron.

I dropped Christy off at her friend Melanie's house. Around 4:30 a.m., I stopped by a convenience store to buy cigarettes, and then checked into the Airway Hotel. I drove to my friend Ron's house. I had no one else to turn to. I was not functioning at all. Whatever he told me I should do, I would do it.

I was me; except I wasn't me at all. I was in shock over everything that had happened. The day had begun with pork chops marinating in the refrigerator. Then Drunk Dad kicked Christy's body all over the house and raped her practically right in front of me. Then I made a choice to get my dog and some toothpaste and wound up killing the very man who had once given me life. I couldn't believe any of it. I had seen him on the couch with my own eyes, but I still couldn't believe he was dead.

I flipped out.

I had dreamed about killing him. I had wondered what life would be like for me if he were dead one day. But this wasn't real. This was worse than any nightmare I'd already lived through. I wanted to go back. I would've done anything to undo that day.

What I had done couldn't be real.

Except that it was real.

I had never done anything more wrong in my entire life.

Yet I made it worse.

I asked Ron what I should do. He said he'd throw the gun, shells, and case into the Meramec River. His girlfriend, Theresa, overheard the plan. Ron didn't have a car, so I left him mine. I called Jason to come get me. He picked up my sister first, then me. We went to Hardee's. I tried to stop crying long enough to explain what I needed. Jason knew something had happened, but he didn't know what or how. I told him only that my father was dead on the couch—someone had shot him, and I needed help.

Jason agreed to take us back to our house on Eminence Avenue, and go up to the door to "find" Thomas Lannert dead. I would run to the neighbor's house to report the crime. Jason ran to the front door, but he couldn't bear to look inside the house. I could. I was inexplicably drawn to it. I couldn't *not* look. Nothing was real. I had to see.

My whole body shook.

I doubled over for a second, wondering if I would pass out or throw up. I got myself together enough to run to Mrs. Custer's house to tell her someone had broken into our house, and my father was dead. She called the police while I cried. Jason was around somewhere; Christy was right there with me. I started losing my breath. I was hyperventilating, and I recognized the feeling because sometimes this happened during Dad's most violent rapes. I couldn't breathe, and I couldn't find air anywhere. Then I started to panic.

Mrs. Custer brought me a wet rag to put on my forehead. I tried to calm down, because Christy was becoming hysterical. My main concern at all times was my sister.

The paramedics and police arrived.

My jig was up fast.

The police took Jason, Christy, and me in for questioning immediately.

I didn't hear his statement, but apparently Jason gave us up upon arrival at the station. At that time, he didn't think I'd done it. But because of conversations he'd overheard, he thought I had paid someone to do it—someone like Ron.

Christy and I became suspects immediately, so mug shots were taken. Christy and I were separated briefly, and I didn't know where they took her. I figured she was in an office nearby experiencing the same harsh treatment. Officers fired questions at me, each one cutting into my core.

My head filled like an intricate, silken web. I couldn't see through my thoughts or make sense of them. I was spinning. I thought I might pass out, but I didn't. I was too shocked to cry. I had no tears left for my father or myself. I'd already bawled for hours. I was too cold inside to speak. I had to sink into a quiet, safe, imaginary place.

While in that place, I beat myself up for what happened. I was supposed to take care of my sister. *Stacey, look what you have done,* I thought. *She never ever should've gone back to that house. I never should've done what I did.* My heart beat nearly out of my chest thinking about what would happen to Christy. There was no reason for us both to get into trouble for this. This wasn't her doing. I vowed to get her out of police hands any way I could. I would say or do whatever police wanted as long as they'd let Christy go. She was still fifteen years old. She still had time to get her life back together. I was already broken; it was far too late for me. No matter what, I knew right then and there that I would take the rap—all of it—if I could.

I sat in the interrogation room with Detective Tom Schulte and Detective House. There was a jail cell right outside the interrogation room. Christy was handcuffed to the cell; I could see her through the small window. She was crying hard.

They let me go out and talk to her. She cried harder. The officers came over to me and yelled at me to stop talking to her. I went back into the interrogation room. Then they let me go back out. The same thing happened a few times before they kept me in the room and questioned me. I didn't want to speak. After all, anything you say will be held against you. While I was waiting to be questioned, I asked to speak to a lawyer.

Detective House said it was a holiday, and they were having a hard time reaching one.

"I'll just call one," I said, looking at the phone in front of me. I hoped they'd at least give me a phone book.

House swiftly removed the phone, and I didn't see it again.

Then the questions came at me like angry swarms of bees.

"We know you killed him, Stacey."

"Why did you shoot your father and say it was a break-in?"

"Tell us now, or your sister will be in big trouble. You don't want her in more trouble, do you?"

"We know you did it."

"Think about your sister. You could help her get out of this mess if you just confess."

"We know you used his .22."

"We know. You did it."

I heard their voices, but eventually I didn't see their faces or their mustaches or their hairy arms or polyester-blend pants. My mind went numb, and I couldn't feel anything anymore in my body. My mind went to the same place it had gone when my father hurt me. I could be there without really being there.

One man's voice broke through my cocoon. Detective Schulte asked the other officer to step outside of the room. "Look," he said, "I know it was you, or I know it was your sister. I know things have happened in that house that never should have happened."

He was sent to get the confession. He was stern but compassionate. I knew he knew I'd been abused. That's what he was alluding to, anyway. I knew he could tell, and I was ashamed and horrified. I wasn't at the point in my life where I am now. I could barely tell a guidance counselor that my father hurt me, and when I did, it didn't matter. The word *rape* was not yet in my vocabulary. It was too heavy, harsh, and loaded. It was too embarrassing and dirty. I could barely speak, let alone tell a husky stranger—a man—what I had been through. I didn't have the words.

But I could relate to what he wasn't saying. I could understand what Schulte was implying. All I was able to say was my father "hurt" me. And what did those words mean?

Schulte told me he'd help me if I did the right thing. He said things would be all right.

He made me feel like all of this could go away. He made me feel like it wasn't too late.

I was able to listen, but I still didn't say much to him. I uttered, stuttered, searched in my tangled head for what I was supposed to say.

Here is how I remember it.

Schulte went on, "If you don't take the blame, it's going to look bad for your sister." Looking back, I can see he was trying to get a confession from me because I was eighteen and easy to prosecute. She was fifteen, and it's harder to punish a minor.

"You need to look at her," he said. "She's stronger; she's stockier. You're thinner. People will understand if you tell the truth."

He was right. Christy was broad and strong. She looked darker than I did, too, with her black eyeliner and tougher clothes. I was super skinny with chicken legs. My hair was cut in a conservative bob. Based on physical characteristics, she looked like the sister who could've done it. She looked more capable.

Schulte was kind, and he suggested that he knew I had been abused. He said he would help me if I helped him. Meanwhile, House doggedly pushed me to admit guilt.

I finally answered, "I'll tell you whatever you want. Just let her go."

They said they would let her go if I cooperated. So I tried to do whatever they said. I would've done whatever they said anyway. The last thing I was looking for was more trouble.

"If you feel bad about what happened, then tell us everything right here, right now," House said. They were doing this good cop–bad cop thing on me. "If you don't tell us, it's because you're cold and not remorseful."

House took my lack of tears as coldness. Neither of them really understood me. They didn't get that an eighteen-year-old can be devastated beyond tears. Part of my pain—my shock—was pure remorse, and that's why I agreed to their demands. They told me I could still do the right thing by going back to that house. But really, they wanted me to confess there.

"I'll go back, but I don't want to go into that room," I said. "Please don't make me go into the living room."

I was losing my mind at this point. My thoughts were broken; my body quaked inside. My emotions ran so high I became numb, and then police officers with video cameras began buzzing around me. Ever since I was eight years old, I had been the master of the poker face. If I cried or showed emotion when things went horrifically wrong, then things just got horrifically worse. I reverted to the behaviors I knew.

I needed someone to tell me to do the right thing. What was the right thing? I had no one but these officers to talk to or confide in. I didn't know a soul to call. I needed a lawyer, but I had been led to believe that wasn't an option.

Obediently, I went back to St. John.

I chewed gum. I chewed it hard and fast, hoping maybe I'd feel something. Maybe I wouldn't look like I was going through the worst twenty-four hours of my life. At that moment, I truly wished I'd pulled the trigger on myself instead of him.

On the way there, in the back of a cop car, I just chewed and squinted my eyes as my insides went dead. By this time, my short blond hair—usually so neatly combed, curled, and teased—splayed out in front of my head at least three inches. It was fried, the kind of hair a girl has when she's trying to look crazy. Or when a girl has not been given a brush before or after her mug shot.

I worried about what was going to happen at that house. I had a sense that he was still alive, and he was really going to kick my ass this time. I felt my father all around me. I could hear his voice and smell his skin. I could hear the sound of him swallowing. There was no way he could really be dead. In my mind, he was very alive. He was still terrorizing me.

I worried about my dog Caitlin. I had dropped her off with a friend in the middle of the night, and I needed her warm, forgiving fur. She was my only comfort, and she was so far away. I had nothing.

The police wanted me to be as uncomfortable as possible, and they were succeeding.

I worried about what was going to come out of my mouth. If I spoke, what would happen? I didn't want to be the girl who'd been sexually abused by her father since she was eight years old. She was a helpless, shameful, and stupid victim. I didn't want to be the young woman—I couldn't believe I was really eighteen—who loved her dad but hated her abuser. That woman made no sense. I didn't want to be the teenager who was abandoned by her mother over and over again. She was angry and scared. I didn't want to be the protective older sister who would have done anything to keep her little sibling safe.

She was a murderer.

I went with Detective Schulte to my house. The cameras went on.

"I decided that he did not deserve to live," I stated blankly into the videotape as per Schulte's exact instructions. I would never get the chance to change what I said, or to put it into context or to show the tears that the jury would want to see.

I not only told Schulte what happened, I showed him, too. I did it while his people followed me around with big black VHS cameras. I crept into the basement window where I could slip right in without my father hearing me. I showed him where I picked up the gun in my basement bedroom. He didn't notice the two bullet holes above the couch. He didn't notice the broken window blinds and cracked bedroom doors or other signs of physical struggle all over that house. So I just kept doing what I was told. I showed him how I walked up the stairs with that gun and set it on a ledge that pointed at my father's sleeping body.

My father's body was still there on the couch.

That was enough.

That is enough.

A Different Kind of Gumbo

Schulte told me he'd let Christy go if I did what he said. I had parroted back his every word over and over—even on tape. But Christy was still in custody. She was sent to juvenile detention. I couldn't do anything else to help her. It was a devastating feeling. After everything I had done, I still had no control.

I was formally arrested. I had to stand in front of a blue background and hold up a black sign that said St. Louis County Interrogation plus my name and a bunch of numbers. I barely remember the camera flashing or the people shoving me from room to room inside police headquarters.

I was delivered to Clayton Jail at 11 or 12 p.m. on July 5. They fingerprinted me and took me upstairs to a dark, solitary cell with just a bed and a toilet. I got to my cell around 2 a.m. I had been awake—mostly hysterical—for well over twenty-four hours. I fell onto the plastic mattress on top of a hard metal bunk. They didn't even make the beds at Clayton Jail—there were no sheets. Inmates stayed for only short periods of time while they waited to post bond or be arraigned.

I had never been so exhausted in my life. But I still had the energy to be a little scared. I didn't have the full realization that my dad was gone. I didn't fully believe that he wouldn't show up and rape me in the night. But then a guard locked my door and walked away. When I heard the key click, something clicked in my head and my heart.

I was safe.

From him.

I had to be locked up to finally be free.

I fell asleep. I had two hours of the most restorative, most complete rest I'd ever had in my entire life.

The truth was on record.

I had told a police officer that I had been abused. I had told a police officer that I had killed my father. For the first time in my life, I didn't have to hide. My reality was no longer a dirty secret; it was no longer a tangled web of lies.

Officers woke me up at 7 a.m. for my arraignment.

I went before a judge to hear the charges against me. I was charged with murder in the first degree and armed criminal action. The bail was set at $750,000. I was expected to plead guilty or not guilty.

I hoped for a miracle. I hoped there was some way I could claim I had acted out of self-defense. I knew it was naïve, but I hoped that I could prove to someone that if I hadn't killed him, my sister or I would have eventually been killed.

I pleaded not guilty.

The gavel went down. I still had not seen or heard from a lawyer.

I was transferred to St. Louis County Jail. At the time, the facility was located in a western St. Louis neighborhood called Gumbo Flats (now Chesterfield Valley). My jail was known as Gumbo. All the criminals—and now I was one of them—were processed through Gumbo or Workhouse. Workhouse was the nickname for the city jail.

I had a lot to learn—and fast. Jail was a huge holding tank—up to forty criminals were housed in open units fenced in by hard chicken wire. They weren't private, but we had sectioned-off cells to sleep in with six to twelve bunks to a cell. Gumbo was like a gangster movie. In a matter of hours I was exposed to a different side of life from anything I had ever seen. I was booked, held, taken to court, and plopped into my new home. I was in a state of shock. I just remember thinking, *Oh my God.* My senses were dull yet overstimulated all at once.

On the first day, I was blessed to meet a woman named Kim. She was about fifteen years older than me. TVs were on in the common room filled with twelve to twenty-four random women. My story was on the news constantly, and each time I heard my name, I winced. I felt like crying, but I didn't dare do it there. I wasn't stupid. Jail was no place to show weakness. Kim kept coming around to tell me, "It's okay honey. You come sit by me."

I didn't leave her side. Later on that evening, she said something that made me laugh. It was the first time I'd smiled in two days.

Apparently, this big, hefty girl sitting across the room thought I was laughing at her. She got up off her fanny, ran across the room, and hit me upside the head. I didn't get a chance to react—not that I would've known what to do—because she ran away and sat right back down.

I didn't know what to do. Kim told me to forget about it. I was terrified. I told the guards that I couldn't sleep in an area where strange women clobber me for no reason. That night, I got moved across the hall.

I was even more scared there because I had no Kim. The inmates were starting to know who I was from the television. The news briefly mentioned allegations of abuse, but thankfully, the news was vague. Still, these women were cruel. Even though I came to find out most of them had also been sexually abused, they taunted me. Criminals look for the easiest way to hurt people, especially a newcomer. I was called "Daddy Fucker" and "Daddy Killer."

I just tried to stay out of the way until I started to feel again. The problem was, I couldn't feel.

As soon as a new inmate arrived, the guards gave out an ugly mustard-colored uniform—a short-sleeved jacket with big clear buttons and huge elastic-waist pants. Anytime we left our cell, we had to wear the uniform. The costume was embarrassing.

I was scared—and bored beyond all sanity. Gumbo's rules included twenty-three-hour-a-day lockdown. We left only for meals, church, or recreation. We got to stretch our legs for recreation three times a week for an hour. My first few days were excruciatingly long. I had no idea what was in store for me there. Gumbo was just a holding cell for women while they waited for and went through their trials. Most were there for just a couple of weeks, maybe a month tops.

But my trial didn't take place for nearly two years. The lawyers kept asking for extensions for this or that, and the judge kept granting their requests. My original judge stopped working on my trial, and I got a new one. Due to all the paper shuffling, I would reside in Gumbo longer than almost anyone else ever had.

Christy arrived to save me. She came from juvie in late August. At just fifteen, she had been certified as an adult to stand trial for conspiracy to commit murder. We were inseparable against the users and gang-bangers and thieves who seemed so foreign to us. It took us a few days to realize that we weren't so different from them. We were criminals, too. Meanwhile, it took us exactly eight seconds to figure out that we had to start defending ourselves physically. In jail, one beats or gets beaten. I left that part up to Christy. If anyone hit either of us in the back of the head, Christy would kick her ass. Christy would not stop till she won. Nobody messed with Christy or her older sister.

We shared our locker, where we were allowed to keep snacks. I got $10 a month from Mom, and so did Christy. Together, we had $20. We used the money for soap, shampoo, Baby Ruths, and Snickers. I needed cigarettes and decent shampoo. Ten dollars wasn't enough. I struggled without money in jail, and so did Christy. But our mom wasn't exactly opening her wallet to help us. We didn't call her to tell her what had happened—our grandmother did. Then, it took Mom a month to visit us from Guam.

She did not have money for an attorney. We had to use the public defenders. And she didn't have money to give us to live. You needed more than $10 per month. These were only minor reasons my relationship with her was strained.

Shortly after Christy arrived at Gumbo from juvie, Mom came to visit both of us. We were in the communal visitors room while another inmate, Kathy Tucker—she was huge—was also finishing a visit. She sat next to me, keeping her eyes on us.

This was Mom's first visit since Christy had arrived at Gumbo. It was the first time she'd faced her daughters together. Christy and

I sat on one side of the table, and Mom on the other. We all held hands.

Mom still wanted to know what happened. She wanted answers, but we wouldn't tell her anything.

I thought, *You weren't there for us. I don't have to spill my soul to you.* I just stared her down. I knew her side of the family was bad-mouthing me. I knew Dad's side thought I was Resident Evil. Mom had clues that something bad was happening, but she chose to ignore them. I felt I had told her enough in the past. I'd be damned if I was going to tell her any more.

Mom started crying.

"Christy's in jail! My baby's in jail!" she said, sobbing. She wiped her eyes with her hands.

We were well aware of our situation, and we had cried enough about it in private. We had nothing to say. We were silent, just listening. That's when Mom lashed out at me.

"Look what you did to your sister!" Mom screamed. "Look what you have done, Stacey."

She took me by surprise. I was heated.

I said, "Look what I did?!" I thought, *I'm here doing everything I can to take the punishment myself.* I stood up. "Fuck you. You want to look at what *I* did? Really?!" I almost added, *You're the one who wouldn't let Christy come to Guam! You were the only person who could've done anything to help.* I held my tongue, but I couldn't hold back my body. I lunged across the visting room table at her. I didn't know what I was going to do to her.

Kathy Tucker grabbed me by the back of my shirt. She swooped one arm around me and picked me up in midair. She carried me to the door of the visitor's room. She opened it and dropped me inside the inmate quarters. Kathy said to cool it because officers would lock me down for a stunt like that.

"Everyone at that table was disrespectful," she said. "Don't let it get the best of you. You should never let yourself lose control like that again."

She was right. But I was still hot. I could not believe my mom could be so cruel and clueless. It occurred to me that I had killed the one parent who ever bothered to help us. As evil as Dad was most of the time, he knew how to fix things. Sober Dad was smart and made problems go away. Sober Dad paid when Christy hit the barn. Sober Dad paid for counseling sessions. Mom—in any form—always made things worse. The irony made me feel like puking right then and there.

I tried to pull myself together. It took a few minutes to convince myself to cool down and stop the nonsense. I told myself that Mom wasn't worth my energy. I told myself to swallow my tears—and quick. After all, if I wanted to make a bad day worse, all I had to do was cry in the chicken coop.

I didn't speak to my mother for a couple of years after that fight. If she blamed me so completely, then I had nothing to say to her. I wouldn't call her. I wouldn't let her come visit me. What was the point if we were just going to fight? Why bother if she was just going to make me feel more worthless than I already felt? I went through the days, weeks, months, and years of jail without my mother. I navigated my way through the legal system as a young adult—completely alone. I didn't receive any advice from anyone in my family, other than now-sixteen-year-old Christy, as I went about the business of being charged with murder in the first degree.

I sent my mother yearly birthday cards. That was the most contact I could manage to have with Deborah.

Alone

After I gave the police my confession, I was heartbroken that they still kept Christy in custody. They couldn't question her, though, because at the time she was only fifteen, and still considered a minor. A parent had to be present. Dad was dead and Mom was in Guam, so the police called Marilyn Paulson. My grandma arrived and sat in the interrogation room while the police grilled Christy. Christy told authorities what they wanted to hear. She told them I had killed Dad for his money. She even wrote it out in a statement. She did this because I told her to, and she was fifteen. She didn't know any better. She didn't know that Dad had been raping me for the last ten years. If she was suspicious, I didn't know, because we never talked about it. I kept her safe from all of those horrors. Of course she knew what Dad had done to her, but I didn't want her to have to tell it. She shouldn't be forced to admit that.

So she didn't. I told her to take a plea bargain, avoid a trial, and get out of the system as soon as she could. I told her from the moment we were in police custody to do or say whatever the authorities wanted. I instructed Christy to say bad things about me if necessary. I wanted to take the blame.

Her job was to get out of there.

Her statement against me eventually got thrown out in court. It wasn't admissible because Grandma Paulson wasn't a parent, and Grandma had no legal right to be in the room.

But Christy got another chance. She was offered a plea bargain that would keep her from going to trial. If she pled guilty to conspiracy to commit murder, she'd get only five years. In lay terms, this means she made a plan—along with me—to kill him. She did noth-ing to stop his murder. This is not how either of us personally viewed the crime—I had no idea I would do what I did that night, and nei-ther did she.

I supported her wholeheartedly because they were talking about life without parole for me, and they were offering her just five years. "Take it!" I told her over and over. "Take it now!"

She was conflicted. She didn't want to incriminate me any more than I wanted to be incriminated. We were both confused. We were two very young people just trying to do the best we could in a com-plicated situation. In the end, Christy didn't really have another op-tion. If she pled not guilty, she'd start traveling down the same road as me. She'd have to admit to being raped and be humiliated in court. After that, God only knew how many years of hard time she'd have to serve.

She took it. By January, Christy was gone from Gumbo jail. She wound up serving only two and a half years in prison at Renz Cor-rectional Institution in Cedar City, Missouri. I was happy with her decision. It didn't matter what had started the whole mess or what had created it; the outcome had become my responsibility. I was the older sister. I had a chance to keep her safe after I'd failed so miser-ably in the past. She'd be fine in prison. If she mouthed off, she could back it up with her fists. Nobody messed with Christy. Then when she got out, she would be safe from our father. Her well-being was something I could hold on to. I did not care about myself. I had noth-ing left in me. I had no sense of self-preservation or self-esteem. I was just a robot. The only fight I had in me was for her. The courts were lining up a hard life for me, and I didn't want that life for her. When all was said and done, Christy got out when she was eighteen. She even had her GED.

I was offered a plea bargain, too. All I had to do was stand in front of the judge and say I committed the crime for monetary gain. The sentence would be fifteen years.

The prosecuting attorney wanted me to say I had killed my father for his money. Attorney Chris McGraugh, my public defender, tried to convince me to take it so I wouldn't have to go through a long trial. With the plea, I would go straight to prison, a much better place than godforsaken Gumbo. Maybe I'd be in the same place as Christy. He loved to dangle the fifteen years in front of me—it was a lot better than a life sentence. I might have to serve only twelve years if I got out on good behavior.

I thought about it for about five seconds.

I would never agree to a false plea bargain.

I knew going to trial meant losing. After all, I had entered a not-guilty plea to a murder I'd already confessed to. I knew I was staring down a life spent in prison. But I also knew that I had already made too many wrong choices. I had covered up my past and I had lied about the gun and the crime.

If I was ever going to be free, this was my time.

Obviously, I wasn't getting my physical freedom back. But I didn't care about that. Emotionally, I could still make things right. I had to take a stand, and I did.

My case was headed to trial.

I was often pulled out of the monotony of jail for questioning, hearings, and meetings with my court-appointed lawyer. He would try to build a case based on battered spouse syndrome or maybe insanity. But to do so, he had to prove that I was abused.

A court-appointed psychologist started asking me questions. The psychologist recorded my story. I even told him about the time my grandfather had tried to touch me. To verify my story, the counselor called Grandma Paulson. Grandma told the psychologist—basically telling the whole court—that I was lying. She said Grandpa never touched me. She had visited me a few times up to that point, but then she stopped.

In a letter, Grandma Paulson said I was trying to destroy her family. She wrote, "How dare you make accusations against my husband."

She said all I had done was tear all the relatives to pieces. She told me to take back what I had said about Grandpa.

I wrote her back a nice letter. But I did not take back what I had said. For the first time in my life, I was committed to telling the truth.

I did not hear from her again. My letters to her never came back, but I'm not sure she read them. We haven't spoken in almost twenty years.

Learning About Courage

The heavy chicken wire that enclosed our common area was painted a terrible almond color. The paint yellowed from all the cigarette smoke and was flaked off so we could see the rust underneath. We had nothing to do all day but chip off the paint with our fingernails. The steel-grate wire fence was supposed to hold us temporarily—before inmates went to prison or, for the lucky few, home.

Without Christy there to defend me, I was scared at times. Christy and I tried to keep in touch during her incarceration, but it was difficult. Just one other person bothered to have contact with me: Tom Wilson.

He found out the day after the shooting. A friend called Tom W. to tell him to turn on the TV. That's when he heard the story of the eighteen-year-old St. John woman who was accused of fatally shooting her father in their home. Tom was in shock.

After Christy had left for Renz prison, I received a letter from him. He was already in navy boot camp. He said he was happy he finally had a pen pal. Tom W. wrote that while he had no idea what I'd been through, he did believe I was a good person. He told me to always remember that. He asked if he could talk to me. I hadn't heard anyone's voice from the outside in months. I was allowed only one phone call once a week on Fridays at 4 p.m. I just didn't have anyone to call. Now, all of a sudden, I did. But to save me money, he wound up calling me every week at that exact time for months. It didn't matter where he was or what he was doing, he was there on the phone for me. Tom W. was my only link to the outside world. He provided much-needed warmth in my life.

We became closer. I had always loved Tom W., and I had always truly respected him. But this time things were different with us. It was just like when we dated for those two weeks back in high school—only more mature and intense. We talked about boot camp and all the tough things he was going through. We discussed our lives and hopes and dreams. We told each other how we felt. I couldn't believe how easy it was to tell Tom W. everything. He was a gentle man with the patience and kindness of a saint. But he also liked to bend the rules when he could get away with it. He was funny.

We discussed us as a couple early on. I wanted him to live his life and do all the things a nineteen-year-old should be doing. I never wanted him to feel tied down to me. After all, I was going nowhere. But we were clear that if a miracle happened, and if I came home, I would be with him. He seemed to be in love with me, and I was in love with him.

Our tryst kept me sane and alive, but it was bittersweet. It was the carrot dangling in front of me that I could never have.

Sometimes, I couldn't take the pressure and the loneliness and the nightmares. Sleeping only got harder. I hadn't made any friends. I missed Christy. I started having flashbacks during the day and especially at night.

As my trial date came closer, I became more distressed, and the prison system was quick to prescribe psych meds. Prison staff weren't interested in helping prisoners work through their issues. It was easier to just medicate us. I wasn't offered psychological counseling. Licensed psychologists saw me only when I needed to be analyzed for legal documents. Those people wanted to know every detail of my life, but they did not offer support or advice.

The psych counselor at Gumbo prescribed Vistaril. Such sedatives were quick fixes that made us prisoners easier to deal with. Vistaril turned me into a total zombie. And I wasn't even sure it helped me sleep better at night, but I'd get in trouble if I didn't take my pill. Obediently, I swallowed the drug every day until I got street-smart in prison—I learned how to pretend I was taking it without really swallowing. Then I would hide the Vistaril and use it to make friends. There were ladies out there who actually wanted to take that drug. I did that only for a little while—until I told them I didn't want it anymore, and they finally listened.

In jail, the truth hit me. For the first time ever, my mask was off. I no longer had to pretend that I was the good daughter with good grades. I didn't have to be perfectly thin with the right hair and eyeliner. I didn't have to please my father. I didn't have to lie to my mom, pretend that everything was okay, and act like I didn't blame her. I didn't have to be just fine anymore.

I wasn't just fine, and admitting that to myself—and to the world—felt good.

No matter what had happened in my past, I was who I was.

Women at the jail started reaching out to me, especially the older ones. They saw me as a kid, a kid who killed her dad after being molested by him. They noticed I had no visitors. They noticed I had only public defenders. No one in the world was helping me. With Christy gone, I needed to accept friendship when it was offered to me.

There was one thing I needed to do to make me feel better. I needed to open up, to have conversations. I needed to stop looking inward all the time.

I shared a bunk with an older woman named Sandy. She tried to give me a few dollars to buy candy and snacks.

I wouldn't take it at first. I was still working on the whole opening-up thing. I also didn't want to take her cash and then owe her a favor later.

"Take the money," Sandy said. "I have extra, and I want you to have it."

After a few rounds of this, I asked her, "Why?"

"It makes me feel good to share it with you," Sandy said. She was short like me, and she had kids my age. Then she sat me down to teach me a jail lesson. "If you don't have the food others are eating, and you want those snacks, you're going to feel resentful. Eventually, you'll lie or steal to get what you want. I've been lying and stealing my whole life. I don't want you to have to go through that or feel that way. So I have extra money; I'm going to give it to you, and I want you to just take it."

Inmates did leave their lockers open sometimes. I would eye their Snickers bars, my mouth watering. But I never once thought of taking their food. If you steal from a woman in jail, you might get yourself killed. Still, I got the gist of what Sandy was saying. I had shoplifted before, back in the eighth grade. Maybe there were feelings inside of me that I didn't understand. Something started to change in my heart.

I decided to take a chance. I accepted her money.

She thanked *me* for letting her help me. She explained that her own daughter wouldn't even speak to her. She was my cellmate for seven months before she got transferred to the Texas prison system. I think she was doing time for possession. Her girlfriend (and I do mean her girlfriend) was Kathy Tucker. Kathy was my six-foot-tall protector. Kathy would get released—but not for long. She'd wind up right back in Gumbo because of her problems with drugs.

All of a sudden, I started getting bullied a lot. Without Christy to stand beside me, I was terrified. This skinny girl named Diane had it in for me. Calling her ugly would've been giving her a compliment. She had a gold tooth, a high-pitched voice, and black hair with blond tips, done up in a cone shape. She'd yell at me from her bright red lips.

"Little bitch!" she said.

I would turn real fast in the other direction and walk away.

Kathy pulled me by the arm gently and said, "I'm getting ready to teach you how to take care of yourself."

"I know how to take care of myself," I insisted. "I just ignore her. I don't pay her any attention."

She said, "That won't work. You gotta learn how to stand up for yourself. She just called you a bitch, so you walk back over and tell her you don't appreciate that."

I was terrified of Diane, and so were most sane inmates. Kathy gave me an encouraging shove on my back. I took in a deep breath and walked in Diane's direction. I just hoped she wouldn't beat me up too badly.

I told myself I could do this. I had braved worse enemies. I told Diane, "You just called me a bitch for no reason, and I really do not appreciate that." I was a total WASP. I knew I stood looking like I'd come straight off the tennis team. But still, I kept going. "I've never done anything to you, and that was uncalled for."

Diane's neck started jiving back and forth, and she was getting ready to open her mouth. But instead of getting smart, she just said, "I'm sorry."

I turned around to Kathy, and I had a whole different attitude. I'd never felt so confident in my jailhouse life. Only later did I realize Kathy had been standing behind me the whole time, arms crossed, giving Diane a menacing look while I spoke to her.

Regardless, I was starting to learn the rules of living inside.

We formed a weird little family. My jail mothers Sandy and Kathy looked out for me. So did my other cellmate, Paula, a grandmotherly woman who wore her silver hair in a ponytail. She was getting ready to leave Gumbo and knew I'd be there awhile. She taught me how to crochet so I could make my own money.

Crocheting was hard! I messed up over and over. But Paula had an infinite amount of patience to sit with me and show me how to do it. I kept practicing after she left, and I finally got the hang of it.

Every night at 8 or 9 p.m., we all got tea. It was hot in the winter and iced in the summer. The iced tea came in those cheap plastic tumblers that sweat all over your hands. Everyone always wanted a cup holder to put on the tea tumbler. I got to the point where I could crochet one in ten minutes flat, and I would charge inmates $1 per huggie.

Being in jail was expensive. I was charged $64 for each of my crimes, which my stepdad paid. And then there were incidentals. No one wanted to use the county soap or shampoo. So the whole time I was in jail and then in prison, I crocheted for money.

I was so bored, and I certainly had the time. Paula had shown me the basic stitches, and I learned the rest from a pattern book that was on the book cart. I taught myself more and more intricate projects. I was a perfectionist. I'd get a huggie halfway done and rip it all out if it didn't look right. I liked being able to make something from nothing. I'd picture something and see it come alive underneath my hands. Plus, making things reminded me of Grandma Lannert. She used to crochet afghans for us.

I graduated into making little heart pillows that the other inmates liked. The edges were lacy, and I stuffed the pillows with ripped-up bed sheets. In jail, they were always passing around sheets. (Later, in prison, I got only one sheet, and I was screwed if I lost it.) It took me about twenty minutes to complete one pillow, and I'd sell it for $5 or $8, depending on whether I liked that person or not. All the bad-mouthing in jail drove me crazy. If a woman was trash-talking other people in front me, I knew she was talking about me, too. Those types had to pay $8. Sometimes, I could tell when someone was being all nice to my face because they wanted me to make them a pillow—for $5.

When I wasn't crocheting, I learned every card game in the world. Gumbo didn't have a library, but I read every single book on the pushcart. I learned how to trace and spent hours making designs. I also started tracing art on envelopes. I believed, like Paula, that I should pass down what I learned. When I saw someone come through jail who looked like she needed an extra hand, I'd sit down and start teaching. Though I probably wasn't as patient as Paula, I tried my best.

The hours were incredibly long in twenty-three-hour lockdown.

I thought a lot about God. I was mad at Him.

We had gone to an Episcopalian church for a short while when I was seven. Christy and I liked bible school that summer. But other than that, I hadn't grown up in church at all. I did know about Jesus, and I believed.

As I got older, I had called on God for help, but He was never there for me. So I stopped asking. I was upset with religion. I couldn't understand why God was letting so many terrible things happen in my life. How could He stand by while my life was a living hell and my father was raping me? I'd lost hope; I didn't want anything to do with this sort of God.

Jail made me rethink religion. There, I started believing in God again because I didn't have anything or anyone else. The only counseling I was offered was with a nun. I took it. I started seeing Sister Judith once a week. We sat at a little round table in the chow hall. She was older and had soft, white hair, plump, rosy cheeks, and a sweet smile. She wore glasses, a black head covering, and a plain-colored skirt. I told her everything, not sparing a single detail.

I told her I was mad, and I told her all the reasons why I was mad. At God. At my parents. Mostly, at myself. She taught me about visualization. She pointed out that we all have a free will, and we make our own choices. There were choices and then there was God's will. She made a lot of sense out of the mess that was my life. She told me to trust in God and just let Him take control of my life.

So I did. Even though life without parole was hanging over my head, I trusted. I said the Twenty-third Psalm, and I gave up and let go. I wasn't at peace with my decisions or my future, but I was able to let Jesus help me carry my burdens. I had to believe that when the time was right, God would open a door for me.

I was doing *The Courage to Heal Workbook* then. The second psychologist I saw gave it to me after her evaluation. *The Courage to Heal* is a 463-page tome on how to make life better after sexual abuse. The ideas in it blew me away. It was the first time I heard that what my father did to me wasn't my fault. I didn't believe it yet, but I started thinking about it. The workbook really got me thinking. I'd seen myself as my father's victim my whole life, and here was this book calling me a survivor instead. The psychologist said I had to turn in at least two homework assignments to her each week. I mailed them, thinking it was part of my court-ordered psych evaluation. I found out later that she was just doing this to help my personal healing.

I devoured the book and the workbook that went along with it. In the workbook, I had to write answers to questions I'd never even considered before, questions such as:

What is still unsettled for me?

How can I cope with my feelings in healthy ways that do not hurt others?

How can I forgive myself?

Can I make the decision to heal?

The experience opened me up—not much, but a little bit. Because of what I was learning, I was able to connect with my mother again. If she wrote me, I was able to write back. Through that course, I learned that no matter what she had done or not done, Deborah was still my mother—and despite her shortcomings, she was the only mother I would ever have, and she loved me. I wasn't getting another mother, so I knew I had to love her, too.

Freeing Christy

Two weeks before I went to trial, in October of 1992, Christy was released from prison. She was lucky to serve only two and a half years of her five-year sentence. I was relieved that she had her life back. Her freedom validated everything I had done. It had been for something.

Christy went to live with Mom and John, but that lasted only about five seconds. John was too strict for her. The three of them couldn't get along. Christy just wasn't happy there. She lived with Aunt Deanna and then on her own after that. She was wild and hard to keep track of.

She had a great body, and she wasn't ashamed of it. So by the time she was nineteen, she was working at Hooters. She did that job for several years. She'd send me pictures of her hugging one of her sugar daddies in Vegas. She went through a string of guys who were overpossessive jerks.

She began partying hard when she got out, and I thought she had a problem with drugs and alcohol. She almost became a drug addict at one point, but thank God, she didn't quite get there. I didn't know everything that was going on as she spiraled downward. In the beginning, she didn't come to see me, and she didn't want to talk to me.

I missed her, but I wasn't mad at her.

I understood how painful it was for her to see me in prison. She would even say so.

"I just can't think about you being there," she would tell me if I caught her on the phone. "It makes me feel so bad."

"I'm here so you can be happy," I'd tell her. "Go out and have a good life. Stop getting into trouble. Knock it off."

I told her if she threw her life away, then my life meant nothing.

We both knew I was right, but I realize now that she was carrying a heavier burden than she could bear. Mostly, she hadn't received any rape counseling—she still hasn't. She was still suffering from our father's abuse. She didn't say so, but I could tell. Then she had me to contend with me. I know she missed me, and I know how guilty she felt because I was still behind bars.

To top off the mess that was Christy's life, she had no guidance. There was no relative to show her how to be a productive and happy adult. She must've felt so alone. I couldn't help her anymore. The only place she found any comfort was in her bad relationships with men.

She was so lost for so many years. I saw her every now and then and always hoped our relationship would become constant instead of distant. But that didn't happen until many years later, not until she became a mother.

Although Christy couldn't talk about what our father did to her, I was proud of her when, despite her problems, she donated her portion of Dad's estate. Shortly after her release, she received $90,000, and she sure could've used that money. But instead, she split it into three chunks of $30,000 each and gave it all to charity. She chose a children's hospital that specialized in noninvasive testing for abused children, a battered woman's shelter, and an organization for abused children. She didn't want a cent of his money.

My Trial

Motion in limine. I had no idea
what the term meant before I was charged with a felony. But in my
late teens, I became familiar with many Latin legal terms. My public
defender, Mr. McGraugh, was kind to me. He was firm and businesslike, but he had sympathy for my story. At times, he seemed truly
sorry about my plight.

I was twenty years old, and I still couldn't use the word *rape*. I
couldn't tell Mr. McGraugh how I got a scar on my wrist. I couldn't
tell anyone what Tom Lannert did to me on my eighteenth birthday.
I couldn't explain the details of a lifetime of abuse because I didn't
yet have the vocabulary. I was just starting *The Courage to Heal*, and I
didn't believe there was good inside myself. The words—*rape, molestation, fellatio,* and *sodomy*—were dirty. I still viewed myself as weak
and worthless for letting such unspeakable things happen to me. So
Mr. McGraugh didn't know all that much. If he had known the sever-
ity of my abuse, maybe he'd have wanted to move mountains for me.
Maybe he would have seen me as more than just another troubled kid
who needed a public defender. He did want to help me, but I didn't
give him enough to go on. My words could only scrape the surface of
what really happened between me and my father.

Mr. McGraugh filed motions in limine before the start of my trial
requesting that certain pieces of evidence be introduced to the jury.
The prosecuting attorney, Mr. J. D. Evans, filed his own motions that
worked to block bits of my story. Mr. Evans's boss was the prosecuting attorney of St. Louis County, Robert McCulloch. Mr. McCulloch
doggedly went after me, calling me a bald-faced liar. He believed I

killed my father in cold blood for his money; he wanted me punished to the full extent of the law.

All of the motions took forever to make their way through the legal system. Then my original trial judge was replaced with another, the Honorable Steven H. Goldman. I had been in police custody—in a jail notorious for its twenty-three hours a day of lockdown—since July 5, 1990. My trial began on October 27, 1992.

I was in big trouble. The prosecuting attorneys could have shown sympathy and given me a lighter charge—anything other than murder one. But according to Bob McCulloch, my father had never laid his hands on me. It didn't matter that Wendy, my former babysitter, and a psychologist testified that I was abused. It didn't matter that Detective Schulte believed I was abused. Schulte was never called to testify. The prosecutor had him removed from my case.

Mr. McCulloch believed that Thomas F. Lannert was a "drunk and violent man, but that didn't make him a rapist."

Mr. McCulloch was famous for being skeptical about sex crimes. Even when a high school principal had sex with three of his students at Hazelwood High School, Mr. McCulloch refused to prosecute him because the victims could offer no physical proof. He didn't take the girls at their word, and the principal got only 120 days of time. In a way, Bob McCulloch seemed to relate posthumously to my dad. They both belonged to the Good Old Boys network in St. Louis. They were both members of the Missouri Athletic Club. The Edge, my father's favorite bar, was a big meeting place for the judges and lawyers. In my gut, I felt that Bob McCulloch had it in for me.

Meanwhile, my lawyer, Mr. McGraugh, did what he could. He filed in vain to use self-defense in my case. That motion was denied because neither my sister nor I was in immediate danger when the crime took place. The victim—my father—had been sleeping. The public defender's next option was to try a battered spouse syndrome defense. The state of Missouri had just adopted it for use in abuse cases, but battered spouse didn't apply to me. I was not the wife, and Missouri had no provisions for abused children at that time. Mr. McGraugh had only one more option for me: insanity.

The judge allowed the jury to hear some evidence of my father's abuse. Then a court-appointed psychologist went on the stand to say I suffered from post–traumatic stress disorder, which can happen after a person experiences life-threatening events. Symptoms include nightmares, flashbacks, and feelings of detachment. According to another expert, I suffered from dissociative disorder, a condition that caused me to lose memory, awareness, and functioning for periods of time. It meant I could detach from my body and leave reality to cope with abuse.

I didn't like these psychiatric terms, but they definitely described me.

Yet, they were not enough to prove my insanity. What I did was completely, heartbreakingly insane. I just wasn't insane when I did it.

Mr. Evans tried to show how I planned and plotted the murder. He brought Jason to the stand. Jason knew my father had money, and he had overheard the conversation I had with Ron when I said I wished Dad were dead. I had been planning a hit, Mr. Evans suggested.

This part of the trial nearly made my heart stop beating. Yes, I had spoken those words to Ron, but that wasn't why I pulled the trigger on the night of July 4. I had done that on my own. I had never considered having my father killed. The allegation made me want to vomit, and there I was stuck with it on the public record.

Mr. Evans showed further evidence to damage me. He had copies of checks I had written, forging my father's name. But of course I forged his name; I ran our household. I had a small moment of victory when my attorney pulled out proof of my dad's signature okaying the monthly bank statements. Those documents proved that Dad knew I was writing checks, and I was obviously doing it with his permission. I did not want the jury to believe that money had anything to do with my crime. That was the one character scar I refused to live with. The jury didn't know I had rejected the plea bargain—the one that offered me fifteen years of prison for saying I killed him for monetary gain. But I knew I had rejected it; the lawyers knew it; and the judge knew it. I wasn't walking down that road of lies and deception anymore. Taking the plea would've been the cheap and tawdry way out of my already desperate situation. I wanted to be a better person, and I had to start somewhere.

In his closing arguments, Mr. Evans told the jury I was in full control of myself when I shot my father. He stated that I knew right from wrong. He proved I was not legally insane at the time of the shooting.

The jury deliberated for five hours.

I did not freak out while I waited for their verdict. The days during the trial weren't that different from the last seven hundred or so I had spent in Gumbo. I spent a little bit of time with my mom—she and John had moved back to Illinois by this time. She had watched the trial when she was allowed to—after giving testimony on my behalf. Her side of the family hated me, and they blamed my mother for letting things go so wrong. Dad's side attended the trial, glaring at me the whole time. Only John sat behind me every day. He said, "We failed you before, Stacey, and we're not going to fail you now."

Mom and John were it. While we waited, my mother gave me a Twenty-third Psalm prayer pamphlet, and I focused on those words of comfort and hope. I told myself, *Okay, God, you're getting ready to take me on a journey. Here I am, Lord. Do with me what you will.* Maybe I would be in prison for the rest of my life. I would leave it up to God.

On October 30, 1992, I was found guilty of first-degree murder. In December, Judge Goldman handed down the mandatory sentence of life in prison without the possibility of parole. In his posttrial report, he wrote, "The sentence is severe for a twenty-year-old. It is also somewhat surprising considering the sexual abuse by the victim's father . . . a conventional life sentence would be more appropriate from a comparison standpoint."

In a conventional sentence, the guilty party gets to make her case before the parole board after serving a certain period of time. Even Charles Manson got the possibility of parole. But not me.

———

When he learned I had been found guilty, Grandpa Paulson marched over to my mother's house with everything she had ever given him—Father's Day presents, photos, cards—in a box. He dumped it at her front door.

He told her, "You left your man. You left your daughters. You're no daughter of mine." She did not speak to him again until he was on his deathbed, many years later.

With that gesture, the entire Paulson side of the family cut her off—and me, too. Mom was heartbroken that I'd just received a sentence of life without parole. She was eaten up with guilt that she could have prevented it, and now she was denied the comfort of a family to fall back on.

Instead, they blamed her.

Instead of sympathy, nearly all of the Paulsons built up a huge wall. Then they threw her—and me—to the other side.

A New Life

To serve out my life term, I was sent to Renz Correctional Institution, where Christy had been. It was out in the middle of nowhere on old farm property. The building looked like a white-concrete symmetrical high school, except the perimeter was circled with high fences, and a water silo towered from the back. I headed to a small building on the property for reception and orientation where new arrivals were given white jumpsuits. I had to spend two weeks in R&O for medical and intelligence testing before I could go into the general population.

I was thrilled.

Anywhere was better than the house on Eminence Avenue.

Anywhere would be better than Gumbo.

Upon arrival, I was strip-searched, a procedure I was familiar with from Gumbo. We were strip-searched before each visitation and after. We also got strip-searched whenever officers cooked up a reason. It was a degrading, time-consuming ordeal. We had to remove all of our clothing, then squat and cough three times. The squats were deep bends that made my legs sore. If we were hiding something in our natural "purses," squats and coughs would supposedly expel buried items. Only women could conduct strip searches.

Male officers would pat-search us before and after visits—or whenever they deemed necessary. We had to take off our coats or jackets and stand with our feet and arms spread wide apart like da Vinci's Vitruvian Man. The officer would run his hands through our collars, down our shoulders over our arms and back underneath them, then down the sides of our ribs and the center of our breasts. With the back of his hands, he would lift our breasts and search under them, following the bra line to our backs. Next he would search our waistbands, circling our waists, slide his hands down the outside of our legs, and search our ankles. Then he would bring his hands up the center of our legs stopping short of the female triangle. If a perv did the pat search, he'd just barely stop before getting too close to our vaginas. If an inmate complained that an officer was too touchy, she'd go straight to the hole.

I never complained.

I was pleased to see so many familiar faces at Renz—in R&O and out on the grounds. I must've known one-third of the women there from my two-year stint at Gumbo. We weren't all friends, but that didn't matter. People knew me, and they knew I'd already done hard time. Right off the bat, I had a little bit of respect. I remember some girl who wanted to kick my ass just because I was new. Then she realized who I was and backed off, saying, "No, it's Stacey Lannert. She's okay."

Women I'd been friendly with—the ones who bought my tea huggies for $1—smuggled cigarettes and Little Debbies to me. R&O wasn't so bad, even though we were locked down. We had only one hour of recreation, and we had to walk everywhere in a single-file line. In the cafeteria, I got my first prison scare. A three-hundred-pound black woman named Big Faye worked on the kitchen line.

When I walked past her one day, she said, "You're so pretty. You're going to be mine."

That was just great, I thought, I'd have to be Big Faye's bitch when I went into general population. I was concerned. The inmates knew I was coming, and they knew what I'd done. They were just waiting to find out what kind of person I was.

I walked into population on the first day with my head held high. I didn't show my fear—and nobody messed with me. It helped that my sister had been at Renz for the last two years. She had been released right before my trial. Christy had already done the dirty work—she kicked everybody's ass that needed kicking. Even though I could barely say boo to a bulldog, I was protected by the Lannert reputation. Smuggled cigarettes and Little Debbies—welcome gifts—kept coming.

A gay couple, Jazz and Josie, had been Christy's prison "mom and dad." A woman who took on the role of the man in a couple was commonly called a bull dyke. Homosexuality is different in prison—it's everywhere. When I caught sight of Jazz, I ran up to her and started talking. A woman named Patricia saw us together and told everyone she wanted to whip my butt. Patricia, it turned out, was Jazz's new girlfriend. Jazz explained it to me: it's disrespectful to talk to a woman without her girlfriend present.

I didn't understand at first. I said, "Patricia shouldn't be worried. I'm not gay."

Then Patricia thought I was dissing homosexuality. We worked it out, and nobody tried to whip me. But I watched who I talked to from then on, and I learned that just about every time you opened your mouth to these women, you got yourself into more trouble.

Almost immediately, lesbian protectors hit on me. They thought I might need a hand at my new home. Arrangements could have been made to guarantee my protection. I firmly and politely declined their offers. I recognized these games, and I didn't fall for them. Anyway, I didn't need help. I knew a few people, and I had a little bit of money. I already had the advantage.

Well, as long as I didn't run into Big Faye.

It took me about five seconds at Renz to learn that there aren't just prison rules; there are also prisoners' rules. To survive, you had to follow the code of conduct.

1. If you're not a child molester, you don't become friends with a child molester. Same goes for baby killers. You

don't talk to them. You don't become friendly with them. You don't hang out with them. They are the prison targets, and people are always messing with them. If an officer picks on a regular prisoner, she'll take it out on a child molester. Everyone sees themselves as above child molesters and baby killers. Those women are forced to form their own sub-culture.

2. You don't tell. You take it. If someone asks you to hide their contraband duffle bag while they get searched, you do it. If you wind up getting caught with the duffle bag, you take the violation.

3. Keep to your own. Find a group of women who are just like you and stick with them. There are no gangs in the women's prison, but there are groups. You can be friendly with women who are different—race, religion—but nothing more.

Caseworkers were like parents. Their job was to help us when we needed it and to dole out punishments when we received violations. Everything you wanted, needed, or got in trouble for came from a caseworker. Mine was aptly named Miss Case, and she was a tough old bird. She knew my sister, and Christy had given her caseworker a lot of headaches.

Miss Case said to me, "We're not going to have problems out of you like we had out of your sister, are we?"

"I hope not," I said.

We didn't have rooms there; we had cubicles. They were more like horse stalls. Miss Case said I would be sharing my horse stall with a woman named Sabrina Kinsey.

Renz had six wings with eighty or ninety women to a wing. We were packed in and exposed all of the time. There were no real walls in our cubicles. Two women shared a cube with only enough room for a bunk bed. No one wanted to sleep on top because there were drop-down fluorescent lights that were barely dimmed at night. You had to sleep with a pillow or towel over your face for darkness. On the top bunk, you could see everyone—eighty or ninety people—and there was absolutely no privacy. I was new; I got the top bunk.

Sabrina

Miss Case thought Sabrina and I would be a good match. She was sixteen when she went in, and she was about my age. Her grandmother had been killed, and she and her boyfriend were involved somehow. I didn't judge my new roommate for what she'd done. One of the things I learned going in: don't judge others; what I had done was just as bad if not worse. Everyone in prison had her own story—her own private hell.

When I walked into my new cubicle, the one I would be sharing with Sabrina, I stared at this beautiful—really beautiful—girl with shiny dark hair all the way down to her butt. Her past didn't scare me; her mean expressions did.

Upon arriving at Renz, I had a court order that I was allowed to bring my personal effects. I showed up in Sabrina's room with way more stuff than the average new girl. I put down my first box. The top flap stated, "1 of 6."

Sabrina stared at the numbers and said, "Ahhh, just fucking great."

I didn't say anything. I thought, *Here we go. My first day, and I'm going to get my ass beat.*

I wasn't stupid. I could see how small the cubicle was. The bunk beds, smaller than twins, took up most of the space. With the two lockers, there was barely enough space for both of us to stand up at the same time. If I wanted to get to my locker, she'd have to sit down on the bed or move out of the way. Even I didn't know where all my stuff would go. There were only two lockers, and I got one.

Sabrina pointed at my locker. "You better be creative because that's all the room you get."

Women were walking up and down the hallway—the cubicles were right on top of each other. One of them pulled me out and whispered, "You better be careful. Sabrina's a witch. Like a real witch. She casts spells and stuff. She's Wiccan."

I thanked her for the inside information and went back to unpacking while Sabrina studied me. More of my property arrived. I received my huge black trash bag. It was filled with tampons, literally a thousand of them. At Gumbo, tampons were free, so I had stockpiled them. I'd always heard you could trade things—especially cigarettes—for tampons. I was ready with my currency.

I turned to Sabrina. She frowned, and I was afraid she would cast a spell on me, but I needed more room. I bucked up and asked her: "Can I use some of the space under your bed if I give you twenty tampons?"

Her stare was blank but she nodded yes.

I tried to ignore her. I stared at the real bed I would be sleeping on. I didn't care if I had to take the top bunk. At least I got a comfy bed with a mattress. Gumbo had only hard plastic mats. But after the first night, I realized I wouldn't be able to enjoy my mattress. Sabrina had put a hard wooden board underneath it. Prisoners could request boards if they had back problems. But Sabrina used it to cover the springs underneath my bed. Our bunks were so close that her long hair would get tangled in the metal wires when the top mattress sagged.

That bed board was so hard, I could barely sleep on it.

Sabrina and I were not friendly. She pretty much ignored me. She had a TV at the end of her bed, and she wouldn't let me use it. I didn't have enough money for my own thirteen-inch set yet. When prisoners watched their TVs, they had to wear headphones. Sabrina never shared her headphones with me.

After fourteen days, I went to Miss Case.

"I don't like my cubicle mate," I told her.

She shrugged her shoulders; she was too busy for me. She said, "I thought you two would be good for each other because you're both young lifers. Sabrina never gets into any trouble, and I thought you could learn from her."

"But we really don't get along. Can't I at least make her take off the bed board?" I asked.

"Yeah, you can make her take it off, but then you'll have to deal with her attitude." Piles of paper and inmate folders surrounded her.

"I want to move," I said.

"You can't move for ninety days. I put you there because it's the best place for you." Then she put down her glasses, and added, "You can't move, but she can."

Sabrina was waiting for me when I got back from Miss Case's office.

"What did she say?" Sabrina asked.

I was sick of her crap. I said, "That bed board is coming down, or you can move. I'm not living for the next ninety days like this."

"All right," she said, laughing at me. She took the bed board down.

Sabrina wasn't so bad after all. She'd just been waiting for me to stand up for myself. I had to earn her respect. I had to earn everyone's respect in prison in big and small ways. Sabrina and I stayed cubicle mates for the majority of the fourteen years we spent together.

Jennifer

I was happy to be at Renz. I had much more freedom than I'd had at Gumbo. We could own up to twenty outfits—jeans and tops that didn't show our belly buttons. We could walk outside freely for a few hours every day. We had jobs. It was like a city. The canteen was in one area; the kitchen was somewhere else. We even had a cosmetology department. Old Renz was clean, structured, and comfortable—at least it was better than any other living arrangement I could compare it to.

People were getting to know me, and someone said I needed to meet this girl named Jennifer Fair. Even before we met, people said we would like each other. I found her easily. She lived on the same wing, and we used the same laundry room. I recognized her at the dryer. She was tall and pretty with a perfect body. She looked nothing like a prisoner. While I was doing a load of whites, I walked up to her.

"Hi, I'm Stacey," I said, trying to look cool and not eager.

"I know who you are," Jennifer said. "Everybody knows who you are. Anyway, we're going to be friends."

And we were from then on. Sabrina was socially inept, so I introduced her to Jennifer and her group of friends. Sabrina never went out and did things until I came along. Sabrina nicknamed me "Come On Let's Go."

We formed a tight group. We lounged out in the yard on the weekends. We watched softball games out on the field. Sometimes we'd play, but mostly, we just watched. Every Friday in the gym, there was free roller skating. We were almost always there from 6 to 8 p.m. On

Sunday, the officers would plug a VCR into a big-screen TV. Different housing units would watch movies at different times all day long. We could bring our own popcorn and sodas.

The best part for me: the yard was always open.

Jennifer and I often went out there together, and one day she said, "You're happy to be here."

"Yeah, I am," I said, trying not to think about the last five years of my life.

"People here aren't used to happiness," Jennifer said. "People look at you and scowl. Anyway, why should you be so happy? You're twenty, and you have life without parole."

I just shrugged my shoulders. I didn't know what I was so glad about. I didn't want to get into it with her. How I finally felt free. How a jail cell had been better than home and the cubicle was way better than the jail cell.

"I'm just saying," Jennifer added, "it's not in your best interest to look happy."

Who Has the Power?

I wasn't happy all the time. For one thing, a messed-up officer named Miss Wilby had targeted me. She was in her fifties, and she looked like one of those mythic centaurs, half human and half horse, because her butt projected out so much. I have never seen a human being built like her since. She picked on me all the time. Every day when we came back from work—my first job was in the yard—we had to get pat-searched before we could go into the building.

Everything we owned had to be okayed and on file at the property shed. I wore this gold cross necklace every day, and I had the proper court order for it. Wilby knew this. She had seen the necklace, and she had seen the file many times. Yet every day when I came in from yard crew, she sent me to the property shed to get a photocopy of the court order showing that I was allowed to have and wear the necklace.

Other days, Wilby would get me on something else: "Where'd you get your shirt?"

My mother had sent me all the stuff I was allowed to have, like personal T-shirts, pants, and soap. "It's on file," I answered.

"Go get a copy from property," Wilby said.

I started calling her Wildebeest.

One day she did a random search of my cubicle—officers did that whenever they felt like it. She wrote me up for having two extension cords and two blankets. I really had only one of both—as per the rules. The others belonged to Sabrina, and she had found the extras on Sabrina's bed. She was just after me.

Wildebeest sent my only blanket, a cheap gray state-issued thing, to the laundry. She took my cord, too.

When she left, I found Sabrina and told her she needed to get rid of her extra extension cords and blankets right away—like immediately. She passed them off to one of our friends for safekeeping for a few hours while I went to the captain.

I told him, "I've only been here a month, and this officer harasses me every day. She confiscated my extension cord and my only blanket. All I've got is a radio, a light, and one state blanket. Now I've got nothing."

Captain called Wilby in. He asked her to bring him my extra extension cords and blankets so he could see them.

Sabrina had hidden everything, so Wilby came back to the captain empty-handed. My violation was dismissed. I didn't get to bask in glory for long though. It turned out that I had awoken the Wildebeest. Instead of patting me down after work, she came and searched our room daily. She didn't just look around; she destroyed our little home. She'd take everything out of my locker and spread it all over my bed. Everyone could see what I owned, and I was afraid some of it would get stolen. In the meantime, Wilby found dumb reasons to write violations against me—my first ones.

I finally went to Miss Case. "Wilby is searching me every day, and she's only supposed to search once a month."

She said, "There's nothing we can do about it because an officer has the right to do that."

"Doesn't she at least have to lock it back up?" I asked, trying not to get too worked up.

"No." She gave me the *Oh grow up* stare.

I went back to our room ranting and raving. I was ready to cuss this centaur out myself. Sabrina advised me not to do it. She said she knew how to put a stop to the searches. She set up our lockers real close together, right in front of the entryway. We were skinny, and even we had to turn sideways to get into our cubicles. When Wildebeest came in the next day, she got stuck. She couldn't get her big old behind into our room.

She complained about it to the same caseworker. The caseworker told her that prisoners were allowed to arrange their lockers however they wanted.

She glared at me from then on. She gave me a look like *You beat me this time, but you won't the next.*

Sabrina and I couldn't stop laughing about it. We had trapped the beast.

Captain Miles was a nice old guy. Captains wore white shirts, and he was the shift commander for the officers, who wore blue shirts. Captain Miles called me into his office one day. He asked me, "How's it going?" Inmates never knew captains' and officers' first names.

"Why? I'm just doing my time. I'm staying out of trouble," I said. Something was going on, and I wished he'd stop beating around the bush.

"Well, you're kind of upsetting my officers," he said. He had white hair and a white mustache. He was smiling, so I was able to relax a little. "They've got a bet about who's going to get you into the hole first, and they each want to be the one who gets you."

"Oh." My heart sank. I didn't know what this meant. Was I doomed?

"They're going to push you until they break you," he said, leaning close to me. "I'd hate to see that happen to you. So you stay as calm as you can, and you just comply."

He was giving me advice I could take. I definitely knew how to comply. So when different officers nitpicked me later, I followed their ridiculous, ignorant orders. I never got heated. I never cussed them. I never even talked back.

Captain Miles wasn't done with me yet. He asked me if I liked to run track. I told him yes. I explained that I had gained a little bit of weight in Gumbo, and I ran on the track to get back into shape. Mom had even sent me my high school track shirt. I'd warm up and practice: run, sprint, run. I liked working out.

"A young lifer named Lisa Harris just escaped before you got here," Captain Miles said. "The officers are worried that if you climb the fence, you might get away. You run fast."

Of course, there was an electronic monitor on the fence, but Renz was old, and most of the monitors were broken. He knew I knew that. He didn't have to say it.

"They think you're a flight risk. They want you in the hole."

I was so thankful to Captain Miles. If he hadn't tipped me off, I would've fed into their game. I would've let the officers push my buttons like Wildebeest had. He taught me something priceless: if I react to the officers, I give them power. If I stay calm, they have no power.

Harassment comes from every angle in prison. You can't be too much of a Goody Two-shoes. I had a little game of my own I liked to play.

Sabrina liked to stay inside, but one day, I made her come outside and walk the yard. I told her I was going to practice running, and she should watch the officers.

Run, sprint, run.

They stared at me. The officers around the perimeter shifted in their positions and placed their hands closer to their weapons. Sabrina cracked up. After that, I got her to exercise with me. After our work shifts were over, we ran like hell to keep the officers on their toes.

On May 28, 1993, I turned twenty-one. I wasn't feeling great that day. I had just written an article for the *Survivors of Incest Anonymous Newsletter* entitled "Stone Walls." My mom had been sending me the newsletters, and I read anonymous stories with interest. I had turned in my own account to see if I could find the words. I kept everything general, writing mostly about disassociation. It felt good to start to open up. I received a letter from a woman who read "Stone Walls," Chris Sitka from Australia. She wrote me letters and supported me all the years I was in prison.

But I just didn't feel good about that birthday. I knew it was the first of many I would spend behind bars, and the reality of it was starting to sink in. My only hope was a woman I had just met, my court-appointed appeals attorney Ellen Flottman. She was tall and thin and kind. She seemed to believe in me, and I hoped she'd be able to pull off some sort of appellate magic.

Later that day, Jennifer and Sabrina surprised me. They had bought a cake mix that needed only water and a microwave. They made me cards and a wonderful dinner of burritos and microwaved pizza. They gave me twenty-one presents, each of them equaling twenty-one items. I got twenty-one pieces of paper, twenty-one stickers, twenty-one envelopes, and so on. They even scored a birthday candle somewhere, which was contraband.

When I blew out that candle—and I still wonder where on earth they got it—I wished that my appeal would be granted, and I would one day be free to make my own home.

Sabrina's and Jennifer's efforts meant everything to me that day. We didn't get to crack open any Champagne, but we didn't need any. I tried not to think too much about my future. I stayed in that wonderful moment. I was safe and content.

The Munchies

When you first get to prison, you have to work kitchen or yard crew. Neither of these was a high-paying job, only $7.50 a month. Big Faye was still in the kitchen, so I chose yard crew. It turned out there wasn't much work to do in the tidy gravel yard. We swept it, but that hardly took up a six-hour shift. The maintenance staff did the mowing, after all. Our supervisor tried to keep us busy, so he gave us these big hoses and told us to wash rocks off the cement blocks. I'd stand there and spray for hours. Eventually, I wasn't allowed to do that anymore because the water bill was so high.

So Sabrina got me a job in her department: data entry. It was one of the jobs that paid. My salary depended on my keystrokes. If I were fast enough, I could make $30 to $60 a month to support myself. I entered the data from ambulance reports and hunting and fishing licenses. It was so freaking boring; I hated it. Sabrina did the job while listening to her cassette-tape Walkman. Her fingers flew; mine didn't. I made only $20 a month.

I finally called Mom to complain. I told her I needed only $40 a month, and then I could find a different job that I liked. She said she'd help me, and I went into the laundry, which paid only $20 a month.

Laundry was great. I got to walk all around the campus delivering stuff. My boss, Dick Hickman, was the best. If we weren't paying attention to our folding, he'd hit us with a huge laundry cart, and we'd fall in. Then he whirled us around the room. He was seventy years old and incredibly laid back. He brought coffee, donuts, and bologna in from the outside. Sabrina would stop by to grab a bite. Any food that was left over at the end of the week magically appeared in a bucket outside my cubicle. Eventually, another woman in laundry, Shirley Lute, got jealous and poured water down the dryer engine. When we turned it on the next morning, it started smoking. Shirley tried to cover it up, but eventually got caught and was fined $90. It was a big mess.

I couldn't help but break rules in prison. There were so many of them. If I wanted a fresh tomato, somebody had to steal it out of the kitchen, and I had to pay her $1 for it. I would buy it, cook it in the microwave, and eat it right away, so I wouldn't get caught with tomato contraband. Those first couple of months, I did the same thing with pot. I bought it and smoked it right away so I wouldn't get caught. All my friends did it out in the yard where the officers couldn't smell it.

Drugs are common in prison. There was always a way to do anything you wanted to do if you were willing to take the risk. Every kind of illegal substance was available for a price. Jennifer would get our pot during her visits and bring it in. For instance, there might be a trash can, a good meeting place, right before the visitor walked into the communal area. Another inmate—someone who wouldn't get searched—could reach out and touch someone else's visitor without any supervision. I never did that, but I saw it happen plenty of times.

At the time, I hadn't been there long enough to be scared of what I was doing. I stuck with my friends who'd been there a long time. I trusted their judgment. After all, they kept me out of fights. If someone started picking on me, Jennifer would step in and stand up for me. She had built up respect, so she could do that. Slowly, I learned I had to stand up for myself, too. If I took shit from someone outside of my group, I'd have to continue to take it. I had to mouth off. I was firm and to the point, just like Kathy Tucker had taught me in Gumbo. I figured out that no one wants to throw the first punch. If someone's really tired of you, they'll do something dirty instead.

Jennifer and I had gotten high one day, and some girl was mad at Jennifer over something small and stupid. I can't remember what it was exactly. But the girl told on Jennifer about her pot smoking and threw my name into the tattle.

I was mad at myself for smoking. But even worse, I was scared. Punishments could be harsh.

I'd seen women spit at officers and get slapped with another year of prison.

If someone threw human waste at an officer, they'd get five more years of time. One crazy woman had a five-year sentence and wound up with twenty because she racked up so many infractions.

They couldn't give me more years, but the hole was punishment enough. Once I got there, I was sure the eager officers would cook up something dirty for me.

But I lucked out. My laundry supervisor, Dick, got involved. He found our urine specimens and threw them out. Then he gave me a big lecture.

"Don't do that again," he said in a private spot in the laundry room. He was not smiling.

He told me I had disappointed him, and I knew I had.

I never smoked anything stronger than a cigarette again.

Windows

In the early summer of 1993, it rained hard in Missouri. The rain was fine with me. I was already feeling down because it was almost July 4, the date that haunted and shamed me. I relived all my nightmares on that day.

As it turned out, I was too busy on the fourth to freak out. On July 3, Old Renz flooded, and we had to evacuate the building in a hurry. Officers woke us up in the middle of the night and told us to pack a pillowcase and a laundry bag with all of our essentials. We were being transferred—all five hundred of us. A few buses and vans pulled up. We got on the buses while our stuff got on the vans.

We arrived at Church Farm State Prison near Jefferson, Missouri. They unloaded us into the gym. I walked in with my friends, and we claimed our cots. Women were jammed in everywhere on rows and rows of cots. We'd been separated on different wings before, but all of a sudden, we shared one not-so-big room.

Tensions ran high. I felt like I was living in a bad-ass prison movie for a minute. There was no structure, and I was completely uncomfortable.

Everyone was running low on supplies, and people I had never talked to before were asking me for things. I always said no, and I never borrowed so much as a tampon from anyone who wasn't my friend. My group piled everything together and shared with each other. We never loaned out our stuff, and we tried to stay independent of the drama all around us.

A game called two-for-one is big in prison. If you run out of something, you go borrow it and you have to pay it back double. Nothing good ever came out of two-for-one. I stayed far, far away from it.

But I did get caught up in racial dilemmas. We'd never had anything like that before. Black girls and white girls stuck to their own, but we didn't fight. That is, not until we arrived at Church Farm.

My problems came to a head when a black clique ganged up to kick my ass. Their group had completely taken over one of two large bathrooms—the only one with hot water in the shower. I didn't realize what was going on, and I walked right into their restroom and took a shower.

When I came out, four women were ready to jump me.

Jennifer came to my rescue. She ran up to the leader of their group, a woman named Clarisse. Jennifer made the case that I didn't know. I hadn't done anything on purpose. Clarisse said they didn't like me because I trespassed and also because I kept to myself. But she took mercy on me and called off the ass kicking. She told her friends to leave me alone and find someone else to pick on.

I had never been so relieved. You'd best believe I went to the bathroom with the cold showers from then on. Soon after that, the prison officials got us out of the gym. We moved into the men's work dorm, and they tried to make life more normal for us. We had wings and cells and more of the living conditions we were used to. We were just crowded, and Church Farm was older than Old Renz.

Everything about Church Farm was gross. The men were still on the property, but they had been sent to the other side, so we didn't mix with them. Those guys kept their facility filthy dirty. It's the inmates who are responsible for cleaning and caretaking, after all. The guards and officers just stand around and watch; we prisoners are the ones who run the prison. The Church Farm men didn't care how they lived.

Meanwhile, Renz was still flooded. The situation was so bad that the facility was finally condemned. We were disappointed that we would never live there again.

But we did go back. In shackles and handcuffs, we got put on a bus back to Renz to collect our belongings. We had to climb through mud and water, and pack up all of our stuff in garbage bags. The smell was moldy and awful. Some people's stuff was completely ruined, but I lived on the second floor, so my belongings were fine. Our stuff was delivered to us in the dorms at Church Farm two weeks later, and we tried to get into a routine.

Many women had lost their stuff and didn't have even basic items like underwear and deodorant. So the prison allowed every one of us to receive a home box—that's when someone from the outside sent us necessities. Mom had already sent me one when I got out of Gumbo, so I didn't ask her for anything. I asked Tom W. if he'd get some things together for me.

He said he didn't mind doing it at all, which was sweet. I gave him a list, and he mailed me a few of his T-shirts. He also shopped for a few small sports bras. He said they were easy to find. He gave me hope and reassurance that love might still be possible for me.

Our physical separation was definitely difficult. My position was obvious. Meanwhile, he was traveling all over the world with the navy. He sent me a photo and wrote me a story about himself separated into three people: Me, Myself, and I. Each one split up to search the globe for the perfect girl. When Me, Myself, and I came back home, they had all found the same girl. That girl was me.

His love was the best thing I had going for me. The second best thing was my appeal, which I was gearing up to file with Ellen. Of course, I wasn't sure what would happen to me, but I had a lot of hope and confidence that something good would come out of it. I often repeated my trial judge's statement in my head: "A conventional sentence would have been more appropriate under the circumstances." If I could just get the possibility of parole, I felt like I could get out of here one day before age sixty.

After receiving our Old Renz property, we began settling into the institution. They doled out jobs. I was told I had to work in the kitchen, and I was hot about it. I had already done yard duty, my mandatory job. I was done with entry-level, crappy prison positions. My manager didn't care. Times had changed, and the old rules didn't apply at Church Farm. I had to work in the kitchen from 4 to 11 a.m. At least Big Faye was not there. She had gone home.

I never ate in the dining hall. I used all my money to buy food from the canteen, like frozen pizza. I hated the dining hall. I had to wear state grays and a gross hairnet. The kitchen stunk like rotting food and bleach. Add to that, I didn't know how to cook anything more than a box of Hamburger Helper.

I was assigned pots and pans. I hated washing dishes with a passion. The kitchen manager, Dennis, was pretty cool. I told him I didn't know how to cook, and I'd be damned if I was going to wash a dish.

"It's just not going to happen," I said.

He didn't like what I said, but he listened. He gave me the job of opening big industrial-size cans of food with this huge industrial can opener. You lower down the can, put the blade into place, and crank a large handle around to open a can of green beans that would feed a hundred people. Once I opened the cans, I'd pour the contents into a big pan and deliver it to the cook. I'd pull onions and potatoes from the storeroom. My job was called the runner. I got the cooks what they needed.

The storeroom had a surprise in it for me—a small window that opened up to the outside. This window had no screens and no bars.

I told Dennis I couldn't be a runner anymore. "I can't do this job," I said. "I have life without parole, and you're asking too much of me to go near that window every day."

He told me, "Tough. Deal with it."

I went to Jennifer about it. I told her Dennis needed to take me out of the kitchen immediately. The temptation to try to escape was just too much for me to handle.

"This is fucking nuts," I said. "There's a window there that leads to freedom. I have the most time here, and they put me in that room."

"Shut up," Jennifer said. "In two weeks, we're going through that window."

My heart raced. I wanted nothing more than to be free. I wanted some sort of life back. But I never lost my sense of right and wrong. I knew going AWOL was a bad idea. While it's hard to punish someone sentenced to life without parole—they couldn't just tack on time if they caught me jumping the fence—an attempted escape doesn't look good during the appeals process.

I thought about it long and hard. I talked to Mom about it during one of our visits. She and John had moved back to the St. Louis area by this time and were living in Edwardsville, Illinois. It was a few hours away from Church Farm, and she visited me about once a month. Not all of our visits went well, but that didn't matter. She still showed up.

This time, I told her everything. I told her I'd need a source of money if I left. I asked her what I should do. She cried. She said I was going through my first appeals, and I needed to think about that. She asked, "What kind of freedom are you going to have? You'll always be on the run. I'll never see you again, and I need you in my life."

I didn't cry, but I took her words to heart as my friends Jennifer and Vicky plotted their escape plan. I had a huge battle with myself. *Should I stay, or should I go?* In the end, I told Jennifer and Vicky I didn't want to go, but if they needed anything from me, I'd help them.

On the big day, I had to report to work at 4 a.m. Vicky, who also worked in the kitchen, was going to start her shift as usual. She was supposed to wait for Jennifer to go through the breakfast line. Jennifer would be wearing her grays; when she came through the line with her tray, she'd find a hairnet for her behind the big milk container. So the two of them would walk into the kitchen as if they worked there—no one would even notice—and pop out that window.

Jennifer grabbed the hairnet and walked into the kitchen at 5:30 a.m. Vicky wasn't there. She had already left at 4 a.m.

The storeroom window opened with a little V hinge. Vicky had already taken a broom handle to it and busted it all the way out. The window was wide open when Jennifer climbed on a bucket, slid through it with a little push from me, and dove out into the yard at Church Farm. Then she hopped the fence.

I was a little stunned and numb. It was hard for me to stay put in that kitchen I hated while my friends took their freedom into their own hands. But it was a turning point for me, too. I told myself, "Whatever happens to me, happens. God doesn't want me to hop out of that window."

I looked to God because I was tired. I had strayed and smoked pot; I had helped them hatch their escape. And, of course, I had done far worse than that, or I wouldn't have been at Church Farm in the first place. I was starting to come to terms with myself and who was to blame for my situation. I was to blame, and more than anything else, I wanted to make things right if that was still possible. I had tried doing things my own way, and it was time for me to step back and let God take over. I wanted to stop feeling so bad for what I'd been through and what I'd done. I hoped that one day, someone in this world would say that they understood. That couldn't happen if I continued to make wrong choices. The Bible says, Come to me all who are weary, and I will give you rest. I was weary. I placed my worries on Him. I asked for forgiveness over and over again. I searched; I thought; and I found peace in my decision. Though years later, on bad days, I would think to myself, *Damn, maybe I should've gotten out of there when I had the chance.*

At 7 a.m., we had count. Then the guards knew Jennifer and Vicky were gone. They locked down the entire institution. They put out an all-points bulletin (APB) and called the Missouri Highway Patrol.

They asked me several times if I knew anything. Officers wanted to know if Jennifer and Vicky had given me money or drugs to help them out that window. They even made me pee in a cup, and it came back clean. They wanted to know where my friends got money from—you can't escape without money. They wanted to know who was picking them up. I told them I knew nothing, no matter how much they harassed me. Not snitching felt like the right thing to do, plus it gave me a good reputation.

Within four hours, officers had collected both of my friends and put them in custody. Their ride on the outside never showed up—he decided he didn't want to be their ferry to freedom.

I saw the police bring them through security in handcuffs. Jennifer and Vicky went directly into the hole. When you escape, you automatically go to the hole for one year. Church Farm's hole was co-ed, so my friends stayed there for only one week. Then they got transferred to the hole at Chillicothe, the nearby women's minimum security prison.

All the long-timers—like me—were immediately fired from kitchen duty because that window was still wide open. They finally decided that, yes, there was a security risk in the storeroom. I was happy to be fired; it was fine with me. Three days later, they woke us up in the middle of the night. They called a few names, mine and Sabrina's included, and told us to pack. We were getting transferred to Chillicothe, too. They did it at night because the phones were off, and we had no way of letting anyone on the outside know we would be out. They didn't want any more escapes. We were going somewhere more structured; Church Farm provided too many opportunities for trouble.

Chilli

Chillicothe was a cool new place. It was like a day-care facility compared to Church Farm and Old Renz. I never thought I'd get the chance to be at a minimum security prison, especially this one. Chilli was known as the resort of Missouri prisons. Meanwhile, the guards must've figured minimum was better than no security, which was the situation at Church Farm. Whatever the thinking, I was glad they decided to move me.

Chilli didn't even have razor wire around the fence. It had real rooms, not cubicles. There were no open wings where women could constantly spy on each other. We were allowed to sit outside all day long if we wanted to, not two hours in, then two hours out like at Old Renz. I could actually play tennis outside on real tennis courts. It was such a nice facility. Plus, I ran into old friends from everywhere at Chilli.

Sabrina was in a completely different housing unit—I was on 5, and she was on 2. We both put in requests to be in the honor dorm. We had both been infraction-free for one year, so we were eligible.

I took a three-mile walk every day when I wasn't working, and the weather was nice. I had an AM/FM Walkman. I didn't get good reception on my radio outside, only inside, so I used a blank tape to record songs off the indoor radio, and then I'd pop it into my Walkman while I cruised along the field. I could pretend I was free for those few precious moments. I could feel free in my own clothes. At Chilli, we were allowed to own twenty-four tops and twenty bottoms, including shorts. Of course, I had many more outfits than that—we all did. I had different kinds of T-shirts and jeans to wear on a daily basis. I only had to wear my prison uniform at work and during visits. Under the circumstances, things couldn't have been much better.

My job was cosmetology clerk, and I made $50 a month. There was a cosmetology school where offenders were trained to cut hair. Most of us went there to get our hair done. Some of the cosmo clerks before me used to take bribes in exchange for appointments with the best haircutters. My boss advised me not to do that. I liked my job, and I didn't want to get fired. But if my friends wanted their hair done, I'd do them favors. A woman might come up to me and tell me she was having a visit on Saturday, and could I get her on the list? If I liked her, I'd say, "Sure." If I didn't like that person, I'd say, "I'll see what I can do."

That's the thing about prison. If I needed something, I never went to the staff. I counted on the other inmates. In every department, we ran the place. The officers just stood around and watched.

A woman named Tanya Goings also lived in the honor dorm. She had heard about me and she knew I stayed out of trouble. So when her roommate left, she asked me to move in. I said yes immediately. I had been living with a tiny girl named Too Short who never had any money and was constantly eating my food. Too Short wasn't all there. I needed to make a switch. Before long, Sabrina made her way into the honor dorm, too, and she lived across the hall. Honor dorm was cool. We could have our own sheets, comforters, curtains, and rugs.

Tanya was great, and we immediately became really good friends. She was about fifteen years older than me, and she was like a sister. She was in for murder. She had been involved in a love triangle and had killed her girlfriend's husband. Tanya was gay. She was self-assured, respected, and kind. I liked to make fun of her sandy blond

Farrah Fawcett haircut and her outdated 1980s gl
you get stuck in the moment you went into prison
nitely the case for Tanya. The styles changed, but

Tanya did all the cooking and cleaning in ou.
in exchange for my taking the top bunk. My lazy butt didn't mɪnu.
Tanya had done eight years already, and she knew how to cook all
kinds of things. The honor dorm had a refrigerator. We could buy
three Tostino's frozen pizzas a week and actually store them. Each
woman was allowed to buy one box of Tyson fried chicken, two burritos, and other stuff per week. My friends and I—Tanya, Sabrina,
and some others—would buy our limit of food and share. We pitched
in to have Sabrina's pizza on Monday, my chicken on Tuesday, someone else's pizza on Wednesday, and so on. We felt like a family, and
we had a lot of fun.

Tanya's job was institutional activities coordinator. She had access to free hygiene supplies, and she'd come home with free soap,
razors, and shampoo that she shared with everybody. She had a
heart of gold and made me laugh all the time.

The doctors at Chilli told me it was time for my annual Pap smear.
I reminded them that I'd just had one during R&O less than a year
before. But they'd lost the paperwork, so I had to go through a whole
new gynecological exam. When the results came back, they showed
some abnormal cells. The doctors didn't really tell me what was going
on; they just called me back in and did a biopsy. A few weeks after
that, in January of 1994, I found out I had an early stage of cervi-
cal cancer. Medical informed me that I would need treatments—
cryotherapy—which they'd do in about four weeks.

I couldn't believe it. I was unusually skinny, but that was my only
symptom. I just couldn't keep weight on no matter how hard I tried,
and I wasn't hungry. I was shocked. How could I be twenty-two years
old with cancer?

I told my friends, who were sympathetic. I also had to call my mom. I was allowed to make collect calls. I started crying as soon as I heard her voice.

I said, "I have cancer!" I thought I was so strong—I worked out all the time, and I didn't do any drugs or alcohol. And there I was: sick.

"I can't believe this," Mom said. "My baby! This on top of every- thing else." She sobbed during the whole conversation.

She came up for a surprise visit that weekend. They called me in my room and said to come down, so I threw on my uniform and put my hair back.

"Why are you here?" I asked, knowing she'd just driven three hours to Chillicothe. For once, I was really glad to see her.

"Because I just needed to be with you," Mom said. John was by her side.

Their support meant the world to me. They were showing me that when things got bad, they would care enough to come find me. Mom and John might not have been much, but they were all I had. They were stepping up.

I had another visitor around that time. My attorney, Ellen, came by to let me know my appeal had been denied. I had cancer, and I had lost my first appeal. I was no longer living it up at my new home in Chillicothe. Reality was starting to sink back in. I felt completely defeated, and a new sadness overwhelmed me. The words *life without parole* became more real. I had been denying that prison would actu- ally be my life, the rest of my life.

Ellen explained the complicated legal reasons why the appeal was denied.

"Stacey, your appeals are always going to be denied," she said.

I didn't want to cry in front of her. I tried to stay strong. I don't like to wallow in problems; I like to fix them.

"So what's next?" I asked.

"We can put together a clemency package." Ellen was always very gentle with me. She was businesslike and lawyerly, but she seemed to actually care about my case. She had long sandy brown hair that was always beautiful and she wore blue suits. She often visited me pregnant. Throughout the years she worked with me, Ellen had four kids.

She explained that the governor grants a clemency. An advisory board could recommend my case to him. Then he would decide whether to grant me a reprieve or a commutation of my sentence. We would have to write a convincing clemency package. I would need to write out everything that happened to me, how I'd tried to repent for the crime, and what my plans were for the future. I would need to find others to write glowing recommendations. I would need to prove the allegations of sexual abuse in the package. She would write the legal parts.

We had time. Clemencies are granted only every four years— sometimes eight—when a governor is about to leave office.

I told her to sign me up.

Part of me lost hope when I lost the appeal, and another part of me wanted to buck up and fight. Either way, my legal issues were only going to get more complicated. It wasn't fair for me to keep stringing Tom W. along.

If I had come home on that appeal, I probably would've been with him. I could see myself marrying him. But the years were passing, and I was still sitting on life without parole. I cared so much about him. I loved him and needed him in my life. But this situation wasn't fair to him. And it hurt me, too.

He came up for a visit, and we had a discussion about us. We had said from the beginning that if my appeal didn't free me, we should break up. Not that we were literally together, of course. But we lived with the hope that we could be a couple. Now our hopes were dashed. It was time to be realistic. He was disappointed and upset at this visit, but he agreed. We needed to just live our separate lives for a little while. We needed to try to forget about each other.

We were able to sit outside under a tree. There weren't any officers around, and he held me and kissed me while I cried. I had visions of us hanging out on some back porch after a long day of work, but picket fences were not in our future. Instead, we were surrounded by wire fencing, sharp and cutting. We said good-bye gently and kindly.

I wanted him to have the opportunity to meet someone, fall in love, and have kids. He just wasn't going to be able to do those things with me. We didn't call or write for at least a year after that.

Tanya

Four weeks passed, then months, and no one from medical did anything to treat my cancer. Every day, I lived with this knowledge. I knew cancer cells were inside, and I imagined them eating my cervix alive. It was a terrible, worrisome time, and I couldn't do anything about it. I complained to my caseworker that I needed the doctors to give me those treatments. She told me she'd see what she could do.

It was my mom who finally freaked out about it. She called the prison and persisted until she got through to a manager. She cried on the phone, saying, "My daughter has been through rape, PID, a murder trial, prison, and now you're letting her sit there with cancer? You're not doing anything about her cancer?"

The next day, I got a call from medical to schedule the appointment. My mother surprised me. She wasn't one to rock the boat, but she did, and she made something happen. I thought, *More power to her.*

For my cryotherapy treatment, I had to wear a thin paper robe while they inserted a probe in me. The doctors used low temperatures to freeze off the cancerous part of my cervix. I went only one time. They warned me that pieces of my cervix would slowly fall out onto pads. It did. It was scary and gross. But afterward, my Pap smear came back clear. After Mom got me cryotherapy, I was cancer free.

That left me more time to focus on my clemency package.

Tanya helped me. We settled into a relationship that was really close and tight. I needed her companionship. We had a special bond and love for each other—her nickname for me was Little Girl. When the officers weren't looking, I could hug her in a place where physical contact was strictly prohibited. I could lay my head on her shoulder while we watched TV. I hadn't been able to touch another person in years. I loved Tanya with all my heart. I didn't care if inmates thought we were together. If anything, I encouraged it because Tanya was respected, and being with her offered me protection. She and I knew the truth: I wasn't gay. But we had a relationship outside what traditional friendships might be. We were closer and more trusting. She helped me keep my humanity intact.

I had to put my life on paper, and it was hard. I didn't want to write the details of the first time my father played Touch Tongues in the basement with me. I didn't want to write about the time he pinned me down next to our wood-burning stove. I didn't want to write about my eighteenth birthday. I had gone out of my way not to think about such awful things, even though the scenes still haunted me nearly every day. And there I was with an assignment: tell your story—the whole story—and give it to your lawyer for the whole world to read.

Tanya reminded me that I needed to get it out. "Writing will be good for you."

She held me when I cried. I cried a lot during those months. She'd say that I was a good person, that what happened to me wasn't my fault. She kissed me, and I let her. I had this longing for connection and touch. It was something so genuine and so needed. She held me again and again as I continued to break down. She loved me, and I loved her.

When I'd have a hard time with my mom—and we still fought sometimes—Tanya would tell me to let go of my anger. I would ask her how. She would tell me she didn't know, but I had to try.

She snuggled with me. She listened.

She's the only person who knew I still heard his voice almost every night.

———

I loved my job as cosmo clerk, but Tanya thought I needed to push myself a little harder.

"I know you're comfortable there, but if life were about comfort, nothing would ever get done," Tanya told me. "Take care of yourself and make sure you're okay; then everything else is a perk."

She got me a job working at Shiloh Lure making fishing lures. I was on the paint line, dipping lures in paint, putting them on a tray, and flipping them back over. At least I wasn't just sitting there dotting the eyes on the fish. I was up moving around. I worked ten hours a day, four days a week at $5 an hour. That was $100 a month even after taxes and Social Security were taken out. For the first time, I could afford extra things like clothes and college classes. I liked having money. Tanya had been right.

I did the job for a year when something strange started happening. I woke up one morning and felt a twitch around my right eye. I didn't pay much attention to it. It twitched all day. That night, it became hard to smile. My face felt tight. I thought it was from dust or some strange thing. The next morning, I was unable to smile or close my right eye. The right side of my face was paralyzed.

I went to the doctor immediately, and he thought I was on drugs. I finally convinced him that I hadn't taken anything in years. Then he thought I had experienced a stroke. But tests revealed that wasn't the case. He said I had Bell's palsy, a condition that paralyzes the face due to inner nerve swelling. No one knows the cause or cure. He paraded me around to all of the nurses to show them my unique condition. I felt like a freak. I took medications and steroids, and my blood pressure was constantly monitored. When I wasn't working, I went to the library to read about this weird condition.

The other offenders teased me. Everyone wanted to have a look at Stacey. I had to tape my eye closed when I slept, and I couldn't close my mouth to swallow. I was embarrassed about something I couldn't control. I felt trapped not only in prison, but inside my body.

The only thing I could do to help myself was exercise my face—something another inmate showed me to avoid getting strange wrinkles. At first, I couldn't make the slightest movement with my facial muscles. But after weeks of stimulating them, the muscles began to loosen. My eye began to flutter—it wouldn't yet close—but any movement overjoyed me.

My friends encouraged me to keep exercising my face. It was weird, but it worked. About six months later, my face returned to normal. I was lucky.

Mostly. About the same time, Tanya got to go home. I was so excited for her to get her freedom back; she had been talking about it for months. She had served her sentence and behaved impeccably, and now her time was up. I was truly happy for her. I was just sad for me.

A Caged Bird

After that, my mom was convinced that the paint fumes from Shiloh had caused Bell's palsy. She told me she'd send me money if I quit that job. Tanya also started sending me money. Mom and Tanya kept in touch regularly on the outside. With their help, I quit the fishing lure factory and took Tanya's old job as the IAC. But there wasn't as much donated stuff anymore. I didn't have a lot to do.

By this time Jennifer Fair had been out of the hole for quite a while, and she'd even made her way up to the honor dorm with Tanya's help. She became my new roommate, but I still missed Tanya every day. Plus, Jennifer's close friend Lisa Harris, her codefendant on her case, had been captured (she was the young girl who had escaped Renz right before I arrived) and was in our room all the time. Lisa and Jennifer were best friends, and sometimes there wasn't much room left for me. I was starting to feel more and more lonely.

To stay busy, I was elected president of the Missouri Women's Association—we did everything from taking pictures to making sure inmates had gifts to give to their children when they visited. Moreover, the new prison superintendent wanted Chilli to open up a new pizza parlor. My new job was to manage it. We got our own space—not even near the kitchen—and I ran the place. I ate a lot of pizza.

I was still working on my clemency package, and I started taking a *Courage to Heal* class offered by a volunteer. With no one to turn to, this was one of the hardest things I'd tried to do. Even though I was familiar with *CTH,* I had a hard time facing the realities of what it proposed. Healing was just as painful as living through the abuse.

It hurt so deeply sometimes that it was just easier to try to forget about it or act like it never happened. But I'd hear Tanya's voice in my head telling me to keep on going. So I did.

Through all the reflection and written exercises, I found it much easier to forgive my father than it was to forgive myself. I stopped trying to figure out why he did it. I didn't know why. Sure, my grandfather might've been an influence, but he didn't make my father turn on me like he did. My father turned on his own. And the truth was, I had absolutely no idea why. I struggled with letting either one of us off the hook. Not only was I a sexual abuse victim, I was also a murderer. I told myself I could overcome these labels. But it was going to take awhile.

I read *I Know Why the Caged Bird Sings* by Maya Angelou for the first time.

When his wing is bruised and his bosom sore,
When he beats his bars and would be free;

Just the title of the book changed my life. Then the words inside opened my eyes. I was a caged bird, and I still had a voice. It dawned on me that my soul, my life, and my spirit could be beautiful despite the bars and fences. This book helped me go easier on myself. I wrote to Tanya about it. We wrote letters and spoke a few times a week at first. But sometimes our contact only made me miss her more. She was living her life, and I was truly happy for her. But her new life was nothing like her old one, and we were slowly, naturally drifting apart. I exercised more; it helped me work out all the pain and anxiety.

Then a phone call came on November 17, 1997. I knew something was wrong because I got called out to the desk and the assistant superintendent handed me the phone. This wasn't protocol for receiving phone calls.

The super said, "Make sure your mother knows this isn't allowed."

My mom was crying hysterically, and of course, my heart skipped several beats.

"Tanya's dead, honey," Mom said, barely audible.

She'd been free for only one year, and she died from an aneurysm. It happened just like that while she had been going about her day.

I was heartbroken. I literally cried for weeks. Jennifer and Sabrina tried to console me, but I couldn't bring myself to smile. I couldn't pretend that their attempts were successful. I stayed by myself so I could sit with my sadness.

I was totally alone.

My mom sent me Tanya's funeral program. There was a picture of her as a beautiful and innocent little girl with two long blond ponytails. A poem was enclosed called "Safely Home."

Roberta

I became withdrawn and closed off. What was the point of making friends if they were just going to leave—or worse, die? Jennifer was off with Lisa all the time, and Sabrina was starting to do her own things. If I did open up, I decided, it would only be to a lifer from them on. Even so, I preferred to stay by myself, to completely withdraw. People started to think I was a snob. But I just couldn't communicate.

I had a teddy bear I'd received early on. We weren't supposed to have them anymore, but mine hadn't been confiscated. It was kind of grandfathered in by the officers. I was a grown woman, twenty-five, and I'd just hug that bear and pray to God.

I smuggled in a live bunny once and a frog I found outside. I just wanted to take care of something; I was so lonely I wanted something to love. I missed the dogs from my childhood—Max, Prince, and Caitlin. Like every other dream and hope in my life, those animals had been taken away from me. Even Caitlin, after being rescued that night, was hit by a car shortly after I went to jail.

One person broke through my barrier. My friend Roberta Gunn was a godsend. I met her after a bad haircut from the cosmetology department. I'd gotten my hair frosted and permed, but the girl who did it completely fried my hair. I had to cut it all off like GI Jane after that. It grew out a little, and the next cosmetology student cut it lopsided. Someone in another housing unit told me about a woman on the other side of the wing who actually knew how to cut hair. I found Roberta, a woman with long red hair, and asked if she could fix it. She did. That was back when we were allowed to have our own scissors. She had a good pair.

I had not been smoking for about a year at the time, and I was living in a nonsmoking room with a woman named Debbie. For no clear reason, I started up again, and I was always going to Roberta's to smoke with her. We started becoming friends. She missed her baby back at home, and she was still heavy from baby weight. We talked a lot about exercise and our families. Like me, she had a lot of unresolved issues with her family. We'd give each other advice and just listen. In prison, it's hard to find someone you can trust and depend on. At the time, all the talk was about the new prison, called Vandalia, that was opening up soon. It was closer to her family, so she was transferring. So I didn't know how long we'd stay friends. I wasn't sure about Vandalia yet, though it did offer computer courses we didn't have at Chillicothe. Vandalia was closer to my sister and mother, too.

But Chillicothe wasn't the day-care center it had been when I arrived. It was changing. A new warden had arrived and was starting to take away our privileges—for instance, we couldn't have many street clothes anymore. We had to wear our grays all the time. We could no longer have scissors. Everywhere we turned, something was being taken away.

It felt like a real prison.

I did a lot of volunteering, and I was the canteen rep as well as the dorm rep. I didn't like these changes one bit, and I decided to try to do something about them. The warden said he was going to keep making changes until we proved we could stand together. He didn't like all the backstabbing and tattling that went on. He came from a men's prison that had a different set of rules: if men have problems, they take care of them—they don't tell.

So on the down low, a few of us organized a peaceful prison protest. One day, to prove we offenders could stand together, we didn't go to lunch. Only 32 out of 650 people showed up. We did a great job, and we proved our point, that we had some power. We could disrupt the status quo in a calm and civilized way.

The warden was pissed, and so were the other prison officials. He told us he was going to keep making changes, and this time they would be hard changes. The staff must've been pretty freaked out by our protest.

To keep us from rising up against them again, they shipped half of us en masse to Vandalia. I volunteered to go.

Vandalia

Visitors enter through the front gate at Vandalia. Offenders are processed through a separate entrance in the back. In August 1998, we arrived in three large white vans, mine holding about twenty inmates. One van was filled with just inmates' property. I had a hard time leaving Chillicothe because it had been my home for the last six years, and for most of those years, it was like living in a kiddie camp. The place didn't even look like a prison. I thought Vandalia might be easier to deal with because we would know exactly what was expected, whereas at Chilli, the new warden was flexing his muscles and taking away new freedoms on a daily basis.

A car met us at the front of Vandalia, and we followed it around back. A razor-wire fence slowly opened, and we got a look at the large red buildings with floodlights pointing down from every direction.

My friend Shelley said, "Oh my God. Why did we volunteer to come here? What did we just do?"

My thoughts echoed hers. It was such an impersonal, overwhelming, unwelcoming facility. *What choice had I just made? Was this really my new home?*

Jennifer was with me, too. She smiled her beautiful smile and said, "Well, at least I won't be alone."

I nodded my head.

Jennifer said, "Toto, I don't think we're in Kansas anymore."

"No shit," I said as I looked at the compound with the brightest lights I'd ever seen.

After the four-hour ride, they unlocked the vans and took us in through a back hallway with buzzers at the entryway. The building was new—that was the only refreshing change from the bug-infested penitentiary I had just left. The tile floor was made of random patterns of soothing colors—mauve, seafoam green, cream, light blue, and tan. The randomness of the tiles drove me insane because I liked order. I could look at those floors for hours and never find a pattern.

Each building had four wings and a central rotunda. The officers were enclosed in a small, round desk area within the rotunda. They were not protected by glass. This central space had computers and monitors as well as a control panel for the officers to buzz open the doors—not our cell doors, but the main door to each wing.

Glass windows ran all along the outside of the wing walls. An officer could sit in the rotunda and see what was going on in the wing dayrooms and hallways, which were video monitored.

When I first entered a wing, I noticed the large open area called the dayroom. I could see upstairs and down the hallway. Inmates from upstairs and down congregated in the dayroom during open hours. There was a phone room with two blue collect telephones that we could use. On the other side of the hallway was a small room that contained a TV; only downstairs inmates could go in there. The upstairs TV area was not enclosed.

As I looked down the hallway, I saw a utility room with a large sink where we could find our mops, brooms, and other cleaning supplies. On the opposite side of the hall was a laundry room with a washer and dryer; each floor had its own facility.

The shower area was off to one side. We had five showers in our bathroom, tiled in small bubblegum-pink squares. The color made me nauseated if I stared at it too long. The showers had a small curtain rod and a bench for our belongings—all in bubblegum. I found out that the water never got very hot, and the pressure always sucked. I couldn't move the showerhead, so I had to find the one that pointed down and didn't spray me in the face. I grew to prefer shower number three. If someone was in the shower, we had to call our place in line. Jumping the line was grounds for a fight. I never jumped the line, but I got cross if someone jumped over me.

My room was down the hallway on the first floor. It locked from the outside with a key. It had a beautiful new maple laminate door with a three-inch window running down the top half and a brass doorknob. Four beds lined the walls, two along each side. White metal frames held a hard plastic mattress filled with some unknown substance. Each bed had a blanket, sheets, and one pillow. We were allowed to order our own blankets, so I got one that was light blue and embroidered with my name so no one could steal it. We were allowed to have a small personal area rug, and mine was light blue. We had a cream-colored stand-up metal locker next to our beds. A footlocker was shoved under each bed. Everything we owned had to fit into these two areas. We hung our towels on the side of the tall locker. I ordered a royal blue one. The only items we were allowed to have on top of our lockers were a Bible, a cup, and two picture frames.

At the foot of our beds was a small metal tray that held our TV. We could watch it only during certain hours and not during count. We'd keep them on during count anyway and just listen for the officer to walk down the hallway. We could usually hear the guard's keys; if not, someone in the room before ours would cough as a signal to turn them off. I would watch my TV with my toe on the power button so I could flip it off quickly.

In the center of the two beds against one wall was a stainless steel shelf for electrical appliances. I kept a dual deck tape player, Walkman, curling iron, and blow dryer there. The walls were creamy white cinderblock. I counted the blocks in the room over and over again.

In the middle of the room was a laminate table with T-bar legs and seafoam green plastic chairs. At the end of the room was a large window with two-inch-thick metal bars three inches apart. There was no way to fit through that window, and I considered every angle.

I thought the large red buildings looked like holding barns. They reminded me of the Bob Evans restaurants, and to this day, I cannot eat at a Bob Evans.

I knew a lot of people at Vandalia. Most of the faces—staff and offenders—were familiar. But my closest friends were Jennifer and Roberta. I was still having trouble opening up to people. At least I liked my job; I worked in recreation as a clerk, and it was peaceful. I liked it because I could work out as much as I wanted, usually an hour a day plus lifting weights. Exercise took away some of my loneliness, and I got too skinny there for a bit. I didn't care; building up my body felt good. The population elected me as the Recreation Council representative twice, and I liked having extra responsibilities. We got to help decide what types of tournaments to hold, which new games to buy, and what equipment, like treadmills, we wanted.

My roommates were random, and I really wanted to live with Jennifer Fair. So Jennifer cooked up a story; she told my caseworker that I had anorexia and we needed to live together so she could make sure that I ate. Her plan backfired. I got sent to the hole for a psych eval for being too thin. Down in a small, single room, all they would give me to wear was a paper gown. I froze my ass off with no mattress and hardly any food. I was miserable. In the middle of the night, a kind officer gave me an extra paper gown to cover up with. But the next morning, the next shift officer took it away from me. When she did, I asked her if she wanted my blood too because those were the only things keeping me warm.

The warden came down in the hole to do a walk-through. He asked me if everything was all right. I told him no. I said I was here for a psychiatric evaluation, and they had only twenty-four hours to evaluate me so they'd better hurry up.

I was totally bluffing—I made up that rule off the cuff. He bought it, though, and called the psychiatrist. None were on duty, so the warden let me out immediately.

Thank God. And that was the end of anyone worrying about me getting too skinny.

Reaching Out

While at Vandalia I met a wonderful man named James Head. He was the principal of a local high school, and he came in to talk to offenders so he could help troubled girls at his own institution. I had taken the *Courage to Heal* class twice and had done the workbook a few more times on my own, but I hadn't actually spoken about what I'd been through.

And here was this man asking me all kinds of questions—along with teachers from his school. He wanted to know what he could do to make a difference. I was able to briefly describe my situation to them. I spoke about my abuse, my helplessness, and my anger. When we finished, I felt off kilter—totally off balance. These were people I didn't know, many of them men. Afterward, Mr. Head wrote me a letter saying that he was highly impressed with me. He thanked me for taking the time to share my story with him.

His approval and validation made all the difference. After all those years, I finally decided that if I wanted to help, I had to be honest. I had to reach inside myself and find that truthful place. The whole experience spoke to the heart of me.

I was selected as a member of the Outreach program, which was similar to the famous program called Scared Straight designed to deter juvenile offenders. Along with a few other offenders, I sat on a panel speaking openly and honestly to troubled girls about sexual abuse. The idea was to keep them from following in our footsteps. I knew—and they knew—there were better ways to deal with even the worst situations. A lot of men listened, too—usually criminal justice students—but I got used to it.

Scott Kinter was in charge of Outreach, and he would ask all the kids in the room to point to the prisoner who had been pushed to the point of killing her abuser. I was small, and I had short blond hair. I guess I just didn't look like a murderer, and they always picked me last. The kids would be surprised. And Scott would drive home his point that anyone could make a really bad decision.

We worked mostly with at-risk juveniles, but sometimes college students came in. I would tell my story, and I was amazed I could do it. Afterward, the adults would tell me they appreciated my candor. I was told that I exceeded their expectations, and that felt good.

Most important, the kids responded to the program. I would talk to them one-on-one, and they were just like me at that age. They struggled to even speak. I was able to pick out the ones who were abused just by looking at them. Victims stand a certain way that is intimidating but also vulnerable. Their eyes are dark, angry, and haunted.

I got so good at picking out the abuse victims that I could tell who they were by asking them one question: What is your favorite room in the house?

Most answered the kitchen, which was a good sign. That was the center of the home, and it meant they spent a lot of time with their parents. If they told me they liked the living room, I asked them why. Usually they said it was because the TV and video games were in there. That was a clue that the child was cut off from her family, and she might need further evaluation.

But if an at-risk child told me her bedroom was her favorite place, she was usually a child abuse victim. She liked to be cut off from the family, and she was trying to find safety in her own space. At the very least, that answer indicated the child's family situation was probably not good. I could also tell by her body language—the way she turned or looked down at the ground.

One girl came in from Kemper Military Academy. She was twelve or thirteen with short brown hair. She started off a real smart aleck. When a kid acted that way, we'd take them off to the side to talk to them. Something about this girl got to me, so I said, "I'll take her."

She had a chip on her shoulder that I recognized—kids have that chip for a reason. She had a lot of sadness and anger built up inside her with no place for it to go. I told her about me and why I was in prison. She started crying, and that was a pretty good indication that something was going on in her world.

I asked her if there was something she wanted to tell me. She said there was abuse in her background. I told her we needed to get her some help and that she needed to tell her teacher. She said she couldn't.

"Do you care if I do? For you to be able to get help, we have to tell an adult who can help you, because I can't," I said to her.

The girl agreed to let me help.

Her teacher was there that day, and I spoke to her. The teacher spent some time with the child right away. When they got back to Kemper, they filed a police report against her abuser, and the man was arrested. I was able to help two other young girls prosecute their abusers through Outreach.

Eventually, I became the volunteer president of Vandalia's Outreach program. It got me in touch with what I had done and where I had been. It was like counseling for me. For the first time, I started to feel like I was healing. I'm not sure who got the most out of Outreach: the at-risk youth or me.

It was 1999, and we were working hard on my clemency petition. At the end of 2000, Missouri governor Mel Carnahan would be leaving office. We had to get my paperwork in so his advisory board could read it. Then hopefully it would land on his desk for a yes or no. As I knew well, the legal system takes time.

Ellen was doing all she could. She had created a Web site called FreeStaceyLannert.org so others could read my story. She also had another idea up her sleeve. On a visit, Ellen brought a stocky, forty-something law student named Mike Anderson to meet me. He was working on a clemency project, and she thought he might be able to help with my case. But he had to believe in me first. He told me that if he didn't buy my story, he wasn't going to work on it. I could tell immediately that Mike was the bulldog that we needed. Ellen was the calm, straitlaced lawyer who wasn't pushy. Mike blasted me with questions, and he just kept to the facts. He was very forceful. But at the end of the interview, he said he'd be honored to work with me.

For my package, I had written several journal entries of my most horrific memories. I had written healing poetry. I had written out my plans for the future, which were to get a degree and help others who had suffered from sexual abuse. We included all of my prison accomplishments—participating in forty-seven acts of volunteerism, holding positions, and serving on committees—things I had done even though I had no hope of release.

Ellen and Mike gathered affidavits from my mother, Christy, and a member of the jury, Ann Albers. I told them about Detective Tom Schulte and how he had believed my abuse—I told them to contact him. But they didn't think much of it at the time. Ms. Albers's words were especially influential:

"I was a juror who sat for and heard the case of *State of Missouri vs. Stacey Lannert*. During deliberation, it was the consensus of the jury that the jurors believed Stacey had been sexually abused by her father, Thomas Lannert. Further, it was the consensus of the jury that the sentence of life without parole was too severe and harsh a sentence; however, the jury was not provided an alternative to the sentence of life without parole. It is my personal belief that the sentence Ms. Lannert is presently serving is too harsh for the crime for which she was convicted. I believe Ms. Lannert deserves commutation from the sentence of life without parole."

Tom Wilson wrote a letter describing my character. Psychological evaluations were included. Meanwhile, Ellen and Mike wrote the legal prose beautifully. She wasn't even getting paid to work on my case at this point. She was putting together my eight-hundred-plus-page clemency petition pro bono. That's why she brought on Mike.

Another Missouri law student, Robert Hegadorn, wrote his law school thesis on my case. It detailed all the reasons why I should be granted clemency and was published by the Missouri Bar Association.

All we were asking was that my sentence be commuted to a conventional life sentence with immediate eligibility for the consideration of parole. We filed the package in July 2000.

As fall rolled around, Ellen was getting word from Governor Carnahan's office that he was favorably considering my case. But he was currently running for the U.S. Senate against John Ashcroft, so we would have to wait until that race was over before he'd give any definite answers.

I had never been more excited in my life. I felt like I had a chance. I let my hopes fly high even though I knew I needed to be careful. I just thought I had it that time. The clemency package was strong; Carnahan was a good man and a great governor. He was showing interest. I didn't protect myself; I didn't think I'd get hurt.

I didn't think Governor Carnahan would be fatally wounded in a plane crash. He died on October 17, 2000. I was watching TV in my room when breaking news interrupted my show. He'd been in a small plane flown by his brother. It was devastating for the state, and he was the favorite for the Senate seat. I was in shock.

I was really sad that he died. I felt guilty for being disappointed for myself. It was a tragedy that affected his family, the state, and the whole country. I was hardly at the top of the mourning list, but I couldn't help it. My hopes faded, and I was sad for myself.

I was ashamed to call Ellen and ask her what this meant for me. I worried that it would be wrong to speak of my needs when someone so important had died. But I had to know what she thought. I stood in line for the phone, and by the time I got one, the room was empty. I was thankful to be able to talk privately for once because I knew I was going to cry. And if the other women saw me cry, they would know what was going on with my clemency. Under no circumstances could I show weakness.

Luckily, she was at her desk, and I got to speak to her. She was sad and disappointed, too. For the last months of the term, Roger Wilson would be taking over until Governor-elect Bob Holden took office. Wilson had already said he would not be giving out commutations.

I would have to wait four more years to submit my petition again.

Going Public

In January 2002, we got word from Governor Holden's office. He had seen my clemency petition already. Ellen and Mike came in person to deliver the news. We went to one of the private visiting rooms just for attorneys. It was tiny, and their presence overwhelmed me that day.

Mike spoke first. "Holden's people said they just got into office, and they hope to win reelection. That could mean seven and a half years before they consider our case."

I knew this was how it worked. I kept listening.

"His advisory board says the only way he'll be able to release you, Stacey, is if you get public support behind you."

Ellen interrupted Mike. "That means you have to go public."

I didn't have to think hard about that one. I immediately said, "But I can't!"

"You have to," Mike said, pretty much ignoring me. "Look, the best thing we have going for you is you. When people hear you and see you, they believe you. The only way we can get you out of here is by you helping you. All you have to do is be yourself."

They might as well have told me I needed to sprout wings and fly to Mars. "I don't want to do it," I said. No way was I speaking more than I already had about what I'd been through. I was ashamed and afraid of my past. I thought they were crazy. "I can't do it," I added. I had spent most of my life building walls around myself for protection. It was one thing to let a few people in through Outreach. It was a whole different story to tell thousands of people—maybe more—about my story.

I viewed Mike as my protector. He promised me he would be very careful in handling requests to speak to me. He told me I could do it because he wouldn't let any reporter hurt me.

I thought to myself, *But I'd be opening myself up to this huge amount of pain. How can you protect me from that?*

I wasn't myself during that meeting. I felt cold, shivery, and withdrawn. They didn't quite understand what they were asking me to do. But if they thought it was my only way out, I knew I needed to at least consider what they were saying.

"How would we do it?"

"We don't know," Ellen said. "We're going to look into it."

By the time they left, I had said yes, I would go public with my story if that's what it took. I felt nauseous the rest of the day. In my heart, I knew what had happened on that July 4. I knew what choices I had made, and I knew they were wrong. I knew I had to stand behind my actions and why I had taken them. I committed one of the worst crimes a person could commit—I took the life of someone in my family. Most people couldn't even begin to fathom why a teenage girl would do that. I did it because I was sexually abused, and I didn't know if I wanted to say that out loud to anyone ever again. Speaking it, would I be able to live with myself? I'd be opening myself up to so many questions. Was I prepared to answer them?

I just wasn't emotionally ready. It had been ten years since the crime. I fought my demons every step of the way. In prison, people would ask me, "Would you do it again?" I feared that question. What was the right answer? Back then, I would've said, "Yes, I'd do it again to protect my sister." But a small part of my conscience was rising up and saying, "Wait, maybe I wouldn't have."

It's funny how life works. Shortly after that conversation with Mike and Ellen, a reporter from *Glamour* magazine called Mike. She had found me on FreeStaceyLannert.org, and she wanted to travel from New York City to Vandalia to do an interview.

Mike called me, prodding me to do it.

I said no.

He prodded me some more.

I said yes.

Next thing I knew, I was sitting across the table from a reporter, Kristen Kemp, and two cameramen in the private visiting room. I told her as much as I could. I told her what I had written in the clemency package. I told her about how Dad killed Christy's cat Buttercup right in front of us. It was hard. I couldn't warm up. I couldn't believe I was giving information that would end up in a national magazine.

Kristen interviewed me slowly; we talked several times after the first big interview in person. She was patient. She wrote a story that wasn't slanted for me or against me—she told the story straight down the line. But one thing was clear: she believed me.

God works in strange ways, and as painful as it was, I knew I had done the right thing. After the *Glamour* article came out, Montel Williams called.

Pressing

Montel wants me to do what?"
I asked Ellen on the collect phone.

"They're going to interview you from prison and do a live satellite interview on the show." Ellen sounded eager. She wanted me to do it, but only with the best intentions.

"No," I said. I hadn't experienced much fallout from the *Glamour* article. It wasn't like offenders read fashion magazines. My mother and sister had seen it, and they approved, though uncomfortably. The article included details about their lives, too.

A popular television show would be entirely different. TV reached more people. Everyone where I lived would not only see me on TV, they'd be glued to my episode. It was too much for me to bear.

"No," I repeated.

"You can't say no, Stacey," Ellen said. "Unless you want to stay in prison forever. Then go ahead and say no."

Mike called with the same spiel. He got me to say I'd think about it.

I reread *I Know Why the Caged Bird Sings* that night. It's a fast book that I devoured time and again. I thought, if Maya Angelou can go public about her abuse by writing this book, I should find the strength to do it, too. I thought about Oprah Winfrey, who was outspoken about a family member who sexually abused her. She had helped so many people by being honest. I drew inspiration from those women. If they could do it, so could I.

The next day, I agreed to do the show. I was so nervous that I slept less soundly than usual for weeks until the TV crew showed up

in January 2002 with their mikes and wires and cameras and questions. Under many security restrictions, Montel and I were put in a
dark room while his crew worked in the background. He made me
feel like he really cared, and he focused just on me. Instead of asking
me things in chronological order, he would come back and forth to
different topics, making it easier for me. It was overwhelming to have
him there. But it felt good to tell him everything, just everything—
more than I'd told *Glamour*. I got it all out, and I cried. The experience
was very hard. I tried not to be embarrassed at what I'd said. And I
tried even harder not to be embarrassed at the spectacle I had caused
at the prison. I did not like to draw attention to myself.

After the interview, Montel's producers contacted my mom and
District Attorney Bob McCulloch. God help me when I thought about
what those two might say. At this time Detective Tom Schulte was
speaking out, too. The man who had taken my confession was going
public saying (a) I was abused and (b) the punishment did not fit the
crime. I wondered where he had been all those years, but that didn't
matter. He was there now, and I was thankful.

Five agonizing months went by until *Montel* aired. In the meantime, I did an interview with the show *Primetime Live*. All of this was
happening to me so quickly and by God's grace—without my being
proactive. Kristen had found me in a Google search. Her *Glamour*
piece led to national TV shows. It was surreal how things had happened, and how fast they happened. I was a nobody before January
2002.

On May 7, 2002, the episode of *Montel* aired. That day, I had two
hours in the morning, two hours in the afternoon, and two hours
in the evening that I could walk in the yard for recreation. I stayed
outside all day with my Walkman on. I knew the time was getting
close to 4 p.m., airtime, and I thought that when I went back inside,
my life would be different from then on. I had made it through the
magazine interview, but now people I knew and didn't know were
going to see me. They were going to hear my story. I expected to be
treated differently.

I was embarrassed and ashamed when I walked into the housing unit around four o'clock. I had to come in because it was almost count time, or else I would've stayed far away. I held my head down, but I could hear that every single TV set was on. As I walked down the hallways to get to my room, I saw my face on the screens. It just hurt so much because those people were going to know in detail what I had let happen to me. They could use my vulnerabilities against me. It was dangerous to be so vulnerable there. After the show, no one said anything to me about it. I stayed nervous.

The next morning, a few people mentioned that they saw me on *Montel*. I didn't know how to answer, so I just nodded and put my head back down. I went to rec to work out. I was teaching classes by this time—I was certified in prison—and I really enjoyed helping others reach their goals. Exercising got me through that time. I did whatever I could to keep my mind off the publicity.

I wondered how on earth I'd let Ellen and Mike talk me into it.

A few days later, I was sitting at a table in the dayroom for mail call. We had to be there, but I wasn't concerned about it. I rarely received mail. The officer called "Stacey Lannert" over and over again. I kept getting up to pick up my letters—I must've stood up twenty-five times. The mail was from names I didn't recognize. I sat down and opened the first letter:

"Hello. My name is Sharon. I saw you, and I went through the same thing. Thank you for telling your story. Now I might be able to tell mine."

The next letter was almost the same: "Thank you for telling your story. I have one that I need to share one day. Love, Michele."

A special woman named Kristi Knotts contacted me and put up an online petition that eventually gathered more than ten thousand signatures on my behalf. A man from Australia, Graham McAllister also saw the show, and he offered to take over my Web site, FreeStaceyLannert.org, when Ellen became overwhelmed with it. I couldn't believe the support I received—from total strangers. Jean Hensley Besner was inspired to start her own movement in Canada, gathering signatures and getting nuns to pray for me.

All that time, I thought I was doing something just for me because I wanted to go home. I needed publicity and public support to get myself out of prison. I didn't realize that I was actually doing something much bigger. Because I'd gone through so much and lived to tell about it, I could make a difference in people's lives. The letters that came for days and days made it okay for me to be me for the first time in my life. Maybe my speaking out really did help people become more aware and less ashamed of sexual abuse. That was a new and empowering thought. I started to think that we could all stop being victims and start being victors. It was enlightening. The encouragements I'd read in my *Courage to Heal Workbook* were finally making sense and coming true for me. I was shocked at this transformation. I didn't have to be embarrassed anymore. The whole world knew the real me. Even the prisoners were supportive; not one person gave me any trouble about what I'd said on TV.

For the first time, I had nothing to hide, and I started to feel a sense of freedom.

Puppy Love

I had high hopes for my clemency package. I still had a few years to wait. Holden wouldn't be leaving office until 2004, and that was only if he didn't get reelected. I had to find constructive, healthy, and happy ways to pass the long days of prison.

But I was still me. I stuck to my own handful of friends—by this time, our group included Sabrina, who was at Vandalia for a while before her release. I was introverted mostly—except when I was teaching step classes or volunteering to lead bingo or take pictures for the photo committee. If I didn't get too close to others, they couldn't leave me, hurt me, or worse, die on me.

Then there was all this talk about the dogs. One of the prisons in the state of Washington had a service dog program where inmates trained canines to help homebound people become more independent. Janet Cole, the founder of Canine Helpers Allow More Possibilities (C.H.A.M.P.), called Vandalia to see if the women and the facility would be interested in letting her come. The director of training, Mary Ruth, would be coming in, too.

Dogs? Most of the women—like me—craved love and companionship. Many of them—like me—were also dog fanatics. Of course we were interested! But I was cynical. There was a lot of paperwork and red tape to go through. In prison, things get messed up really quickly for the dumbest reasons. Surprisingly, prison officials thought bringing C.H.A.M.P. onto our campus was a good idea.

In July, the first strong, friendly dogs arrived. I was interested, but I didn't trust the program. It was too good to be true. I was afraid that if I got involved, it would be taken away. I didn't know if I could handle the heartbreak of losing another dog. All it would take to get C.H.A.M.P. kicked out was one person breaking one rule. But I watched Janet and Mary work from afar. They were amazingly kind and patient. Mary was truly a dog whisperer. And the dogs were going to help people in need. Everything about the program appealed to me.

The first two dogs at the prison were golden retriever puppies named Finders and Keepers. My friend Jennifer started training Finders and brought him over to me in the yard. I petted him and looked into his happy eyes. They were the first dogs to stay with inmates twenty-four hours a day for training. I thought, *Okay, that's it. I gotta do this. I gotta give it a shot.* I had a hard shell around my heart, and I would have to take the chance that it would crack.

I had to fill out an application to see if Janet and her trainers were interested in me. They liked my application, which included many recommendations, and brought me in for an interview. They convinced me to quit my great job at the rec center. I was hired along with eleven other women—many of them my friends. Four people already had their own dogs. I got the fifth dog right after I was hired.

Before I could get a dog, they had to train me. I even had to spend time in a wheelchair, so I would understand what our clients' lives were like. I dedicated myself to the program and to my dog, a beautiful white lab named Tory. He and his crate moved into my cell. I had to move the table out of our room, and I put him underneath the window. My roommates didn't mind—they loved the dog. He was with me twenty-four hours a day, seven days a week. He went everywhere with me. If I went to work out, Tory came, too. If I was teaching aerobics classes, he'd lie down and wait for me. Sometimes, just for fun, I'd tell him to get up because he knew how to follow some of the class moves. He could side pass while I did the grapevine, and everyone liked that. Tory could walk forward to a count of four, then walk back. He'd stay by my side doing aerobics until I told him to lie down.

My time with Tory was just wonderful. It lasted only a year. Tory was such a joy; he taught me as much as I taught him. I learned about patience, pride, and the ability to let go.

He changed my view of forgiveness. I made a ton of mistakes training him. I would say the wrong words, give the wrong hand signals, and send him confusing messages by accident. I would become impatient, frustrated, and upset when he would not perform the way I wanted him to. But I was a softie.

I would give him a command—something he knew darn well—and he would just sit there and stare at me with his big brown eyes, waving his thick tail. I knew he was laughing at me inside. Eventually, I learned to laugh back. I didn't have the heart to correct him because I loved him and didn't want to scold him. I let him get away with all kinds of things.

Mary Ruth, the training director, took me aside and said, "You need to be more firm with Tory."

"I can't; it hurts me to correct him," I said.

"I understand that, but you aren't being fair to him. Tory needs your leadership, not your acceptance. If you do not correct him, you are not leading him. He will not understand why he is being corrected by me for doing the same things you let him do. You are hurting him instead of teaching him," she explained.

That was a hard one to chew on. I had to step up and be a leader or walk away from Tory. I didn't know if I could stand the look of betrayal in his eyes when I gave him his first correction. What would happen when I told him to sit and he ignored me, causing me to physically pull up his collar to make him sit? I asked him to sit again, and he ignored me. I did the gentle correction, and he got the message. I reached down slowly and pulled up on his collar so his rear end would go to the ground. His eyes were mad at me: *How dare you punish me*. I was big bad Stacey there for a minute. He wondered where his treats were, and where was the fun Stacey who played with him? I asked him to sit again, and he did it.

Then we played his favorite game, tug-of-war, and all was right in Tory's world again. Tory forgave me instantly, no strings attached. The stunning realization that this dog could forgive me so easily filled my heart. If this wonderful and simple creature of God had the capacity to forgive me, I had to ask myself, *Who was I* not *to forgive?*

I had to ask God to help me forgive my father and myself. God grants forgiveness and forgiveness means freedom. I didn't have to forget, I just had to cut myself some slack. I needed to show myself loving-kindness and realize that, yes, I made a tragic choice. But finally, after taking a long, hard road, I now knew better.

I loved that dog, and letting him go to his new owner, a handicapped woman named MJ, was one of the hardest things I've ever had to do in my life. He had grown from an untrained puppy into an excellent service dog. In the morning, he would come out of his crate totally happy and full of energy. He wagged his tail and wiggled his butt. He'd pick up a bone or toy to show it to me. He always snorted. I would miss that snort more than anything else.

He was my heart, my joy, and my serenity. But Tory gave MJ something I didn't have—freedom. I knew I had done right. I had helped another. Tory also gave her friendship. I tried not to be selfish, because she needed him even more than I did. But when he left, I cried so hard. Mrs. Ruth found me and gave me a big hug. A woman named Nola videotaped Tory's first meeting with MJ, and their connection was close immediately. It warmed my heart to see them working and bonding together. Still, there was emptiness in my heart that took a long time to subside. This time, though, my heart didn't harden. And I knew I would be okay.

I agreed to train more dogs. I was good at this job, and I lived for it. I trained numerous dogs during the following years of incarceration, and each one taught me a specific lesson.

For example, Nelson, Tory's little brother, taught me how to survive graciously. When he was in a puppy home—a volunteer was keeping him—he was attacked and nearly killed by another dog. I took to him immediately, scars and all. I begged the C.H.A.M.P. staff for the opportunity to train him to help me get over the loss of Tory. Nelson not only survived, he thrived. He made me realize I didn't need to control my future again. Things turn out okay; everything is in God's hands.

Shadow, like Tory, taught me the power of forgiveness. C.H.A.M.P. rescued him after his owner died. He was a stray, hanging around his master's home, when a neighbor shot him. Even with a bullet in his leg, he still loved humans. I needed to learn to still love people, and I did.

Thor taught me patience, humor, and acceptance. He was one goofy golden retriever. He liked to play all the time; training him was often futile. Accepting him for who he was—instead of who I wanted him to be—set me free.

Another Good-bye

Sabrina had been my best friend, my roommate, and my partner in crime for more than a decade. Sometimes we had been close; other times, we drifted apart. But we had always been there for each other. She had my back if I needed anything—from a shoulder to a cigarette. We had trained dogs together through the C.H.A.M.P. program. Selfishly, I hated the thought of being in prison without her. At the same time, I truly wanted her to have a good life. I wanted her future to be wonderful and fulfilling.

Sabrina was getting her chance. Even though she had a life sentence like I did, the parole board was letting her go. I wasn't jealous about that. I was just hurt that she would no longer be a presence in my life. She could dream big, and I couldn't.

A few days before an inmate left, we always threw her a going-away party. It wasn't a party-party because we couldn't have food or drinks. But all of the person's friends would gather in the yard and give speeches or say nice things. We always waited until the last second to have the party because leaving is so emotional. When prisoners say good-bye, it's forever. Sabrina wouldn't be allowed to visit me until she had been off parole for five years. Because she had a life sentence, parole officers could keep her on parole for thirty years if they wanted to. The point was: people are often saying good-bye forever once they leave prison.

I would miss Sabrina. We all gathered and hugged her and showered her with good luck and good wishes. We asked her about her big plans. Then we went around in a circle, as we always did, and asked this question: "What would you do if you were free?"

I was the only one in our group that day who had life without parole. It only made me hate the question more. Some talked about seeing their loved ones; others wanted to open a restaurant or go to Disney World. I shrank to the back of the circle, hoping they'd pass over me. Of course, they didn't.

Sabrina pressed me because she believed I would be out one day. She said, "Come on Stacey, what do you want to do?"

"When I'm free, I want to go to Walmart," I said. That was my standard answer that made everyone laugh.

"Oh come on, you can do better than that," Sabrina said.

I felt so put on the spot. I tried not to dream about freedom much because it was too heartbreaking. But I could tell by her stubborn eyes that she wanted my answer. So I thought about the epitome of freedom.

"If I'm ever free, I want to go skydiving," I said with meaning. I wasn't scared; that's what I really wanted to do.

Everybody cheered.

Sabrina hugged me and said, "One day, you will."

Nancy Grace

Before Holden left office, I received one more call for an interview, this one from Nancy Grace. At the time, she was a reporter for the *Larry King Live* show. I knew who she was, and I was scared of her. She was mean. I told Mike and Ellen that there was absolutely no way I was going on air with that woman.

Of course, they persuaded me to change my mind.

She came out to the prison with her long, choppy, hard hair. She was as mean as I figured, and she said, "Girl, I will know if you are telling the truth or not. And if you think I'm going to put you on TV so you can sit up here and lie and weaken a prosecutor's case, then you need to think again. If you are a liar, then you deserve to be here."

I just said, "Yes, m'am" and "No m'am" like an obedient girl. The last thing I wanted was trouble with Nancy Grace. I knew I'd hold my own when I simply told the truth.

By the end of our interview at Vandalia, the hard-edged reporter was crying. She believed me. The episode aired, and I was happy with the outcome. I said I didn't understand how I ended up where I did, but that I had made mistakes. She asked me if I still saw my mom.

"Your mom is really all you have," Grace barked.

"Her and my sister," I answered.

"Do you ever blame her or wonder why she didn't save you?" Nancy asked.

"Yes. But I can't. I can't live like that. I can't have all that anger. I can't be mad at anybody. I can't be mad at my dad. I can't be mad at me. I can't be mad at her. I can't be mad at Christy. I can't be mad at my prosecutor—I just want to be free in my heart, in my body, in my mind, and in my soul."

Ellen was a guest and spoke on my behalf. To balance the story, Nancy also interviewed the prosecutor, Bob McCulloch, who went on and on about how I killed my father for his money. Ellen gently corrected each one of his statements.

I thought he looked like an ass on television, and my case looked understandable. It was becoming clearer to other people that his lack of compassion was the reason my sentence was so severe.

A hobby of mine was to make intricate afghan blankets for my friends. I didn't crochet for money anymore, but if I really liked someone, I would make them a beautiful blanket from the best yarn I could find. I sent blankets to Tom W., Christy, Mom, and my mom's friend Robyn. My mom's coworker, Robyn Merschen, had lived a traumatic life, and we became friends through the mail and phone calls. She and her husband, Ed, would come see me on food visits and bring me all kinds of yummy dishes. I made the blankets for my friends in prison and for myself.

I wanted to open up; I wanted to thank the people who'd stood by me all the years I'd been in prison. I started to want to build relationships instead of avoid them.

I'd need those relationships to pull me through. Governor Holden was about to make his decision. I was so hopeful, I almost couldn't contain myself.

Ellen and Mike held a demonstration outside his office around the end of October. Commutations are usually given out at Thanksgiving and Christmas. They got a group of my supporters together— my mom, my sister, Tom W., Ed, and other friends—and they waved signs outside of the state capitol. We all thought we were going to get it. We'd had so much positive publicity—just what his people had asked for.

Governor Holden commuted a few people's sentences, and I could barely breathe waiting to hear from him. Word never came. I didn't even get a yes or no answer. He left office, and my clemency petition had been ignored.

My heart was completely broken.

Yes or No

After I picked myself up off the floor—wasn't I at least worthy of a yes or a no?—I got back to the regular business of being an offender. I trained dogs, I taught fitness classes, and I spent time with the few people who mattered to me. Visits with my mom were still rocky sometimes, but things between us were getting smoother. After many years of figuring out life on her own, Christy was coming to see me again. Seeing Christy was always the best part—even though I worried about her.

I experienced dark moments of depression on and off. I had doubts about my fate more often than I used to. I would be watching TV and see a happy family and think *Damn, why couldn't I have that? Here I am, and I did this to myself.* Sometimes Mike would call and catch me in one of those times. He showed me more kindness than I could imagine. With his huge sense of right and wrong, he'd tell me, "Just imagine yourself floating down a river, the breeze in your hair while you're catching a fish. That will be you one day."

I trusted him. He had run for the prosecutor's office in his hometown of Houston, Missouri, a few years before. The guy running against him used me as a playing card during the campaign: "How can you elect Mike Anderson for prosecutor when he wants a murderer to go free?" Mike was very vocal during that election about my case and why it was important. He stood at podiums supporting me, and he won the election.

I had reasons to stay positive, though it wasn't easy. I had been incarcerated for fifteen daunting years by the time Governor Matt Blunt took office. During his State of the State address, I watched his facial expressions intently, searching for indications that he might set me free. I got a positive feeling about him. He stood there saying that all child abusers should get the death penalty. He seemed like the type of guy who would have sympathy for me.

During his term, Governor Blunt tried to get such a law passed in Missouri before the Supreme Court struck it down. He was serious about child abuse. He understood that molestation was horrific, and that it should no longer be swept under the table. I had more hope than ever.

One big joy in my life was Christy. She had stopped taking drugs and didn't drink much anymore. She'd quit her job at Hooters. She got married and had a daughter named Alisyn on August 4, 2006. I never had a better visit than when I held my niece for the first time.

News about Ali was a highlight of my life as time dragged on, sometimes quickly and sometimes slowly. Prison was no longer fun or adventurous. It was the same old thing with the same old offenders year after year. I wasn't trying to find my way anymore, but I was noticing big changes in myself.

I was healing. In those last three years, I stopped asking why my father raped my sister and me. I forgave him. I started to be kinder to myself. I started to feel I was worthy of a real life, a life outside these prison walls.

There are three things you find in prison. First, you find God. Second, you find forgiveness. Third, you find yourself. I was lucky to find all three. I told God that I was not happy about my predicament, but wherever He placed me, I would do what I could to make a difference. If I needed to go public, I would go public. If He wanted me to train dogs, I'd train dogs. Where God decided to lead me, I would follow.

But I truly hoped He'd lead me out those doors. I hoped for that more than anything else.

Governor Blunt's term was ending at the end of 2008, and he was not running for reelection. I was antsy all year long. He had my new and improved clemency package. We received no word from his advisors; they wouldn't communicate with us except to tell us they were aware of me and my case.

This was going to be it. I could almost feel it. It had to work this time. The governor-elect, a man named Jay Nixon, was a political buddy of my naysayer, the prosecutor Bob McCulloch. If my sentence didn't get commuted this time, I would have to wait four—probably eight—more years for a more sympathetic governor. I would probably be forty-three years old before I got another chance to get out.

It would be putting it lightly to say I got my hopes up.

Thanksgiving of 2008 came and went with no word. I called Ellen, and she sounded just as disappointed as me when she said, "Let's just wait. Give him till Christmas."

Christmas arrived, and Governor Blunt commuted a few sentences. My name was not on his list. Neither Ellen nor Mike had heard a peep from his office. New Year's Eve only brought more silence. I did not get a yes or no from the governor. I wasn't even worthy of an answer.

For about a week, I was the maddest person. I was like, *Okay, this is my life. And nobody even cares enough to tell me yes or no.* I was more upset about not hearing anything because it made me feel so useless, so small. Then I looked around me—at the cement block walls and the nauseating pink bathroom tiles—and I wondered if I was ready for more. Could I take incarceration another day?

I had done good things in the prison system. I had made small differences while locked up. I wanted to make a difference in the real world. I felt ready. There was so much more my soul needed to share and experience. It was hard to keep pushing myself when I was stuck on one square mile of land.

I wasn't going to get clemency. Prison was going to be the rest of my life. It hurt so bad. My soul ached that this was all my life would ever be. I started to experience true self-pity, the kind I hadn't felt since I first got to Gumbo. I was bitter—angry even—about all that was not going to happen to me.

I couldn't even take a razor with me to shower number three because I knew I might get weak and make the long slashes up and down my wrists. I used an electric razor instead. I lived this way for about four days. I sat on my metal bed, and I thought, *I can't live life like this. Every moment can't continue to be a waking hell.* Every time my mind turned to suicide, I asked God to please just let it end.

My friend Chris Sitka sent me a poem that I read over and over. It was written by an anonymous author and called "Things I Hope for You." It stated:

> *I wish for you to be the sun and the moon and the stars.*
> *I hope that you never destroy your whole self when parts of you are hurting.*

I should keep myself whole if I could. I would focus on the sun and stars, and I would tell myself that I still have those things. I'm still here, and there's still something to live for.

I reminded myself that I still had some choices. I could decide what color socks to wear. I could wear my hair up or down. I could decide what I wanted to eat for lunch and breakfast. Every moment in my life was a choice. In knowing I had choices—I could choose how I was going to feel day to day—I started to ponder true freedom. I could be free if I wanted to; the rest was just geography.

God left Moses out in the desert for forty years. I told God that I was ready, too. But the truth was, we don't tell God anything. He tells us. I wasn't happy about my plight in prison, but I had found my salvation there. I couldn't become any more free than that.

My desperate fog started to lift.

I had a dream. I saw the grapevines that surrounded our white picket fence when we first moved into the house in Alhambra. The vines were gorgeous and produced beautiful grapes that my mother used to make jelly. I felt so much happiness in that dream. Then the vines slowly deteriorated, rotting away due to neglect. What was once lush and green became brown and decayed and broken in many places. I felt such sadness and grief. Then I heard a voice: *Do not be sad, those were not your vines to tend. You will have your own vines and if you tend them, they will be beautiful.* My dream put my life in perspective. I was not responsible for my childhood, but I was responsible for myself as an adult. I wanted to tend my vines.

After one of the darkest weeks of my life, I let everything go. I was done. I had forgiven my mom, my dad, and myself. I had life without parole. I could either hate myself because of the choices I'd made, or I could forgive myself. I decided it was time. I was truly forgiven, I decided, and it was done. I gave myself forever to God. I asked him to direct me because I sure as hell hadn't done a good job of directing myself. I surrendered. I felt relieved when I let go of all control.

Then it dawned on me that I was already free. For the first time ever in my life, I experienced peace. I remember what it felt like to breathe easily. I chose life, whatever that might be.

And I was free.

Another Kind of Freedom

The first week of the New Year had passed. I got a message through the officers that Ellen needed to talk to me, and I was to call her the next day at 3 p.m. I thought it couldn't be anything important. She was just checking in on me to see if I was okay. Everyone—Mom, Christy, Tom W.—had been calling or visiting to make sure I was all right since Christmas, when we knew it was over.

I called her on a Wednesday—no big deal.

"Hi, Stacey," Ellen said.

"I just want you to know I'm okay. I'm disappointed, but I'm okay," I shared immediately. Ellen was always worried about me, and the last thing I needed her to do was call the prison and tell them I needed observation. Suicide observation—stripped nearly naked in a padded cell—was the last thing I could handle. So I acted almost cheerful on the phone.

Ellen cut me off. She said, "Stacey, it's not over."

"What?" I had no idea what she was talking about. I did *not* want to get my hopes up.

"Governor Blunt's office called me, and they're investigating your petition. They've already talked to Detective Schulte, and we should find something out on Monday."

I told her thank you. We hung up, and I couldn't breathe.

When I went back to my room, an officer was there helping pack up one of my roommates who was moving back to Chilli. I looked like I'd been run over by a car. I wanted to cry so badly, but I couldn't let the officer or the other inmates see me upset. I had to maintain a straight face that said everything was okay. I sat down.

I looked up, and two caseworkers were in my room wanting to know what was going on. I told them I didn't know, but I might still get an answer on my clemency petition soon. I told myself, *Don't lose it; don't lose it; don't lose it.*

I went to take a shower so I could bawl my eyes out. I needed the release. As soon as I found peace, I found out I might get set free. It was absolutely too good to be true.

I wasn't expecting to hear anything else until Monday, so I tried to calm myself down. It was no easy task. Then three days later, on Saturday, I was sitting on my bed at count time—just what I was supposed to be doing—reading a magazine about the tragic death of John Travolta's son. Over the speaker system, my name was called to the rotunda.

That was unusual. I thought, *Great, I wasn't sitting the right way on my bed during count, and now I'm going to get in trouble.*

When I arrived, an officer told me there was a call for me in the rotunda on the prison phone. That made me nervous, because we're not allowed to receive calls on the rotunda telephone. It was the shift captain on the other end of the phone.

"You want me to do what? And isn't it count time?" I was institutionalized. I didn't like varying from the protocol. I was stunned.

Then the captain said, "Stacey, write down this phone number, then hand the rotunda phone to the officer so I can tell him it's okay. Then go use the collect phone."

All of a sudden, I was in a can't-function mode. This kind of thing happens only when a family member dies. I handed the receiver back to the officer, I walked into the phone room, closed the door, and made my call.

All the women were in their rooms for count, and they were listening in the hallway because I got called to the rotunda. I dialed and reached Ellen.

Ellen answered, yelling, "Stacey!" She couldn't breathe, let alone form words. "We got it!"

"Really?" I said, not knowing if my heart was still in my chest. I laid my head on the little table and started bawling. Sobbing. Trying to control my emotions was of no use.

Ellen cried, too. She'd been waiting sixteen years for this news. "He commuted you to twenty years," Ellen said.

"I don't understand. We were just asking for parole to be added at some point in my life."

Ellen interrupted me. "This means immediate release. The order was given for twenty years but with *immediate* release."

Even under the best of circumstances, I thought I'd get the possibility of parole, and then I'd have to wait at least six months to go before the parole board. I couldn't really fathom it. What she was saying was too good to be true.

She said she didn't understand all of the details herself. She would call me later in the evening to discuss it.

I hung up the phone. I couldn't call anyone else. I closed the door and walked down the green mat into the main hallway where everyone was looking at me. I went into the bathroom. Shelley met me there. As soon as I saw her, I started crying. I hugged her and told her what had happened. She started bawling, too. Within a few minutes, twenty-five women were in the bathroom with me. Some were crying, others were cheering.

An officer called me to the rotunda and asked me what had just happened.

"I just received commutation!"

He shrugged his shoulders like, "Oh well," and waved me back to my room.

In my room, I fell into child's pose with my head on the floor. I sobbed like I had never sobbed before. No one had ever seen me do that. But this time, everyone could hear me, and I didn't care. I couldn't hold myself back.

A girl, Delilah, whose room was kitty-corner to mine, said, "You cry, girl."

As soon as count cleared and I got myself together, the next thing I did was call Christy. She was hysterical with happiness and relief.

Fruit Salad

I had six days until I left. It might as well have been six minutes. On the day I got out, January 16, 2009, Ellen was to pick me up at 8:30 a.m. I chose the early time because other prisoners were getting out that day, too, and I didn't want to hold them up if there were reporters outside. Just after 6 a.m., I took a shower; then I planned to go to breakfast and say good-bye to everybody. But at 7:10 a.m., the captain said I had to leave. I was still fixing my hair, and I told him I wasn't ready. Then I was like, *Okay, who cares? I'm outta here.*

Apparently, media crews were crawling all over the place. The officers wanted to get me out of Vandalia before my story created a circus.

There was a part of me that wasn't ready to go. The release wasn't what I had been expecting. I hadn't had time to wrap my mind around actually going. I felt a moment of panic. I was leaving everything I'd known for the last eighteen years of my life. I was leaving my safety zone and my beautiful dog Emma. And not only was I going, they were hurrying up to kick me out.

I told myself, *You can do this. You can do this.*

I didn't even have a coat. Oddly, I walked from my room to the reception area where they release inmates wearing my grays. It was so quiet. No one was up and out yet. The yard didn't open until 8 a.m. I thought, *I'm never going to have to walk down that path again.*

I started to feel excited. Ellen was there. Only one person was allowed to pick me up, and I thought it was appropriate she be the one. She had brought the street clothes that Christy had given her.

I changed into them in the bathroom in the reception area. I didn't want to wear anything I'd owned inside once I got out. I gave away all of my property except my ratty, much-loved teddy bear and a few photos and poems. I sent those to Christy's house before my release. I walked out with nothing. Literally.

Whenever we interacted in public, we had to wear our grays, and this was the first time in eighteen years I had worn street clothes. I was not immediately identifiable as #85704.

I had on Christy's teal sweater and her jeans. I was not used to the new style of jeans that sat so low on my waist. I wore her black leather jacket and a pair of chunky black boots with heels. I hadn't worn a heel in I don't know how long, and I was afraid I might stumble out the door. But I walked out with my head held five feet, two inches high. It was all utterly surreal.

They made Ellen drive up to the carport and secured the gate behind her car, a green Oldsmobile. So when I got into her car, I was still in prison. She was nervous, too, because for those fleeting moments, we were both locked down.

Then the staff opened the chain-link gate. I held my breath. Newspaper and TV crews lined the sides of the road.

Ellen patted my knee as she drove.

"I'm okay," I said. "Let's go! Let's go!"

My mother was in her car on the other side of the gates, and she followed Ellen's car.

Ellen and I had planned to meet my sister a few blocks away at a restaurant called The Rose. We had called the restaurant a few days in advance to let them know we—and God only knew who else—would be coming. Everyone was there—Mike, Mom, Tom W., Robyn and Ed, my cousin Becky, and others.

The first thing I did was hug my mother—it was the first time I really meant it in twelve years. We knew we had a chance together, an opportunity. Our relationship may never be exactly what I want it to be; we had all made mistakes. But I was glad she was there.

Reporters asked me tons of questions while I tried to say hello to my friends and family. It was impossible to decompress. The restaurant had asked what I wanted to eat when we made the reservations, and I said a fruit salad. The ladies who volunteered at the prison leading our Bible study were the ones who brought it out for me. I started crying. I was too excited to eat, but I loved staring at my order—we had so little fresh fruit in prison.

I went to the bathroom for some privacy, but didn't know how to use it. Mom came in and explained the automated toilets and faucets. Even the towel dispenser was electronic. Tom W. handed me a GoPhone, one of those temporary prepaid cell phones. He wanted me to give out a temporary number to the press, so they wouldn't be able to reach me so easily later.

After our big breakfast, Mike Anderson drove me part of the way to the highway, about five miles. I was headed a few hours away to Arnold, Missouri, to stay with Christy, her husband Brian, and their baby Ali. He put on a CD of Josh Groban and pointed out a bald eagle that flew overhead. He gave me a lecture and $1,200.

"You're free now; make your own choices," he said. "You wanted this opportunity, so don't let it go to waste. Don't ever let anyone put you down."

He told me the money was what people had sent him on my behalf over the years. I ended up using $700 of it for my first car. I thanked him over and over.

Then I switched cars again. I got into Christy and Brian's SUV. It was Brian's birthday, and he joked, "How many men do you know that get a sister-in-law for their present?"

Christy sat in the backseat with me and kept touching me on the shoulder, making sure I was real. We were so happy. Then I asked if we could stop at a gas station with an express mart. I wanted to go in.

"Do you want me to go with you?" Christy asked.

"No, I want to do this by myself." Everyone had been showing me things for an hour and a half. I wanted to feel free, to be Miss Independent. I wanted a pack of gum.

Gum was contraband because offenders could use it to gum up

locks. If we got caught with it, we'd get a violation. Sometimes an officer would sneak us some, but I'd be so paranoid, I could hardly chew it. So it meant a lot to me to buy my own real gum.

I walked in thinking the clerk wouldn't want to serve me. Maybe he'd know I was a prisoner and tell me to get out. I felt like Offender Lannert 85704. Surely, he knew my numbers, too. As it turned out, he barely looked at me, and I bought two packs of chewing gum without a hitch.

I didn't even chew any. I just put it in my pocket and rubbed it every so often thinking, *This is mine.*

Men

I spent my first full day of freedom in Christy's apartment while they were both at work. It was great, and it was weird. I didn't have anywhere to go because I didn't have a car yet. I cleaned and did all of her laundry. I sat in front of her computer all day researching anything and everything on the Internet.

After work hours, my friends—many, like Sabrina, had been released—came and picked me up. All of these people called and stopped by. It was just so much fun. It hadn't yet sunk in that I wasn't a prisoner.

My old friend Roberta had been out for a while, and she invited me to live with her in Pevely, just twenty-five minutes away from my sister. I would have loved to stay with Christy, but her apartment was small, and she had a grown-up life to live. Roberta's house was big, with an extra bedroom in the walk-out basement, so I accepted her offer. She was a good influence on me. She had opened her own hair salon and gotten back together with her husband. She was taking good care of her two kids. They rescued animals, so there were kittens and dogs and rabbits everywhere in her spotlessly clean home.

Every night, Roberta and I spent thirty minutes talking about groundedness, and how much I needed it. She was the amazing person I needed at the time I needed it most.

Ed and his boss, Charlie, helped me get a car, an old beat-up Honda that I loved even though it looked like hell. Charlie's son,

Dustin, worked on it every other week to keep it running. Tom W. eventually got me my own cell phone connected to his plan so it wouldn't cost me that much. Things with Tom W. were great, but we had no expectations. We still loved each other dearly—but this time, in a more adult kind of way. He had a longtime girlfriend he knew from our high school. He was happy, and I didn't want to interfere. I wasn't ready for anything serious with anyone, and I cherished our close friendship. It was enough.

I started meeting guys and dating one or two, but that was very difficult. Even though I was thirty-six, I still knew nothing about men—nothing healthy anyway.

Shortly after coming home, I wanted to visit Dad's graveside. Christy must've read my mind because she called me the day I was thinking about it. She asked if I had anything to do. I told her my thoughts.

She said she would go with me, and she picked me up.

It was so hard seeing his name on a tombstone in a cemetery in St. Louis. The guilt of knowing he was there because of me was overwhelming. I shook and cried. So did she.

Although this was the family cemetery plot, I begged Christy to never lay me there to rest. She agreed and asked for the same consideration.

I never forgot all of the pain that led to July 4, 1990. I never, ever forgot my own guilt. But I forgave him, and I forgave myself. He was my father, and he was supposed to protect me. He did protect me from most things—just not from himself.

I regretted that my father would never have the opportunity to change as I had changed. But I hoped that the good side of him would have forgiven me for what I did. I hoped that he would have been proud of the woman I had become.

I will always be his daughter, after all.

———

While I was in prison I met a man named Elliot Freeman, six-teen years my senior. He had visited me once as part of the Out-reach program many years ago. We reconnected when I got out and started dating. He owned an aikido studio in St. Louis, and he was very patient and understanding. He was good for me in so many ways. All my life, I have wanted real intimacy and close-ness. I hoped it wouldn't be tainted by my past, but sometimes it was. I felt like I deserved love and sex just like everyone else, but it was harder for me. The first time I had sex with Elliot, I left the next morning without speaking to him for a month. His scent over-powered me. I had something of his I needed to return, so I even-tually called him to tell him I was stopping by. He asked why I ran away.

I said, "Your smell was too much for me. Too musky."

"Well, Stacey, we can always go shopping. I'll let you pick out co-logne and body wash that you like," Elliot said.

So we went to Bath & Body Works, and we've been together ever since.

I could give myself to him, but I couldn't snuggle afterward. I would smell something that reminded me of the past, and I would just get up and shower. I still had a lot to work through.

But I cared about Elliot, and I wanted to work through things with him. It was a tender balance because I wanted to be around the strength that a man has; I wanted to be able to lean into it. At the same time, I didn't want that strength to dominate me like it had before. Elliot was great for me. He was a very strong man—strong enough to be gentle.

I couldn't commit to anything complicated, so I called him Mr. Right Now.

When I said that, he replied, "You know, fifteen years ago, you would've destroyed me." He insinuated that only a mature person could really handle me. He was probably right.

———

Mike made good on his promise that I would ride down the water with the wind blowing in my hair. On a gorgeous summer day, he and his wife took me to Big Piney River, which looks more like a creek. They wouldn't even let me paddle. I was instructed to sit back and enjoy. The sun touched my face while fish jumped around the boat. Crickets chirped, and the birds sang.

Facing Freedom

trained a few friends' dogs. I had enough money because Roberta gave me a place to live. Everyone—Mom, Christy, Tom W.—gave me the things I needed right out of prison. I drove around in my beater of a car.

I had never experienced happiness like that. I was free.

When I thought things couldn't get much better, I received a phone call from *The Oprah Winfrey Show*. After much back and forth, they decided they wanted me to appear for my own half-hour segment.

I usually didn't get nervous about the press anymore. I had done *Nancy Grace* again—this time on her own show—after getting out and hadn't batted an eye. This time was different. This was big. I actually had to go shopping for nice clothes, a blue button-down shirt and black dress pants. All Oprah wanted was for me to share my story, and that was my wish, too.

I had started a Web site—now a not-for-profit—called Healing Sisters (www.healingsisters.org) with the mission of eradicating child sexual abuse. If I can't eradicate it, at least I can shed some light on the matter. When Governor Blunt released me, his letter said:

"Stacey, this is your chance to have a positive impact in society and to make a difference in the lives of others. I feel sure that you will use this opportunity to help those that might benefit from the perspective you have gained over the difficult course of your life. Best of luck to you in the future."

I had to do *Oprah*, and I wanted to. She and Maya Angelou had been guiding lights for me for many years because they were so open about their own pasts. So with much fanfare, I boarded that plane from St. Louis to Chicago. I stayed at the ritzy Omni Hotel and used the food vouchers Harpo Productions had given me. I felt like royalty, especially when I got my makeup and hair done in the green room.

I went onto her stage and sat on a comfortable high chair. Oprah sat across from me wearing a black sequined shirt. She played a video of my backstory that almost made me teary. She showed photos of Christy and me when we were kids. She showed photos of my father. Then she asked how I was doing.

I don't remember everything I said—just that I was sorry for what I'd done, and I hoped others would speak up when they were being hurt. I said that child abuse cannot be tolerated, and no one else should make the mistakes I made. People who are abused think of killing their abuser, and while there is power in that thought, the act is actually cowardly. True strength lies in being able to tell the truth about what happened. Abuse is shrouded in darkness because that is mainly where it takes place and where people like to keep it. If we expose sexual abuse to the light of day, we can change it. We can end it. We can expose how ugly it really is.

Oprah nodded her head.

She asked me if my sister knew.

I said, "No, and I felt like I was protecting Christy by taking the sexual abuse in some strange way."

Oprah said, "I understand that."

I leaned forward, closer to her.

She went on. "I really do. I really do." And then she smiled at me.

I was validated, completely. From that moment, I let go of a lifetime of having to defend my thoughts, feelings, and actions. I didn't have to do that anymore.

In front of the world, Oprah Winfrey understood me.

For the first time, I felt redeemed.

Bonds

Mom and I had a huge fight around the time I started doing publicity. She believes she did not know that I was being sexually abused. She still feels terrible every day of her life for letting me down. She admits she made mistakes. After all, she is human. But she says she wasn't aware of the abuse at the time.

She did not like my insinuating on air that, yes, she did know what was happening to me.

I laid the groundwork for our relationship right then and there. I said, "You're going to have to accept how I see the past, and what I say about the past."

She was quiet. She had been crying.

She finally said, "You're going to have to accept me for who I am."

So we agreed to disagree. She could have her view, and I was entitled to mine. We could spend our lifetimes being right and making the other person wrong, but then we wouldn't have each other.

In my mind, Mom is just like me. She wanted what I wanted: happily ever after with a knight in shining armor—plus a couple of kids. I don't want that now, but I did growing up. We bought into the same fairy tale. Both of our fairy tales went unspeakably wrong. But when it comes right down to it, she wanted somebody to love after her divorce. She spent her life looking for happiness, made choices and sacrifices, and did the best she could with what she knew. And she saved herself, which is kind of important. But since the crime, she's been there when I needed her. She moved back from Guam. She chose to side with me even though her family disowned her. She sent me money in prison, and she and John visited me regularly—even when I wasn't nice to them. She has been trying to right wrongs for a long time.

For our first Mother's Day together in eighteen years, we sat down and talked over a wonderful lunch. I found the perfect card that said:

"Even though we struggle, I love you." Inside it read, "I only get one mother in this life and need to be thankful that I have one. I am."

When I got out, I worried that people in St. Louis wouldn't accept me, a convicted felon. I guessed that people wouldn't want to be in my company, and surely they wouldn't want their children to be around me. My release had been all over the news, even before I went on *Oprah*. For a few months, I noticed a lot of whispers and points when I went about life at the mall or grocery store or Taco Bell or wherever.

Because I had only prison identification, one of the first things I did was go to the Social Security Administration office to get a card. I gave the worker my birth certificate and prison ID.

She said, "You look so sweet. What on earth could you have done?"

I said, "Well, I murdered my father who sexually abused me."

She just looked at me for a minute. I think she recognized me, and she smiled. She gave me a temporary card so I could get my driver's license, and she said, "You come right back here, and I'll help you get started."

When I returned in a few hours to pick up the permanent card, she wouldn't even let me wait in line. She handed me my Social Security card, saying, "Good luck to you. Good luck."

After my *Oprah* episode aired, I was even more worried. I had just started teaching step classes at a large local gym and was afraid I might get fired.

Apparently, one of the personal trainers was pointing me out, saying, "That person killed somebody."

Another trainer, my friend, told him, "Then I'd do everything she said if I were in her class."

I was surprised when I got so much support from the members of my classes. They smiled at me and waved. I was embarrassed but pleased. Women would follow me into the bathroom and say, "You're that girl."

I'd say, "Yes, yes I am."

Over and over, I heard the words: "Honey, I'm so glad you're home."

On May 28, 2009, I turned thirty-seven as a free woman. It was just a day; I didn't expect much. After all, I already had the best present I could ever dream up.

But when I walked into Elliot's house near downtown St. Louis, I was truly surprised. He had gathered all of the friends and people I loved in one place. I cannot describe how touching and special it was. My mother, sister, Tom W., and many others were crammed into his house, laughing, talking, eating, and drinking.

We just celebrated; there was so much to be thankful for.

That surprise party summed up why I fell in love with Elliot Freeman. We had just started dating then, but with that party he did something so meaningful—and labor intensive—for me. I realized he was a wonderful man to give me exactly what I had been missing for the past eighteen years—or longer—of my life.

After the party, I was cleaning inside, and he was working in the backyard. I remember looking out the window and seeing him there watering his plants.

I thought, *Wow. I love this man.*

He made me happy; he listened; he made me laugh. He irritated me sometimes, but I had learned things couldn't be sweet without a little bitter. I knew I needed to make a choice after that party. Either I needed to be with him or leave him—wholeheartedly.

I had been calling him Mr. Right Now, and I decided to stop that. I wasn't sure if he was Mr. Right, but I knew I loved him. I decided to stay and to love him with all that was inside of me. He was a good man, and not loving him would hurt me.

A few months later, I accepted when he invited me to move in.

Little Things

Christy came over to our house, and she saw a bunch of old photo albums sitting on my coffee table. I was getting them out for research on this book. She picked up the one with the red cover.

"Are you sure you want to look at those?" I asked her.

"Yes." She was still as determined as ever. She flipped through and laughed at the photos of us as kids. In one I'm dressed in a Raggedy Ann dress, and she's dolled up in a Mickey Mouse outfit—presents from Grandma Lannert.

Then she turned the page and landed on a photo of Dad. She closed the album and put it down.

I gave her a hug. "It's just a picture, Christy. He can't hurt us anymore."

She said, "You're in a different place than I am."

I understood. She remembers only all the bad parts of Tom Lannert—the smacks, cursing, and violence. He was an evil man, but I also remember the good parts of him. Christy doesn't want her daughter to know anything about Tom. I don't try to be Christy's puppet master; I just stand there beside her. I don't walk in front of someone who might not follow, as the poem goes.

I'm thankful that she's finally seeing a therapist. I wish only freedom and happiness for her. In the meantime, she has me.

Today, little things like coffee make me unbelievably happy. In prison, I could only get instant coffee in a Styrofoam cup. My mornings now are wonderful, filled with that rich aroma of a fresh pot I brewed myself. My healing ritual has always been to be outside and watch the sun. Sometimes I'll drink my coffee during the sunrise. It reminds me how everything is renewed. Tomorrow will always come.

I spend my days working on my Web site for Healing Sisters, a registered nonprofit organization that I hope will help other survivors. I go on the site to tell my stories, and I invite everyone else to tell theirs, too. I want to bring sexual abuse out of the darkness and into the light. That's the only way to end this epidemic. One in four girls are sexually molested in the United States today. Former governor Matt Blunt called on me to make a difference, and I hope to fulfill this promise.

I speak on college campuses about what I've been through, spreading my message to anyone who will listen. We talk about the signs that are easily missed and the consequences of making wrong choices. I just don't want anyone to feel trapped like I did; I don't want anyone to walk the same path. There is hope. It's even more true today than when I was a kid: there are organizations and people who care and will help a child who is sexually abused. I hope Healing Sisters grows into that kind of helpful place. I want others to feel the love and support that people have given me.

I stay busy. I teach ten aerobics classes a week. My favorite is butts and guts. I am starting to do more personal training, too. I love pushing my students to their limits and helping them reach their goals.

I still help the C.H.A.M.P. staff when they call me. I sometimes take in their dogs for a few weeks. I've even volunteered for their fund-raisers. Of course, now I have my own dog, too. His name is Coletrane.

My ultimate goal is to go back to school and get my degree. I have to save some money first. I'd like to become a psychologist—working with women who are overcoming their pasts.

Just before my thirty-eighth birthday, I had an idea. But I didn't want to go at it alone. I called my friend Toni to run it by her.

"I am going to get you a present, but I need your permission first," I said. It was almost her birthday, too.

She didn't say anything, so I went on. "I would really like to go skydiving, and I thought you might enjoy it." Skydiving, to me, was the epitome of freedom.

I took her silence as a no. Then all of a sudden she said, "Sure, why not?"

I found a place nearby called Fly Free Skydiving. I told my old friend Sabrina about my plans. She wanted to come, too.

So a few days later, we all drove down there separately for our big jump. I thought for sure they would chicken out. But they showed up, and they didn't look scared. For some reason, only two jumpers were allowed on the plane at a time. So I let them go first; I wanted them to be able to jump together. I watched the small rickety plane climb high into the air for twenty minutes. One at a time, my friends floated out.

They landed with the biggest smiles I'd ever seen. I wanted some of that.

I got into the plane with the crewmember. You have to fly tandem with someone strapped to your back on your first jump. My guy was cool; the plane was not. It crept higher and higher into the air while I looked down. I noticed a huge white cross up on a hill in a private residence. The cross got smaller and smaller. It was the only focal point I had. No matter what, I felt like I could keep my eye on God and know my place on—or above—the earth.

When we got to 10,500 feet, he opened the door. You don't jump out; you roll out. The guy strapped to me said, "Right foot out, left foot out, head back!"

Boom. We tumbled out of the plane. Then we were floating in air. I didn't feel a rush of wind. I didn't feel like I was falling. Instead, the earth was amazingly beautiful. The clouds were right next to me.

"I'm going to pull the chute," the guy said.

Our parachute opened, and the floating sensation was taken away and replaced by something slower and more graceful.

He said, "Do you want to spin?"

"Yes!"

I pulled the cord like he told me, and we did circles.

"Do you want to spin again?"

"No," I said. I just wanted to drift down to the ground. The whole time, the cross kept getting larger and larger. I felt like I was in God's hands. I jumped with total trust and faith that I was going to be okay.

ACKNOWLEDGMENTS

STACEY LANNERT

I am forever in debt to Detective Tom Schulte for going against the grain and speaking out. Thank you.

C.H.A.M.P., Inc. (Canine Helpers Allow More Possibilities) changed my life, and I am grateful. Thank you, Janet Cole, Mary Ruth, Nola Ewers, and Dianne Peters for being first role models and now friends.

I could not have taken this journey without my coauthor Kristen Kemp. Thank you for helping put into words my triumphs and my nightmares. My soul is free because you found my voice. Thank you for gently nudging me to places I did not want to go and for the friendship that led me through the darkness.

I would also like to thank my family who have traveled the ravaged ocean of my life and are still onboard: Mom, John, Christy, my brother-in-law Brian, and my cousins Beka and Nicolette. Thank you for showing me the true meaning of family—for being there no matter what. Christy and Brian, thank you for bringing my beautiful niece into this world and for sharing her with the rest of us.

Elliot Freeman is the man I choose to share my life with, and I cannot thank him enough for his gentleness, patience, and strength. Elliot, you are wonderful, and I truly love you.

While we can never choose our family, we can always choose our friends. The following people are the family of my heart:

Robyn and Ed Merschen: Thank you, Robyn, for your friendship. You kept me sane with our hundreds of phone calls that helped me stand strong. Thank you, Ed, for all the food visits and Scrabble games. I love you both.

Tom Wilson and his family: Thank you for standing beside me. You will always have a special place in my heart and in my life. I don't know who I would be without you.

Jim and Janine Gelker: Thank you for opening your hearts and family to me and for sharing the best dogs in the world, Fozzie and Maddie.

The Swederskas: Thank you for making room for one more.

Kristy Wolske: My newest friend who takes me shopping and is brutally honest about what looks good and what doesn't.

Shawn Fischer: Thank you for your time and help. You're a great reader.

Chris Peanick: Thank you for being there for me—always—with your quiet strength and total love.

Toni Sullivan: You helped me redefine my life, and I am grateful every day.

Bino and Rick: Thank you for just being you and sharing all that you have with me. I love you more than you will ever know.

Sabrina Kinsey: Thank you for being the sister God forgot to give me.

Tanya Goings: You will always be in my thoughts and in my heart. Your star burned bright, if not for long. Thank you for lighting up my life.

Shelley Fossel: You are the one person left behind, but you are never forgotten. I look forward to the time when you will join us soon for your new life. Hang in there, and I will be here when you come home.

I mustn't forget six special people who started out as supporters and have become friends. I would not be free without Chris Sitka, Graham McAllister, Jean Hensley Besner, Robert Hegadorn, Dr. David Camp, and Kristi Knotts. Your time and dedication will always be remembered and appreciated, but it's your friendship that will be treasured.

I would also like to thank Rachel Cohn, who helped guide us down the publishing path and who put up with me during my first glass of champagne. Boy, those bubbles worked fast.

Thank you, Gina Kirkland and Carrie Campbell at Kirkland Productions, my lecture agents, for giving me the opportunity to enlighten college youths about the devastation abuse causes and how to spot it. Thank you for having faith in me.

Our editor, Julia Pastore, has been gracious, understanding, and wonderful to work with. Thank you for your patience and for helping me share my life in a way that I hope is healing and inspiring.

Dorian Karchmar: Thank you for believing in me and helping us to find the perfect home for *Redemption*.

To all of the people who offered understanding and support, thank you from the bottom of my heart. You helped give me strength when I did not have enough of my own.

This book is for everyone who has suffered or is still suffering. My greatest wish is that you find freedom through forgiveness, faith, and most of all, happiness. My transformation did not occur when I was alone. I had to open up and accept help to come alive again. By standing and speaking together, we can all become free.

My life has been difficult but it has been blessed. My greatest gift has been my faith, and I thank God for it every day.

KRISTEN KEMP

Writing this book was like taking a journey. I took a lot of people along with me. Many thanks go to Dorian Karchmar at William Morris, who believed in us from the first second. I am also grateful to Julia Pastore at Random House for her kindness and brilliance as she edited. Thanks to my friend and fellow author Rachel Cohn, who took so much time to listen and to make awesome things happen. I'm grateful also for the unrelenting support of my mentors, Naomi Wolf, and Wende Jager-Hyman of the Woodhull Institute for Ethical

Leadership. Thanks also go to Angel Williams and all of my friends at New York Sports Club in Montclair; I appreciated your daily words of encouragement. Through the most difficult moments in the writing process, my husband, Johan Svenson, showed only love and patience. I love you, I thank you, and I owe you. I thank my three children for their smiles and hugs.

And to Stacey: I finally understand that anything is possible because I met you. For the rest of my life, I will carry your light and your inspiration with me. I am forever changed by my steady, meaningful, and compassionate collaboration with you. You have all of my love and support as you go forward with your next amazing chapters.

ABOUT THE AUTHORS

STACEY LANNERT is a writer, speaker, and fitness instructor. In 2009 Stacey was released from prison where she served eighteen years for fatally shooting the man who raped her from age eight through eighteen. That man was her father. Stacey never lost her ability to love life and learn from it even though she was sentenced to life without parole. The governor of Missouri granted her clemency in 2009, and within six days, she walked out of the prison gates. Stacey had been granted her physical freedom; it was the ultimate act of forgiveness.

Though locked up, Stacey was already emotionally free. Through the power of love and forgiveness, she created a meaningful life for herself from behind bars. She helped troubled teens find strength to tell their stories of abuse through a program called Outreach. She even helped some of them prosecute their abusers. Stacey also trained therapy dogs for handicapped people through the nonprofit organization C.H.A.M.P. While making the world a better place, she was also focused on forgiving.

Filled with compassion, hope, humility, and even wit, Stacey travels the country to share her story with college students. Her topics of discussion include how to spot sexual and emotional abuse and what to do about it; the importance of speaking up, telling the truth, and never being ashamed of who you are; the power of hope, forgiveness, and helping others; and how the legal system deals with sexual abuse and women.

In May 2009, Stacey brought her message to 40 million people when she spoke for thirty minutes on *The Oprah Winfrey Show*. Stacey has also appeared on *Nancy Grace, 20/20, Larry King Live, The Montel*

Williams Show, and many other programs. She has created a popular, active, nonprofit organization and Web site called HealingSisters.org with a message to help other victims however she can. Stacey can share her story. She believes that no one is a victim—no matter what she's been through. As we work on ourselves and work to heal the world, we can all become victors.

She lives in St. Louis, Missouri.

KRISTEN KEMP started writing at age sixteen. Her articles have appeared in *Glamour, Self, Men's Health,* and many other publications. She has written fifteen young-adult books for Scholastic, her most recent is titled *Breakfast at Bloomingdale's.* She teaches classes on writing in New York City and online. Kristen created a community-based parenting blog in her hometown called BaristaKids.com. She currently edits HealingSisters.org. She is a certified domestic violence volunteer care provider. She lives in Montclair, New Jersey, with her husband, twin daughters, and son.